A2 COMMUNICATION AND CULTURE:
The Essential Introduction

Peter Bennett and Jerry Slater

Routledge
Taylor & Francis Group

LONDON AND NEW YORK

First published 2010
by Routledge
2 Park Square, Milton Park, Abingdon, Oxon, OX14 4RN

Simultaneously published in the USA and Canada
by Routledge
711 Third Avenue, New York, NY 10017

Routledge is an imprint of the Taylor & Francis Group, an informa business

© 2010 Peter Bennett & Jerry Slater

Typeset in Folio and Bauhaus by
Keystroke, Tettenhall, Wolverhampton
Printed and bound by CPI Group (UK) Ltd, Croydon, CR0 4YY

British Library Cataloguing in Publication Data
A catalogue record for this book is available from the British Library

Library of Congress Cataloging in Publication Data
Bennett, Peter, 1961-
  A2 communication and culture : the essential introduction /
  Peter Bennett and Jerry Slater.
    p. cm. — (Essentials)
  Includes bibliographical references and index.
  1. Communication. 2. Reading comprehension—Ability testing.
  3. Language and culture. I. Slater, Jerry. II. Title.
  P90.B38 2009
  302.2—dc22   2009022557

ISBN 13: 978–0–415–47160–2 (pbk)

CONTENTS

ILLUSTRATIONS

The following were reproduced with kind permission. While every effort has been made to trace copyright holders and obtain permission, this has not always been possible in all cases. Any omissions brought to our attention will be remedied in future editions.

ACKNOWLEDGEMENTS

'Home Is so Sad' from COLLECTED POEMS by Philip Larkin. Copyright © 1988, 2003 by the Estate of Philip Larkin. Published in the World outside the USA by Faber and Faber, 1988. Reproduced with kind permission.

'Home Is so Sad' from COLLECTED POEMS by Philip Larkin. Copyright © 1988, 2003 by the Estate of Philip Larkin. Reprinted by permission of Farrar, Straus and Giroux, LLC.

'Teens say they like vinyl records over CDs' © 2006 United Press International, Inc. All Rights Reserved.

CAN'T BUY ME LOVE Lyrics by John Lennon, Paul McCartney © Copyright 1964 Sony / ATV Music Publishing. All rights reserved. Used by permission.

'Retailers accused of ignoring Bangladeshi workers' plight', Matthew Taylor, 05 December 2008. Copyright Guardian News and Media Ltd 2008.

Dibb, S. (2005) 'Business Briefs: Checks and Chavs', http://www.open2.net/money/briefs_20051028branding.html, The Open University © The Open University, 2006

Carter, Angela (1998) The Snow Child in *The Bloody Chamber*. © 1980 Angela Carter. Reproduced by permission of the author c/o Rogers, Coleridge & White Ltd., 20 Powis Mews, London W11 1JN.

Here's to the Crazy Ones from Apple's 'Think Different'. advertising campaign. Courtesy of Apple, Inc.

THE HOME FRONT Lyrics by Billy Bragg © Billy Bragg. All rights reserved. Used with permission of Bragg Office and Sincere Management.

'Blair fears curse of the Dome will dash Labour's poll hopes' by Jo Dillon, Sunday 9 January 2000 © The Independent.

'He Ain't Heavy, He's My Uncle' episode from *Only Fools and Horses* © John Sullivan.

The Wild Swans at Coole by William Butler Yeats. Reproduced by kind permission of A P Watt Ltd on behalf of Gráinne Yeats.

'Warwick Ave.' Words and music by Aimee Ann Duffy © 2006, reproduced by permission of EMI music publishing Ltd, London W8 5SW

WATERLOO SUNSET Words and Music by Ray Davies – © 1967 Davray Music Ltd & Carlin Music Corp, London NW1 8BD. – All Rights Reserved – Lyric reproduced by Permission.

WATERLOO SUNSET Words and Music by RAY DAVIES © 1967 (Renewed) DAVRAY MUSIC LTD. and ABKCO MUSIC INC. All Rights for the U.S. and Canada on behalf of DAVRAY MUSIC LTD. Administered by UNICHAPPELL MUSIC INC. All Rights Reserved Used by Permission.

'Colchester: Delight at Tesco plans' defeat' by Gareth Palmer. Used by kind permission of Newsquest Essex.

AQA examination questions are reproduced by permission of the Assessment and Qualifications Alliance.

MOVING ON, MOVING UP: FROM AS TO A2

Figure 1.1 Lake Powel, Utah. 'To see a world in a grain of sand . . .'

(William Blake)

This book is for students of Communication and Culture; more specifically, for those who have completed the AS course and are now embarking on a programme of A2 study. It is certainly a 'text book' in the sense that it will guide you through the specification, advising you on how to fulfil the coursework requirements and prepare you for the examination. However, you will already know enough about our subject to realize that it would be impossible to produce a truly comprehensive volume: one that covered every possible angle and explored every inch of territory. The breadth and diversity of the area make that impossible. What we can do, though, is to equip you as thoroughly as possible for your own journey through the endlessly fascinating landscape of Communication and Culture. The purpose of this introductory chapter is to give you a feel for the distinctive nature of the A2.

How will A2 be different to AS?

One of the key concepts in the AS part of the specification is *identity*. You will have spent a good deal of your time examining the ways in which identity is communicated by us and to us, as well as the intertwining of cultural, subcultural, group and individual identity. The 'ideas that people have about who they are' as we defined identity in the AS glossary are just as important at A2, but now our discussions of cultural practices and cultural products, the meanings we attach to everyday life take a slightly different turn. At this level, there is rather more emphasis on *differences*; differences in behaviour, tastes, habits and interpretations. We want to describe and explain these differences and, most importantly, to relate these differences to power structures in society.

The AS course presented you with tools (remember the 'toolkits'?) with which you could analyse the meanings of day-to-day culture using your own experiences and observations as the 'raw material' for study. You will certainly have been encouraged towards a critical outlook; one in which you develop your own ideas and opinions based on reason, argument and evidence. These will be especially useful skills as you move on to the greater depth and breadth of study required at A2. You will need to widen the scope of your study to take in evidence and examples from beyond your immediate personal experience, for instance by making cross-cultural and historical comparisons. You will encounter a wide range of different views or perspectives: contrasting ways of explaining how things are and why those power differences mentioned above have come about. Not only will you need to familiarize yourself with perspectives, but you will also need to develop your critical confidence in order to evaluate them and test their usefulness in a variety of contexts. These contexts will include many of the cultural practices and cultural products familiar to you from AS: the real or imagined places where we (in Goffman's sense) *perform* our selves. The contexts include some major sites of cultural communication – Places and Spaces, Fictions and Objects of Desire, all of which provide opportunities for further excursions into the meanings and practices of everyday life.

At this stage, we should pause to remind you of some familiar terms from AS, including some terms already used in this introduction. Perhaps they seem a little less familiar if you have just returned to A Level study after a long summer. Just in case they have temporarily slipped from your memory, here are some Information Boxes to refresh the memory.

INFORMATION BOX – CULTURAL PRACTICES ℹ

These are the 'things we do'; the activities that comprise our daily lives. Examples include:

- Greeting a friend
- Attending a class
- Taking a holiday
- Getting dressed

- Travelling on a bus
- Eating breakfast
- Chatting with friends
- Playing a video game

The list, of course, is endless, but our focus is not so much on listing practices but upon understanding the *meaning* of practices. What are the rules or *codes* that guide people's behaviour as they perform these activities? What are the variations between different individuals, groups, subcultures and cultures?

For each of us, our 'cultural belonging' is determined by the degree to which we share an understanding of how to perform these everyday acts. This is what Raymond Williams called a 'structure of feeling': a shared knowledge and understanding of what it means to act in a certain way.

INFORMATION BOX – CULTURAL PRODUCTS ℹ

These are the things we encounter in our daily lives – things as diverse as these few examples:

- An MP3 player
- A pair of jeans
- A hairstyle

- A toaster
- Your bedroom
- A Ford Focus

All of these are material, tangible objects but, just as with Cultural Practices, our particular interest is in the complex range of meanings associated with these things. Objects acquire significance in different contexts to people of different cultural backgrounds. They are represented to us in many ways, so that an important aspect of the 'structure of feeling' described above is the shared understand of what cultural products mean. You will have developed some skills in analysing or reading cultural products and practices as you followed the AS course.

Being critical

In AS we encourage a personal critical approach. This does not mean finding fault with everything, it means developing an open-minded, questioning, evaluative approach to your studies. This continues to be the case in A2, but now you will need to engage more closely with the many ideas, investigations and theories developed by writers in this field in order to apply them to your own studies. This is not to say that your own ideas no longer count; far from it. Your ability to think critically, analytically and creatively is still your principal asset, but this ability is enhanced and developed by your immersion in the ideas and perspectives developed by established writers. Their ideas are not simply there for you to learn, but for you to test, debate and apply in the context of your own experience. In short, your approach to A2 study needs to be informed, theoretical and practical.

An example

As an illustration of A2's distinctive approach, consider an idea that you have already thought about at AS: Goffman's dramaturgical model of self-presentation. What Goffman provides is a way of understanding, or at least describing, human behaviour and a set of comprehensible elements within this approach. We are, he suggests, like actors, presenting ourselves to all the other actors (who also serve as a kind of audience) on the broadest stage of all. We do our performing with varying degrees of sincerity across a range of roles and employ subtly different versions of ourselves to suit the context and the teams within which and against which we play. Not only this but we also try at all times to leave our personal signature, our individuality on our work. This is a very feasible model that engages us with its clarity but it does not simplify, rather it multiplies the potential complexities by introducing numerous considerations. It is useful largely for this reason. If we take T.S. Eliot's claim about human beings and reality ('Human kind cannot bear very much reality') then useful theory lets us 'bear' more because it helps us to see that there is more.

The theories, issues and topics you will meet at A2 are also very much of that kind: they address you, provide you and entice you to go further, broader and deeper. They do this in part by moving their emphasis towards *power* as a key concept and partly by relating to wider culture as well as the self. When first addressed Goffman's theories of self-presentation appear to be exclusively 'personal', since 'The Presentation of the Self' appears to be exclusively about the individual. However the full title of Goffman's masterpiece is *The Presentation*

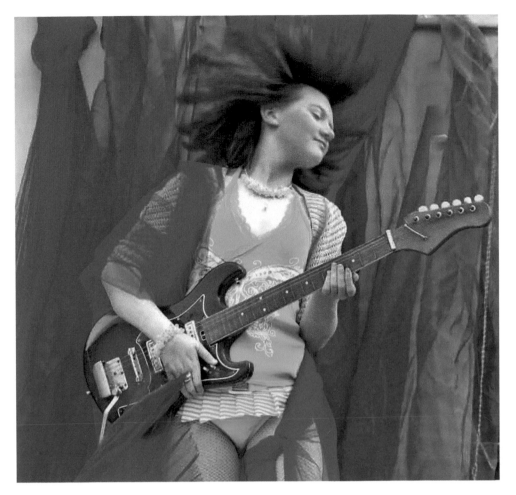

Figure 1.2 Presentation of the self owes much to our role and our audience

of Self in Everyday Life (Goffman, 1990) and it is on these contexts that we shall be focusing in A2. To extend the dramaturgical metaphor we might simply ask of our own performances as cultural actors:

- Whose are the lines we are speaking?
- Who is the author?
- Who or what directs us?
- Who 'casts' us/decides the range of roles?
- What choice of narratives do we have?
- Whose stories are we involved in and in which roles?
- Who determines which 'teams' we 'represent' or within which we perform?

By now, as students of Communication and Culture it is doubtful whether you expect definitive answers to these questions. What you will get however are some possible answers and lots more questions, lots of explanations some of which are hopefully as useful as Goffman's. Orchestrating and eliciting these theories, these further explanations, will be the concept of power. It is the force behind all of the questions above, the underlying complication in a world that would otherwise allow us to exercise unlimited choice about who we can be and what we can do. In some senses it is the difference between theory and practice.

POWER: Power combines the capacity to act with force (influence) with the authority to do this. It addresses all those ways in which individuals and institutions have control and influence over other people and their actions.

In the great majority of societies, power is not distributed equally. Economic resources, political authority and the ability to physically control others are often concentrated in the hands of minority groups who therefore exercise domination over the majority. The exercise of power by such a dominant minority over a subordinate minority also involves the validation of power. As we shall see, many cultural practices and codes of communication contribute to processes where the unequal distribution of power is made to seem legitimate or even natural. These processes lead us to another of our A2 key concepts: *ideology*.

A simple way to exemplify the limitations of our real choice is to use Goffman's categories to identify where power in its various forms restricts or modifies our ability to be free. Think for this purpose of power operating in two spheres:

1 interpersonally between individuals involved in communication
2 culturally as an embodiment of the values of the broader society (for example in relation to such matters as gender, ethnicity or social class).

Goffman suggests that persona and performance are key to the process of self-presentation, that the first stage is about making decisions about how to play yourself. This then of course is linked to role, teams and staging to create the presented self. However, all of this is potentially beset by problems since all of these categories are subject to a power dynamic if only at the level of expectation and expectation is perhaps the most demanding pressure of all. Thus when a situation is described which involves self-presentation (and there is barely a situation that doesn't demand this) we are dealing with a set of conventions which are just as important as those governing the creation of other kinds of text. At one level, after all, we are just dealing with two different kinds of characterization and each has a bearing on the other. Thus stereotypical roles like 'dutiful son/daughter' or 'straight A student' are negotiated through both presentational and representational codes.

ACTIVITY

Expectation is the mother of all cock-ups?

Imagine a simple communication dynamic: the job interview. Here is a situation which makes ideas about self-presentation explicit so that they can be usefully discussed. Usually we do consider how we are playing ourselves in these situations to meet sets of social conventions which imply that playing this game is somehow connected to potential success.

This interview however is not one in which we are involved, it is one we are observing. There are only two participants: the interviewer (A) and the interviewee (B). The other factors to watch are the job (C) and the style of the interview (D). Consider the relationship between these four factors by completing the following table. Consider how far our expectations of the likely job are affected by the other likely job factors.

Interviewer	Interviewee	Job	Style
Male	Female		Informal
Female	Male		Formal
Middle-aged female	Young female		Formal
Middle-aged male	Young male		Informal

This simple activity should clearly demonstrate the significance of power relationships with respect to age and gender. Jobs are not all equal; different occupations enjoy different levels of status and income and these are probably reflected by the way in which you have completed the chart.

> **IDEOLOGY:** Ideology is a concept that explains the asymmetrical (unequal) power relations described above. Unfortunately, there are many different theories and interpretations of ideology (these will be dealt with in more detail in later chapters). A useful starting point is Louis Althusser's description of ideology as 'a system of representations at the heart of a given society'. Peter Barry explains that this definition makes culture 'a crucial vehicle of the values which underpin the status quo in any society. These values and assumptions are usually implicit, often unrecognized, but suffuse all the artefacts and all the culture of a given time.' (Barry, 2002, p. 163) The status quo means 'things as they are', the unchanged position, so we could re-state the proposition as follows:
>
> The meanings and values we attach to cultural products and cultural values are not neutral. They tend to reinforce existing power relations in society. In this sense both cultural practices and cultural products have an *ideological* role.

Journeys, excursions and other trips

This course could be seen as a series of excursions: a virtual, and sometimes physical tour of significant sights and sounds of contemporary cultural life. The A2 programme gives both general and specific ideas about where we should go and then offers us the names of potential reputable guides, but the rest is up to you. What you find will partly depend on how you go about looking. 'Anything is hard to find', claimed The Smiths, 'when you will not open your eyes'. This turns out to be extremely good advice for Communication and Culture students.

We search for satisfaction of various kinds but certainly the satisfaction that comes from exploring and understanding meanings. For such 'journeys' we need our wits about us and our eyes open. We need to be aware that there are many potential barriers (seen and unseen) between ourselves and the 'pure and simple truth' (which Oscar Wilde reminded us was anyway 'never pure and rarely simple'). The tools and attitudes we brought with us from AS will be useful here since they partly prepare us for a 'project' that is ongoing. A proverb of travelling suggests 'It is better to travel hopefully than to arrive' though perhaps a more pessimistic or pragmatic view would be less ambitious: 'It is better to travel hopefully than without hope'. The idea of journey as a metaphor for period of time, an endeavour (like your programme of A2 study), a relationship or even life itself, crops up frequently in contemporary culture. How many time have you heard a film or a book introduced with the words 'Let us take you on a journey . . .'?

We are also reminded, at each turn, of stories in various media since 'journey' is also the shape of the simplest linear narratives. This is not only a series of

Figure 1.3 'Journeys are the midwives of thought.' Alain de Botton, 2002

references but rather more significantly a mode of address for reporting on our lives. 'World is crazier and more of it than you think', wrote the poet Louis MacNeice and it is this abundance that must be checked. Much of the 'cultural work' that we undertake in our day-to-day lives is devoted to turning the mass of disparate experiences into something coherent enough to live with (if not by). We learn from artistic narratives the art of abbreviation, of selecting and simplifying the experience into manageable and comprehensible 'chunks'. Perhaps this is why lessons are easier to learn from films and books than from experience.

Alain de Botton writes very effectively about this in his illustrated philosophy book *The Art of Travel* (De Botton, 2002). In a chapter entitled 'On anticipation' he writes about the relationships between thinking about a place you are going to visit and actually visiting it, suggesting that the former is always going to be cleaner since it inevitably simplifies and selects. This sheds light for us on the relationship between theory and practice with the former having in this context the advantage (and limitation) of a travel guide:

> **A travel book may tell us, for example, that a narrator journeyed through the afternoon to reach the hill town of X and, after a night in its medieval monastery, awoke to a misty dawn. But we never simply journey through**

an afternoon. We sit in a train. Lunch digests awkwardly within us. The seat cloth is grey. We look out of the window at a field. We look back inside. A drum of anxieties revolves in consciousness. We notice a luggage label affixed to a suitcase in a rack above the opposing seats. We tap a finger on the window-ledge. A broken nail on an index finger catches a thread. It starts to rain. A drop wends a muddy path down a dust-coated window. We wonder where the ticket might be. We look back out at the field. It continues to rain. At last the train starts to move. It passes an iron bridge, after which it stops inexplicably. A fly lands on the window. And still we might only have reached the end of the first minute of a comprehensive account of the events lurking within the descriptive sentence 'he journeyed through the afternoon'. **"**

(De Botton, 2002, p. 14)

ACTIVITY

Thought Diary

De Botton's list is in itself a simplification of what goes on in the mind of every participant in a communication act. Much more might have been included. Taking this as a challenge, prepare to write a comprehensive account of the events lurking within the descriptive sentence: 'I had a Communication and Culture lesson yesterday'. Your preparation should consist of a thought diary recording everything you think, feel and see while inside the classroom on the model of de Botton's 'journey through the afternoon'. See how long you can keep this up without losing the plot!

It is in this sense that all theories need to be evaluated in the light of practice. The critical process of apprehending what there is to see is a process very like the processing of everyday life: it must involve selection of details and by implication, deselection. De Botton is again useful:

> **The present might be compared to a long-winded film from which memory and anticipation select photographic highlights.**

(De Botton, 2002)

In a similar way, we inevitably isolate 'photographic highlights' when engaging critically with our material. As we try to make sense of our experiences, the day-to-day life that is the raw material of our study, we find ourselves reaching for analogies and metaphors (like 'the journey') that help us to make sense of things. Unfortunately, these metaphors and analogies are often fully functioning perspectives themselves. In contemporary culture these are often technological: we think of life as 'programmed' or see ourselves as characters in 'a long-winded film'. Like all the other perspectives you encounter on this course these may well be useful but it would be dangerous to think of them as neutral or transparent. The technological determinist Neil Postman summed up the way technologies impact on perception with this simple description of human development:

> **To a man with a pencil, everything looks like a list. To a man with a camera, everything looks like an image. To a man with a computer, everything looks like data. And to a man with a grade sheet, everything looks like a number.**

(Postman, 1993, p. 14)

Just in passing, we may also note Postman's generalized use of 'man' to mean 'man or woman'.

All analogies will ultimately break down and it's as well to know when to abandon them: this is perhaps the point where we are trying to make the world fit the theory rather than the theory fit the world. The twentieth century bred many examples of ideologies that squeezed human realities into their abstract designs. Life ultimately is not a journey, a film, or even a lottery; it's just that there are aspects of all three of these 'activities' that help us to understand something about who we are and what it's like being us. They also constitute useful frames in which the broader experiences can be observed, if not contained. This is also the function of creative work: to frame the world so it can be examined in detail. It is easy to see how we might be apparently 'travelling' through life but perhaps more interesting to see what travelling really tells us about the people we are and the values we, and our cultures, have.

Example: travel as a cultural practice

Perhaps this is the point to move swiftly from metaphor to something more substantial, from intellectual excursions to actual journeys. De Botton again can give us a start if we'll let him:

> **If our lives are dominated by a search for happiness, then perhaps few activities reveal as much about the dynamics of this quest – in all its ardour and paradoxes – than our travels. They express, however inarticulately, an understanding of what life might be about. . .**

(De Botton, 2002, p. 9)

This is an open invitation to talk about 'our travels' as both a series of past events and a series of anticipated things to come. When in AS we talked about taste and the need to have favourite books and films sorted out we were simply talking about basic choices within particular contexts. Thinking about where, how and why we might travel is an altogether more complex set of problems.

ACTIVITY

A Grand Day Out

This work needs to start with a series of declarations which then can be developed and challenged. These two questions are a decent starting point, phrased to acknowledge the issues we have already addressed in AS:

a) If asked and given little time to answer, which place you have visited in a day did you like the best (and is this the same or different to the answer to the task: 'Describe your best day out'?)

b) Where's the best place you have ever been?

Now share responses and consider how precisely 'places' have been identified (Consider for example the answers 'Eurodisney' and 'London' or 'Old Trafford' and 'America').

In Nick Park's *A Grand Day Out*, Wallace and Grommit, aided by a homemade space rocket, make the ultimate excursion: to the moon. They find, as they

Figure 1.4 *A Grand Day Out*

anticipated, that the moon is made of cheese and fighting off the attentions of a demented cooker, revel in the discovery, as famous cheese-eaters, of the place best suited to their 'needs'.

ACTIVITY

Our Day Out

Now work with others to create your ideal excursion, working towards answers to the following simple questions:

Where to?

To do what?

With whom?

How are you travelling?

To approach these questions it might be useful to rank some of the contenders.

continued

Theme Park	Bowling	Ruin
Nature walk	Concert	Cinema
Zoo	Castle	Sporting activity
Gig	Theatre	Picnic
Stately Home	Sporting event	
Museum	Restaurant	

And to rank the importance of these factors:

| Cost | Company | Distance |
| Weather | Educational Value | 'Thrill' |

Our Day Out was a play by Willy Russell, often performed by schools and amateurs about a school trip arranged for a class of 'bottom stream' kids. The kids in question are taken to the seaside. Traditionally school and college trips have higher aspirations. In order to justify the tag 'educational' they direct themselves, often tenuously, towards aspects of the school curriculum or towards accessing in a simple way what AS called 'High Culture'.

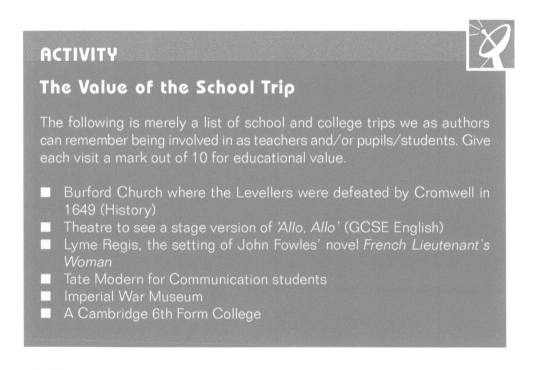

ACTIVITY

The Value of the School Trip

The following is merely a list of school and college trips we as authors can remember being involved in as teachers and/or pupils/students. Give each visit a mark out of 10 for educational value.

- Burford Church where the Levellers were defeated by Cromwell in 1649 (History)
- Theatre to see a stage version of *'Allo, Allo'* (GCSE English)
- Lyme Regis, the setting of John Fowles' novel *French Lieutenant's Woman*
- Tate Modern for Communication students
- Imperial War Museum
- A Cambridge 6th Form College

One very clear element here is the valuing of our History as manifest in surviving physical evidence: from royal burial masks and standing stones to castles and stately homes. Seeing history, as we often do, as collections of plundered wealth hoarded in palatial homes or gifted to a national storehouse like the British Museum is hardly unproblematic. It is as if the anchor 'History' provides a powerful dispensation from such considerations (a sort of ethical 'get out of jail free' card). When asked to admire the paintings in a stately home such as Longleat or Chatsworth House we are being asked to address more than their artistic value: they are 'priceless' in the sense, principally, of expensive beyond imagination. Ask not how they were acquired or what they say about the values of those who often still benefit from them – ask instead when they were painted, by whom and for whom.

If these activities are working as intended, you should by now be getting some notion of how we shall be dealing with cultural codes, products and practices at A2. Now we move on to a more extended activity with a comparative dimension.

'This is where I live'

Examine the images in Figures 1.5a–f from the MTV show *Cribs*, in which various celebrities put their homes and possessions on display for the benefit of the viewing public. These stills are from the 2007 show based on rapper 50 Cent (aka Curtis James Jackson III).

Source: http://www.youtube.com/watch?v=bD1GJRiQlrw

Figure 1.5a From one champ to another. Step inside 50 Cent's Connecticut mansion which he bought from Mike Tyson

Figure 1.5b 50 says this oven still has the packaging on it because he never uses this kitchen. He has six kitchens

Figure 1.5c In his movie theater, Curtis has over 3000 movies available at the touch of a button

Figure 1.5d Downstairs 50 has an indoor basketball court

Figure 1.5e The stripper section of the house. Two poles, a stage, and, yes, a swing

Figure 1.5f 50 claims he can pack about 2000 heads into his fully functional dance club

The show informs viewers that 50 Cent's home includes a collection of 30,000 films for use in his own private cinema and a nightclub especially set up for striptease performances.

What do these images tell us about 50 Cent and MTV's audience. How are the images anchored by their captions? Make use of your AS toolkits and concepts such as representation, value and identity to analyse and discuss this series of images. What do the concepts of power and ideology add to your analysis?

Now look at the images of The Duke and Duchess of Devonshire and their ancestral home, Chatsworth House, (Figures 1.7 and 1.8). What contrasts do you see arising from the previous set of images? What do your contrasting reactions tell you about your own value system? Perhaps you can devise captions for these images that anchor them (a) similar to and (b) different to the 50 Cent pictures.

If you want a further example of this kind of overlap take a look at Celebrity magazines like *Hello* and *OK* and compare them with the family portraits commissioned by aristocratic families in the eighteenth century (and before). These images might all easily bear the collective title: 'Here I am in front of what I own'.

Obviously much of what you are doing above can be reached using the tools and concepts provided by AS. You are addressing issues of representation, culture and value. Perhaps most of all you are assessing the importance of context. However,

Figure 1.6 The Duke and Duchess of Devonshire

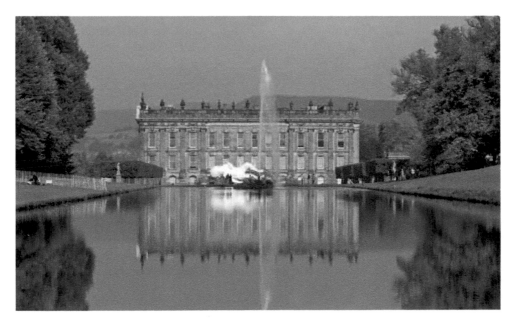

Figure 1.7 Chatsworth House, Derbyshire

Figure 1.8 The dining room, Chatsworth House

as you would expect, A2 will look to push you further by offering you further techniques and explanations. Partly this will be a change of emphasis, shifting from a focus on personal identity to a concern with cultural identity. This requires more than a reading of, say, 50 Cent the celebrity. It requires a reading of the systems of power and representation within which he is defined. It particularly requires an awareness of those systems of representation that enshrine the values of the more powerful and dominant groups in our society. These systems are *ideological*, they contain social and cultural information about how things are 'supposed' to be. As such they are often unconscious and invisible, allowing us to walk through The Tower of London without ever thinking 'plunder' or 'theft'. Interestingly works of art stolen by the Nazis in their temporary conquest of most of Western Europe are still being pursued and returned. How do you feel about the principles of returning works of art to their rightful owners? Could this principle be applied to, say, the British Museum and what would be the consequences?

The issues you have been grappling with in these last few pages should, we hope, have made you confront just a few of your 'taken for granted' assumptions about culture. We all, consciously or unconsciously, subscribe to perspectives, to ways of looking at the world. As the A2 course develops we shall have to confront the idea that there are many contrasting modes of interpretation and that our own personal perspectives are just as much up for critical evaluation as any others. It may well be that you favour a rational, evidence-based (or empirical) approach. It is interesting, though, to consider approaches from perspectives whose starting point lies beyond the text in question or a given situation. These perspectives may take a view informed by a particular or vested interest. So for example, some might see the 50 Cent/Duke of Devonshire situation purely as an issue of social class and economic power and would explain everything ideologically in those terms. Others would see the significant absence of women, and by implication, the nature and status of their roles as 'dancers' or strippers as the primary issue. A third group would consider ethnicity as the essential consideration both in terms of 50 Cent's stereotypical Gangsta posturing (and his contextualization as thus) and in terms of the colonial implications inherent in the acquisitions of leading British aristocratic families.

In the course of time these theoretical perspectives will be developed and to some extent formalized. Here it is enough to acknowledge that to have this set of other ways of seeing can only enhance our own personal response. We are not asked to exchange our view for others but rather to see the process as one which will potentially bear fruit. We can certainly give them names, not least as a way of organizing what we are encountering as we go.

INFORMATION BOX – THREE PERSPECTIVES: A STARTING POINT   *i*

Marxist perspective: this is the approach that sees everything in terms of its economic aspects, and the implications of these in terms of social class.

Feminist perspective: this is the approach that considers gender the significant issue. Patriarchy (male dominance) is seen as an enshrined ideological force that maintains inequality at all costs.

Post-colonialist perspective: this is the approach that sees our society dominated by a mainstream culture that maintains a set of relocated Colonial attitudes. The key relationship is between this 'mainstream' (ethnically white) and all those who are 'other' than this (who are seen as variously 'exotic', 'mysterious' and 'savage').

Not only do these perspectives offer us readings of '50 Cent' and the 'Duke', they also offer us further comments on the AS debate about High and Popular Culture. In some senses, of course, 50 Cent and the Duke are central to that debate anyway, but arguments about the degree to which High Culture represents the views of merely those most powerful can certainly be clarified by Marxist, Feminist and post-colonialist readings. This is an argument about dominant ideology, which John Fiske sums up succinctly as 'white patriarchal capitalism'.

> **DOMINANT IDEOLOGY:** From a Marxist perspective, the dominant ideology is the ideology of the dominant class. The dominant ideology is the set of common values and beliefs shared by most people in a given society, informing how the majority thinks about a range of topics. The dominant ideology reflects, or serves, the interests of the dominant class in that society.

Other perspectives

It will also be necessary to consider perspectives which address the special conditions that have been created by the exponential development of technologies of all kinds. The Canadian visionary Marshall McLuhan foresaw much of this in the early 1960s and gave us a vocabulary and a set of slogans. It was he who coined the phrase 'Global Village' to express the effects of technology on a shrinking world. He also suggested that the mass media were ultimately 'an extension of our senses', an idea (like so many of McLuhan's) that has been given new 'bite' by developments within virtual reality and intuitive technology. Most famously he suggested that 'The Medium is the Message' which again in a world of Xbox and iPod, Blu-ray and Blackberry is enjoying a new lease of life. McLuhan had grave misgivings about the impact of these processes, believing that new technologies irreparably changed the way we think, feel and operate. We can argue about 'think' and 'feel' later but no-one could question the fact technology has changed the ways in which we do things.

In ten years both mobile communication technology and the proliferation of the World Wide Web have changed all of our lives significantly. The very fact that we can access a tour of 50 Cent's (place) home at any time, in a number of formats, untethered to a scheduled TV show called *MTV Cribs*, is in itself the epitome of the new world. Some would argue that within this very act, a significant shift of power has taken place, that the 'age of ideology' is over. When we have so much control, how can we be controlled? However we might equally say that in a media-saturated world of recycled images, whose highest ambition is irony, we have suddenly been given responsibility for making meaning but not the power to do so. In such a world, which some have labelled 'postmodern', the old explanations have begun to break down to be replaced only be a vacuum, what the postmodernist Lyotard called 'A cultural Disneyland where everything is parody and nothing is better or worse'. In the end this is our last word on 50 Cent and the Duke: they are essentially playing the same game where nothing is better or worse.

POSTMODERNISM: This is an approach that sees the inherent confusion and uncertainty of modern living as key to understanding it. It argues that in a world in which reality itself is questioned that overarching explanations have no place. Life is to be seen as a series of negotiations unreferenced to absolute truth — rather it is 'do-it-yourself' pieced together from fragments.

ACTIVITY

Displaced Reality and the Online Hotel Tour

What you are required to do here is a performance but you can choose:

a) Sincere
b) Cynical

The task is to write and perform a voice over for the slides below which constitute an online visual guide to a fashionable London hotel. Think what stories this sequence might tell, with or without lashings of post-modern irony.

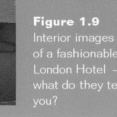

Figure 1.9
Interior images of a fashionable London Hotel — what do they tell you?

A final example: 360° fictions, Sherwood Forest and the legend of Robin Hood

One of the focal points of this A2 course is entitled 'Fictions' (see Chapter 5) where we will be looking further into the structures through which we sequence and process reality. Perhaps Grange hotels would baulk at their virtual tour being described as a 'fiction' since the connotations are superficially of something made up. The structural features of stories, of fictions are termed narratives (another key concept!). Narratives have featured implicitly throughout this chapter as codes, languages in their own right that govern the flow of information; how and when it is given and when it is withheld. Narrative is also, of course, governed by experience, convention and expectation. We never enter these structures without this knowledge, so partly what is happening is a process of confirmation or denial, conformity or rebellion.

Thus when you access a virtual tour which promises a 360° viewpoint, you do so with a significant set of expectations. What it appears to offer is a truth predicated on the saying 'seeing is believing'. In fact what you see is conditioned more by the context than the view. Hence when accessing the 360° view below we are searching for the narrative anchor rather than taking in the beauty of the forest scene.

Figure 1.10 Sherwood Forest: under the major oak (approximation of Sherwood 360°)

Read the anchoring caption and things begin to happen, sophisticated things. Here is a 'real' location (Sherwood Forest) and semi-fictional context (Robin Hood). On the website the camera can be operated (apparently) by the viewer, which almost dramatizes the process since it seems to represent our minute-by-minute response to a landscape at once denotative, connotative and symbolic. 'History' is certainly part of this 'bricolage', as is legend, but representation supersedes presentation. Every generation, it is said, has its own Robin Hood and perhaps it is the filmic and televisual versions that most impose themselves in this adjacent medium. It may be for you that the BBC's recent version with Jonas Armstrong gets most easily superimposed. For others an emblematic 1980s version starring Michael Praed and featuring a young Ray Winstone will always be definitive.

Clearly something significant is being said in each of these cases (and collectively). In the face of the arguments we advanced earlier about dominant ideology supporting those with power in a society, this enduring set of stories might appear to be contradictory. Are these not stories of outlaws with integrity, of supporting the poor in the face of their oppression by the rich, of the redistribution of wealth? Is not Robin the peasant struggling against tyranny aided by the human virtues of courage, loyalty and integrity?

Interestingly Robin Hood stories are found all over the British Isles so Nottingham and Sherwood have no special claim save that made by tourism over hundreds of years. 'Robin Hood' was, almost certainly, a title rather than one man's name passed on from one outlaw band to another, a corruption of 'Robin in the hood' (or the Hooded Man). The hoodie, it seems, has always been the garb of those outside of the conventions, of those beyond the pale. In recent years the moral panic has sometimes reached epic proportions with some schools and colleges outlawing hoodies for little obvious reason. Not since drainpipe trousers and beetle crushers in the 1950s have items of clothing created such a fuss. The association of hoodies and hoodlums in the public imagination overflowed to such a degree that teenagers were asked to remove their hoods when entering some shopping malls. For Robin on the other hand the hood is worn as a distinguishing mask, a medieval Asbo!

ACTIVITY

The Hooded Man

Figure 1.11 Contrasting images of the hood

continued

Consider the meanings of hoods in the pictorial sequence above. You may wish to address this issue semiotically in terms of :

- The status of signs (iconic, indexical, symbolic)
- Levels of signification (denotation, connotation, and especially myth and ideology)
- Meaning-fixing processes (anchorage and relay)

In addition you might like to consider the importance of the following issues:

- Social class
- Ethnicity
- Gender
- Ideas about Englishness/Britishness

In spite of the presence of related stories across the British Isles, Robin Hood is often presented as quintessentially English. In historical terms he is depicted as an Englishman/Saxon fighting against the foreign invader (Normans). As such he is set firmly within an emblematic English rural ideal and within traditional constructions of English ethnicity. Like so many medieval stories his was subjected to a full Victorian overhaul to remove the 'wolfshead' and replace it with a groomed medievalism, more 'olde worlde' than real world. Robin in these stories was both redeemer and redeemed and married Marian in a country church, surrounded by those decent chaps 'The Merry Men'.

ASIDE

Robin and the Saracen

Robin Hood stories come with a shufflable pack of Merry Men, most importantly and consistently: Little John, Will Scarlet, Friar Tuck and Much the Miller's Son. Into this boys' club is allowed only one 'maid', perhaps to confirm that the otherwise 'gay' Robin is all man. However the adhesion of the reusable myth is so powerful that writer Richard Carpenter was able (largely by accident) to introduce a Saracen (Arab), Nazir, to Robin's band in the 1980s only to find that the big film version of 1991, *Robin Hood: Prince of Thieves* (dir. Robin Reynolds) cast Morgan Friedman in this role as if it were a 500 year old myth.

Other versions have stressed the outlaw/vigilante elements and perhaps if we are looking for "a real modern day Robin Hood" it is not to the TV series *Dukes of Hazzard* (from which this theme comes) that we should look. Perhaps it would be more interesting to consider the unromanticized representations of ordinary people fighting back in films like *This is England* (2006, dir. Shane Meadows) and *Outlaw* (2007, dir. Nick Love). Barthes characterized myths as collective connotations, personal responses to signs that were shared with others (thus not only empowering the sign but also connecting the respondents). Robin Hood is such a sign: open, suggestive, comfortably vague and yet entirely recognizable, one into which we are invited and allowed to invest our emotional and intellectual energy. As a sign he is a kind of channel for thoughts about liberty, resistance, courage and a certain kind of savage nobility which we might not express elsewhere. In reaching back to our individual and collective childhoods he is able to revive and reconcile competing thoughts and contradictions and remind us periodically, as Richard Carpenter's TV Robin often did, that "Nothing is forgotten. Nothing is ever forgotten".

References and further reading

Barry, P. (2002) *Beginning Theory; An Introduction to Literary and Cultural Theory* (2nd edn), Manchester: Manchester University Press.

De Botton, A. (2002) *The Art of Travel*, London: Penguin.

Eliot, T.S. (1959) *Four Quarters*, London: Faber & Faber, p.14.

Goffman, E. (1990) *The Presentation of Self in Everyday Life*, Harmondsworth: Penguin.

Postman, N. (1993) *Technopoly: The Surrender of Culture to Technology*, New York: Vantage.

2 THEORETICAL APPROACHES

Communication and Culture, we hope, is an enjoyable and interesting subject to study. Undoubtedly though, it is also complex and can be demanding, as you have already discovered by now. You could be forgiven for thinking that a whole raft of theories (don't worry, they're coming your way) would only make it even more complex and difficult. In fact, the purpose of theory, the necessity for theory, is to make complex subjects *easier* to understand and more accessible. Theories should help us to see patterns, to make connections, to compare and contrast. They should also help you to make links between Communication and Culture and your other studies as well as helping you to formulate your own ideas and opinions.

Rather than spending page after page in justification of 'theory', let's just dive in and hope that the purpose of theory in general will emerge from our explanations of the specific theoretical approaches you will need for your A2 programme of study.

Market liberalism

Most of the theoretical approaches you will find listed in the specification are broadly critical perspectives. But what are they critical of? For the most part, they are theories that find fault in the way things are, the status quo; they see problems and inequalities in the dominant structures of power. Market liberalism, however, is broadly supportive of 'the way things are' and tends to assert not only the economic benefits of capitalism but also its social, cultural and political benefits.

What is capitalism?

Capitalism is certainly a subject that inspires strong opinions and emotions, as witnessed at the frequent anti-capitalist demonstrations (see Figure. 2.1) held at locations around the world.

Pro-capitalist demonstrations, such as the one conducted by a few Young Conservatives (see Figure 2.2), may be less common and less well attended, but

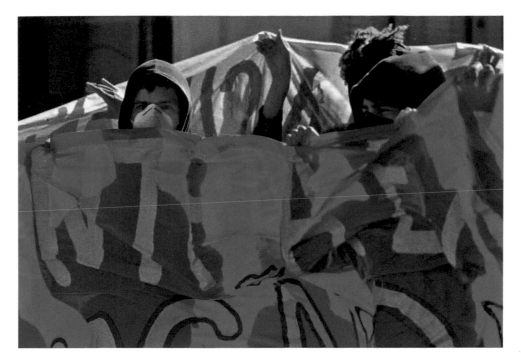

Figure 2.1 Anti-capitalist demonstration in Lisbon, May 2009

this should not disguise the fact that most institutions (for example political parties, corporations and newspapers) are broadly in favour of capitalism.

Capitalism is an economic system that emerged in eighteenth-century Europe to become, by the early twenty-first century, the world's dominant form of economic organization. It is a system in which people are driven to produce goods and services for a profit. The three prerequisites for production are:

- land
- capital (money)
- labour

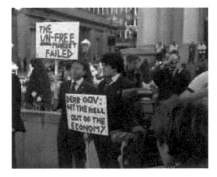

Figure 2.2 Young Conservatives demonstrate in support of capitalism, London, April 2009.

Within a capitalist system, the first two of these, land and capital, are concentrated in the hands of a minority who are able to make profits by purchasing the third factor of production: labour. Land and capital are privately owned by individuals or companies but labour is owned by all of us: everyone has the capacity to sell their own labour. Labour power (which can be either physical or mental) is exchanged for payment (wages). The goods or services that are produced in this way are then sold on the open market; a market in which the majority of buyers (consumers) are those same workers who sell their labour to the owners of capital – the capitalists.

The market is regulated by the laws of supply and demand whilst *competition* between providers ensures that price and quality are controlled. This idea of a 'free market' is right at the heart of capitalism.

So far, we have developed only a simple model of the basics of capitalism, but these basics really are essential if you are to understand the implications that capitalism has for communication and culture and the critical perspectives we shall be discussing later in the chapter. Just to make sure that you have fully grasped these principles, let's try a made up example of how capitalism works.

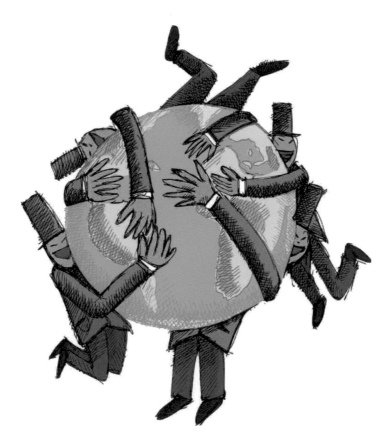

Figure 2.3 Capitalism has become the world's dominant economic system

Capitalism in Action: Flimflam Jam

Two speculators get together. One, named Flim, has land; the other, Flam, has money. They decide to form a company, the Flimflam Jam Company, in order to make profits from the production of jam. Money is invested to build and equip a factory on the land, fruit is grown and other raw materials such as sugar are purchased. Workers are employed for the factory and fields. Flimflam pay high wages to those with specialist skills or knowledge that are essential to the enterprise, but lower wages to those workers who are easy to find and, if necessary, easy to replace.

When Flimflam are ready to set a price for their jam, they have to take various factors into consideration, most importantly:

■ The cost of production and labour. In order to make a profit, the income from sales must exceed these costs.
■ The price and availability of other jams in the marketplace. If there is a shortage of jam, prices will be higher but if the market is flooded, prices will go down. These forces are the so-called laws of supply and demand.

Flimflam decide to produce two ranges of jam: the Flimflam Heritage Thick Fruit Special and Jammy Jam. The Heritage Special is made to the highest standards with expensive packaging to match. Jammy Jam is half the price and competes at the lower end of the market; it aims to be cheap and cheerful. Flimflam realize that selling jam is not just a matter of creating a product – consumers also expect a set of attractive meanings to be attached to the product. For a further discussion of the value of products in relation to packaging, marketing and the expectations of target consumers, see Chapter 6, Objects of Desire.

In a world of leveraged buy-outs, hedge funds and quantitative easing (don't worry, we don't understand them either) this little tale may seem simplistic as well as rather twee, but it should help you to take some important steps towards an understanding of capitalism. We have already hinted that market liberalism involves rather more than just economic principles; it also embraces a set of philosophical and political notions linked to the core idea of the 'free market'. The form of capitalism that endorses the freedom of the market in its purest (or, depending on your point of view, most extreme) sense is usually referred to as 'laissez-faire capitalism'. Laissez-faire means 'leave it alone', so in this form of capitalism the market is allowed to operate in accordance with its internal laws (e.g. supply and demand), without any interference whatsoever.

But who would want to tamper with the market or interfere with its freedom? As far as the market liberals are concerned, the enemy of the piece is the state. For the supporters of laissez-faire capitalism the absolute ideal would be no state intervention at all but most market liberals acknowledge that some 'rules' have to be enforced by the state. In reality, governments have always intervened in the market, Some governments may seek to control wages by restricting pay rises or, alternatively, may intercede to protect low paid workers by introducing a minimum wage. Sometimes, national governments restrict the freedom of trade by passing laws to protect their domestic industries. This would mean, for example, stopping imports from coming in to a country so that home-based industries would not have to face competition from foreign competitors who may be able to produce goods that are cheaper or better quality.

Another way in which the state can intervene is to remove whole sectors of the economy from the market in order to create a 'public sector' alongside the privately owned parts of industry. In the UK, the following institutions are located wholly or partly in the public sector:

- The NHS
- Armed Services
- Education
- The police
- Civil service

- Local Government
- The Roads
- The BBC
- Prisons

Britain, then, is a country that has both public and private industries, otherwise known as a mixed economy. The political approach that favours a mixture of public and private enterprise is called the social market position. There have been fierce debates for many years about this balance, with the Conservative Party generally favouring more emphasis on private enterprise and the Labour Party generally more supportive of the public sector. When the Conservatives under Margaret Thatcher won power in 1979 they set about transforming the public/private balance by initiating a programme of privatization. Many companies and economic sectors were shifted into the private sector in a process that critics called a 'sell-off' of the nation's assets. The coal industry, the steel industry, BT, the utilities (gas, water and electricity), British Airways and the railways all found themselves in private hands over the course of the next decade. Most interestingly, from our point of view, the arguments put forward in favour of privatization were not just economic but also cultural. The culture associated with the public sector was condemned as being lazy, self-serving, bureaucratic, backward-looking and inefficient. In contrast, private enterprise was systematically associated with virtues such as dynamism, efficiency, risk-taking and cutting edge modernity. In this way, Thatcher's privatizations were an economic, political and cultural project. Politics, like advertising, often deals in the assignment of positive or negative meanings.

Market liberalism is by no means confined to the economic sphere. For its advocates, the free market is at the centre of an interlocked set of political values: individual liberty, property rights, freedom of choice and expression. Market liberals also share the conviction that capitalism is best served by democratic and pluralist political systems, i.e. those in which everyone is entitled to vote and there is a genuine choice between diverse parties all competing for power.

Market liberalism: a case study

Let's say that you have chosen to investigate a particular cultural product as an 'object of desire': a digital camera. How would market liberals contribute to the debate about the roles and meanings of this item? Their position would be something like this:

> This camera shows just how much free markets benefit consumers. Competition between different manufacturers is intense and this means that prices keep falling even though the quality and reliability of the cameras continues to improve as each new model appears. Consumer demand means that manufacturers have to invest heavily in research and development so that their products constantly benefit from technological innovation and give something new to the consumer. Design is also important to potential purchasers; buyers want a camera that looks good and feels good as well as doing its picture-taking job efficiently. As a result, manufacturers strive to produce cameras that are desirable as well as functional. Most of the leading camera makers offer a range of models from the basic and cheap to the sophisticated and expensive. The digital camera industry provides employment in manufacturing, distribution and retailing. Factories are located in parts of the world where labour is relatively cheap, so that consumers can benefit from low prices.
>
> The cameras themselves are a source of interest and pleasure to their owners. They enable photographers to express their creativity as well as enabling them to keep a record of events in their lives. Consumers will often want to replace their cameras after a few years even if the model works perfectly because they want to upgrade to a new model with better features. This is good for the industry and good for the consumer.

Figure 2.4 A waterproof digital case study of market liberalism

To summarize, market liberals stress the benefits of

■ free markets
■ free trade
■ competition
■ supply and demand
■ limited government interference in the market
■ pluralist political systems.

As a perspective, market liberalism is invariably optimistic about the potential for capitalism to meet people's needs and to sustain economic progress. The principles of market liberalism are often presented to us not as arguments but as straightforward 'common sense', as if they were forces of nature rather than ideas about how to run the economy and society.

The downturn

Recent years have seen more than a few problems for the world's economies, variously described as the Downturn, the Credit Crunch or the Recession.

This has stimulated some heated debates about the free market and capitalism itself. As we have seen, market liberals extol the virtues of competition and accept that weak or inefficient companies have to go bust, so that those that survive in the market are those that are able to compete most effectively. However,

Figure 2.5 The BBC's 'Downturn' graphic. A familiar sight on TV news in 2009

governments on both sides of the Atlantic have interceded during the course of the economic crisis to prop up failing companies, particularly in the banking and car industries. These spectacular 'bail-outs' have been justified by economists who say that such actions are needed to save the system and to prevent capitalism from going into meltdown. Laissez-faire market liberals, on the other hand, have condemned this sort of government intervention because they believe that the market should be left alone to sort things out for itself.

As students of Communication and Culture our interests are less in the economic causes and consequences of recession and more in the cultural implications. What sort of impact do economic fluctuations have on our cultural practices and perceptions? Perhaps the most serious of these is that many of us become aware that there *is* an economic system and that it is one that has flaws. As noted above, the underlying principles of capitalism are often invisible because they are 'naturalized'. Market liberalism is barely criticized or even scrutinized because it is placed in the same sort of category as the weather or the changing seasons; the sort of thing we may grumble about but which is just 'there', beyond our power or capacity to change. However, when an economic downturn comes along this cloak of invisibility is whisked away. The workings of capitalism and its philosophical underpinnings are exposed, challenged and debated. Alternatives are considered. A fundamental shift in our ways of seeing things and making sense of them takes place to the extent that 'certainties' seem less certain; 'truths' and 'laws' are called into question rather than just accepted.

In other ways, too, cultural practices and habits respond to economic change. Writing in December 2008, Jonathan Freedland reported a dramatic rise in supermarket sales of comfort food:

> **Could that be down to the wintry weather rather than the frozen economy? No. Tesco saw the boom in reassuring ready meals and cosy grub during the period from May to October. This isn't about staying warm, says the store, along with other retailers who've noticed a similar pattern on their shelves. It's about Britons cheering themselves up, padding their tummies as they**

tighten their belts. And notice the dishes in demand: traditional British fare, as if we're fleeing scary global economic forces, seeking refuge in the familiar smells of mum's kitchen and school dinners. 🙶

(Freedland, 2008)

As Freedland and others have suggested, we don't find our comforts in food alone as the recession deepens; escapist films, home-based holidays ('staycations'), reading, gardening and hobby cooking have all flourished as employment and incomes have come under threat. A cover feature in *New York* magazine explores the possibility that harder times have led the city's inhabitants towards a more caring and compassionate outlook on life, more inclined to be considerate towards others than to be self-centred and greedy (Senior, 2009).

It would be a mistake to overemphasize or simplify the relationship between economic and cultural change, but as you go on to use the theoretical perspectives in your investigations of cultural practices and cultural products it would be an even more profound mistake to ignore economic factors altogether.

Critical perspectives: Marxism

Karl Marx died in 1883, so it is perfectly reasonable to ask how the ideas of this nineteenth-century economist and philosopher could possibly be relevant to our understanding of contemporary communication and culture. Marx spent much of his life exiled in England and he is buried in London. The inscription on his tomb includes two quotations from his published works that serve as a good introduction to his ideas and a clue as to why he is still so influential today. The first, 'Workers of all lands unite' comes from *The Communist Manifesto* (1848), which concludes with the words: 'The workers have nothing to lose but their chains. They have a world to win. Workers of all lands unite!' The second quotation is 'Philosophers have only interpreted the world, the purpose is to change it'. These express Marx's view that working class people all over the world have more in common with each other than they have with the ruling classes that oppress them in their own particular countries. Clearly, *The Communist Manifesto* is more than just a critique of capitalism; it is an indictment of capitalism that incites the working classes to seize power for themselves; this is why it has been such an influential book.

Many workers and political activists were inspired by the vision of communism and they struggled for decades to overthrow established ruling classes. One of their greatest successes was The Russian Revolution of 1917 which inaugurated the era of communism in what became the Soviet Union. Subsequently, China, Eastern Europe, Cuba and the national liberation movements in many other countries (mostly former colonies of the western powers) turned to the principles of communism as a model for social and political organization. Marx's view was that a transition from capitalism to communism was inevitable because he viewed

Figure 2.6 Marx's tomb in Highgate Cemetery, London

communism as a fairer, more efficient and more advanced mode of production. However, within just 70 years of the Russian Revolution, communist regimes around the world began to falter. The single most momentous event in this process came in 1989 when the Berlin Wall came down. A fascinating insight into life before and after the wall came down is provided by Wolfgang Becker's film *Goodbye Lenin!* (2003) The wall divided communist East Germany from capitalist West Germany and was a powerful symbol of the Cold War between the western and

eastern powers. Within a few years, the Soviet Union fragmented and new con-
stitutions based on market liberalism and pluralism were introduced in Russia, the
former Soviet republics and eastern European countries such as Poland, Rumania
and Hungary. East and West Germany were reunited. China too, though still
controlled by the communist party, has moved towards some of the key principles
of capitalism such as competition, profit making and a degree of free enterprise.
Where capitalism finds itself under threat in the modern world, the challenge is
more likely to come in the form of political movements that Marx abhorred:
nationalism and religious fundamentalism.

In view of the apparent demise of communism and the triumph of capitalism, why
should we bother with Marxism as a theoretical perspective? The main reason lies
in the explanatory power of Marx's ideas and the ways in which they have been
developed by those who have followed in Marx's footsteps. Marxism, as we shall
see, does not refer just to the ideas of Marx himself, but to a huge body of work
generated by numerous academics, theorists and revolutionaries who have
adapted and developed Marx's ideas. As we shall discover with our other theoretical perspectives, there is almost as much disagreement *within* the perspective
as there is between one perspective and another.

Marxism: the basics

Having filled in some historical and theoretical context, it is time for us to explore
in more depth the basis of Marx's critique of capitalism and the implications for
Communication and Culture. A fundamental principle of Marxism is that all social
institutions and cultural practices are shaped by economic factors. This means
that in order to understand, for example, the family or education or government
or the legal system, we must first comprehend the economic system or, as Marx
would term it, the mode of production.

INFORMATION BOX – THE BASE/ SUPERSTRUCTURE MODEL   *i*

This is really a way of understanding Marx's view of the relationship
between the economy (the base) and the social/cultural sphere such as
family, politics and law (the superstructure). It's rather like a house in which
the foundations (the base) are invisible, but without them the rest of the
house (the superstructure) would collapse. As David Oswell explains:

> In a capitalist mode of production, we would expect to see laws that
> supported the ownership and inheritance of private property and

---

capital, to see political structures that helped to keep in place the embedded power of the bourgeois class that owns capital and to see family forms that allowed the socialisation of offspring into particular classes and forms of labour.

(Oswell, 2006, pp. 158–9)

In Communication and Culture, we study phenomena that are found in the superstructure, but for Marxists we can only make sense of these if we understand their relationship to the forces of economic production; in other words, the base/superstructure relationship. This view – *economic determinism* – has been hotly debated in Marxist theory. Some writers in the Marxist tradition have questioned this iron rule that the mode of production determines everything else that goes on in society. In their view, it is sometimes justifiable to analyse cultural phenomena without reference to economic conditions.

The problem with economic determinism is that it denies the possibility that *anything* emerging from the superstructure has the capacity to change people's ideas or their behaviour. This rules out the possibility that cultural products such as films, plays or books or cultural practices such as demonstrations or political activity can play much of a role in historical change. The difficulties of this position have led many Marxist theorists to take a more relaxed view of the determining influence of the economic sphere on social change. The idea that some parts of the superstructure (i.e. culture) may be partially independent of the economic base is often referred to in Marxist theory as *relative autonomy*.

For Marxists, human beings have always organized themselves in order to extract what is needed from the environment in order to survive and prosper. Historically, modes of production have developed from the earliest forms of hunter/gatherer society (a sort of primitive communism) through societies based on slavery (like ancient Greece) to feudalism and then capitalism. Each stage is more sophisticated and more efficient than the one preceding it. In the section above, on market liberalism, we offered a working definition and account of capitalism which, you won't be surprised to learn, is rather different to the Marxist analysis. A Marxist account would be something like this:

In capitalist economies, one group of people (the ruling class or bourgeoisie) own the capital (money) to invest in factories, offices, machinery, new technology and land; in other words, almost all of the things necessary to produce wealth. The missing ingredient that the bourgeoisie need to produce wealth is the labour needed to create profitable products and services. Labour is owned by the second

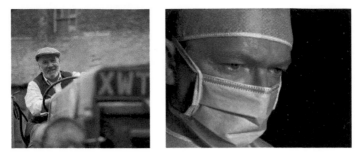

Figure 2.7 The working classes: anyone who sells their labour

(and much larger) group in society, the working class or proletariat. Labour may be physical or intellectual, skilled or unskilled, so that in Marxist terms the tractor driver, the neurosurgeon and the Premier League footballer are all members of the working class.

However much or however little workers are paid for their labour, there must always be a profit margin for the enterprise to flourish. Marx termed this the 'surplus value of labour', the proportion of labour's true value that is not returned to the worker but retained by the capitalist as profit. This fundamental difference in the material interests of the two classes is the crux of a Marxist analysis. It is in the interests of the bourgeoisie to pay as little as possible for labour whilst it is in the interests of the working class to receive the full value of their labour. This idea of a conflict of 'material interests' is discussed further in the next section, but it is important to understand that what Marx means by 'material' here is something that is real or tangible rather than 'illusory'. Workers may not realize that they are being exploited and members of the bourgeois class may not realize that they are being exploitative. However, the exploitation of labour is still in the 'material' interests of the capitalist but not in the material interest of the worker.

Another consequence of the capitalist exploitation of labour is what Marx called *alienation*. Although all workers contribute to the net worth of society, workers under capitalism fail to derive any of the psychological benefits of productive work. Instead of enjoying a sense of control, creativity and job satisfaction derived from their labours, most workers have a purely instrumental attitude to work; it is seen as a kind of 'necessary evil'. Marx identified four different types of alienation experienced by workers in a capitalist system:

1. Alienation from 'human essence'. This is the feeling of being no more than a very small cog in a huge machine.
2. Alienation between workers. Labour is a commodity to be bought and sold so individual workers find themselves in competition for jobs.
3. Alienation between workers and the process of production. Activity at work seems without meaning or purpose .

4. Alienation between workers and the products of their labour. Workers have little or no control over what they produce and hence feel no emotional attachment to their products. In factory production systems they may not even see the finished product.

For a further discussion of alienation and Marxist approaches to the links between production and consumption, see Chapter 6, Objects of Desire. For a more detailed definition of alienation, see: http://www.marxists.org/glossary/terms/a/l.htm

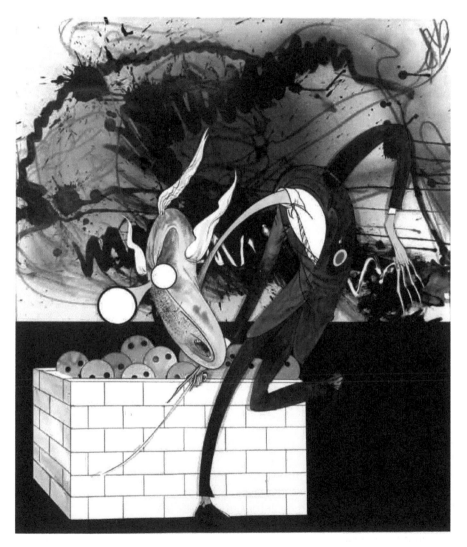

Figure 2.8 Pink Floyd's 1979 rock opera *The Wall*, especially the three songs entitled *Another Brick in the Wall*, alluded strongly to alienation. Gerald Scarfe's illustrations, here of *The Teacher*, reinforce the message

Whilst market liberals value the benefits of competition between companies, Marxists would suggest that there is just as much collaboration as genuine competition. Corporations may compete with each other to gain customers, but more significantly, they work together to ensure that the capitalist system remains intact. Far from working in the interests of the customer, big corporations operate in their own interests by swallowing up smaller competitors in takeovers or by merging with larger competitors to achieve efficiency savings. Instead of encouraging more and more competition, capitalism has seen the concentration of wealth and ownership in the hands of a small number of gigantic multinational corporations.

Marxism, ideology and the 'culture industries'

Ideology is one of the most important (and difficult!) of our A2 key concepts (see Chapter 3). In Marxist terms, though, ideology can be defined fairly simply. It consists of the lies, deceptions and misinformation peddled to the working classes in order to maintain the state of 'false consciousness' which prevents workers from seeing their true or material interests. This concept of false consciousness has proved to be rather vexed and controversial in Marxist theory. On one hand, Marxist revolutionaries may use the workers' false consciousness as a justification for all sorts of tactics to lift the working classes out of the apathy and lethargy which (from their point of view) prevent the proletariat from rising up against the bourgeoisie and seizing power. On the other hand, the concept seems to smack of condescension and a 'blame the victim' mentality. Is it really the case that working people don't revolt against the capitalist system simply because they have been so easily conned by the lies and spin of ruling class ideology? It does seem to be a rather patronizing view of how people are motivated to act.

ACTIVITY

Is Our Consciousness False?

Many Marxists believe that workers are kept in a state of 'false consciousness' by the strength and power of ruling class ideology. But what sort of widely held beliefs are deemed 'false' in this way? Weigh up the arguments for each of the following and see if you can add any of your own examples of so-called false consciousness.

- Some people are born to be bosses and some are born to be workers. We can't all be in charge! It's just the natural order of things.
- Anyone can succeed if they put their mind to it. It's a level playing field and those with the most drive will inevitably succeed.
- Society rewards talent. There are numerous outlets for our creativity. Fame comes to those who deserve it.
- Workers shouldn't be greedy. If they ask for too much pay others will find themselves out of a job.
- Don't rely too much on other people. It's your responsibility to look out for yourself in this world.
- I may win the lottery.

If bourgeois ideology is so powerful, how does it get distributed and who does this 'ideological work' on behalf of the ruling class? Marx himself argued that religion had a key role to play in this process; he described religion as the 'opiate of the people'. Contemporary Marxists are more likely to argue that the mass media have taken over from religion in performing this function. Put rather simplistically, their argument is that:

- the mass media are owned by the ruling class
- the mass media are used to indoctrinate the masses (the working class) into the belief that capitalism and its values are 'good for all'
- dissenting or oppositional voices are largely denied access to the media. Dominant ideology is presented as 'natural'.

In other words, the function of the mass media is not just to make money as an industry but also to serve the ideological interests of the ruling class. Ideology masks the conflict between classes and promotes the view that the inequalities and exploitation of capitalism are simply 'common sense' to which there is no alternative. By extension, we can see that it is not just those cultural products created by the institutions of the mass media that can be seen in this way; we can extend the analysis to *all* cultural products and cultural practices.

This idea that the mass media and systems of cultural production have done a great deal to prevent the collapse of capitalism predicted by Marx was developed by the theorists of the Frankfurt School. This group of intellectuals were active from the inception of the Frankfurt Institute for Social Research in 1923 and their work has been highly influential in Marxist approaches to culture in capitalist societies. Their approach to the ideological role of culture is characterized by Longhurst *et al.* as follows:

> **Through radio, TV, movies and forms of popular music like jazz, the expanding culture industries were disseminating ruling-class ideologies with greater effect than Marx could have envisaged. The further development of consumer society in the twentieth century powerfully aided the process of working-class incorporation by promoting new myths of classlessness, and wedded the working class even more tightly to acquisitive and property owning beliefs. Even oppositional and critical forms of culture can be marketed (consider Andy Warhol, the Sex Pistols and Damian Hurst).**

(Longhurst, Smith, Gaynor, Crawford and Ogborn, 2008, pp. 74–5)

At this stage, you may be reminded of some of your AS Level investigations into the relative values of popular and high culture. The Frankfurt School are (on the whole) highly dismissive of popular culture because they see the 'culture industry' and the products that it churns out as being little more than propaganda for capitalism. This approach leads Theodor Adorno, in particular, to make some damning indictments of popular culture. Listeners to pop music are 'infantile' and fans of the jitterbug dance craze were described as 'retarded', their dancing having 'convulsive aspects reminiscent of St Vitus' dance or the reflexes of mutilated animals' (Strinati, 1995, p. 67). It makes you wonder what he would have made of body popping!

The very fact that popular culture is neither difficult nor demanding and that it offers simple and direct pleasures contributes to its complicity in capitalist ideology. According to Adorno, we crave 'standardized' cultural products because they seem to validate lives that are themselves standardized. At work we are alienated by dull, repetitive and undemanding tasks, but this alienating effect is relieved by dull, repetitive and undemanding cultural products (like pop songs) and cultural pursuits (like dancing). Popular cultural products may seem to offer us freedom of choice and aid self-expression, but for Adorno, this is an illusion; a phenomenon he terms 'pseudo-individualization'. In singing along with a pop song or in recognizing a particular variation on a theme we enjoy the feeling that we are finding expression for our own individual emotions, but in reality we are simply imitating others. Our consumption of popular culture simply makes us docile, apathetic and passive, hence more susceptible to manipulation by ruling class ideology.

Critics of the Frankfurt School analysis of popular culture have argued that it is just too negative and too sweeping in its characterization of cultural products and cultural practices as 'tools of capitalism'. It is difficult to find evidence amongst today's consumers of popular culture of the unqualified *conformity* that Adorno and Horkheimer argued was responsible for adjusting us to the norms and values of the social system. It would be just as easy to find evidence of diversity, creativity and, even, resistance to dominant ideology in contemporary popular cultural pursuits. This is not to say that cultural practices have no ideological significance – far from it. Rather, the critics of the Frankfurt School, still working in a broadly Marxist tradition, have suggested a more subtle relationship between culture and ideology; one which recognizes the active role of consumers and users of cultural products in creating meanings. Another Frankfurt School theorist, Herbert Marcuse, is discussed in Chapter 6, Objects of Desire, with particular reference to consumerism. Useful material on the Frankfurt School can also be found in Dominic Strinati's *An Introduction to Theories of Popular Culture* (Strinati, 1995), Chapter Two and in John Storey's *Cultural Theory and Popular Culture, A Reader* (Storey, 1998).

In concluding this section we shall return to that rather fundamental distinction that Marxist theory draws between the economic sphere and the cultural sphere; between base and superstructure. In a recent contribution to the debate, Scott Lash and Celia Lury have suggested that this distinction needs to be re-examined in the light of changes in modes of capital accumulation (i.e. different ways of making money). Whilst broadly agreeing that the Frankfurt School analysis was useful and correct in the context of its time, they argue that circumstances have changed drastically since the mid-twentieth century and that we need to approach the economic/cultural relationship from a new angle.

> **Our point is that in 1945 and 1975 culture was still fundamentally a superstructure. As a superstructure, both domination and resistance took place in and through superstructures – through ideology, through symbols, through representation. When culture was primarily superstructural, cultural entities were still exceptional. What was mostly encountered in everyday life were**

material objects (goods), from the economic infrastructure. [. . .] [In] 2005, cultural objects are everywhere; as information, as communications, as branded products, as financial services, as media products, as transport and leisure services, cultural entities are no longer the exception: they are the rule. **"**

(Lash and Lury, 2007, pp. 3–4)

Lash and Lury's argument, then, is that the emergence of a global culture industry has transformed the relationship between culture and economy. It is no longer the case that the industry concentrates on the production of objects that can be sold and circulated as commodities. Rather, their efforts are invested in the production of brand identities such as Nike, Disney or Calvin Klein that can be attached to any number of products. The cultural sphere, previously characterized by its association with ideas, symbols and representations rather than tangible objects is now transformed as culture, in Scott and Lury's words 'becomes thingified'. In Chapters 6, 7 and 9 we shall examine some of the techniques used by the global culture industry to create brand identities and turn cultural products into 'things'.

Marxism: hegemony

The Italian writer, Antonio Gramsci (1891–1937) offers a useful slant on the idea that culture can be used as a means of social control to ensure that the ruling classes are able to hang on to their power. The process of incorporating the working class by winning their consent is called hegemony. Rather than relying on physical force (for example, the police or the army) dominant groups exercise control by persuading the proletariat that the form of social organization and power distribution under capitalism is actually in everybody's best interests. We could certainly think of many examples of the naked and aggressive use of force to crush demonstrations, strikes or uprisings, often followed up by exemplary punishments. But the use of force – the coercive state apparatus – is not necessarily efficient or effective. It can be an expensive business keeping a riotous population in order and the use of force is always likely to contribute to an escalation of violence. It is much better to secure the consent of subordinate groups by creating a consensus.

So far, these ideas may seem very similar to the ideas about ideology described above, but Gramsci's concept of hegemony is particularly useful in understanding how a ruling elite goes about the business of winning consent in order to exercise social control. In most societies, the dominant class (or 'ruling bloc', as Gramsci termed them) is likely to consist of a series of alliances between different groups with different agendas. These groups have to be welded together in order to present a united front to subordinate groups. From this point of view, culture is not just a means of winning the consent of subordinate groups, it also has a vital role in uniting the more or less disparate groups that make up the ruling bloc.

Figure 2.9 Antonio Gramsci, the Italian Communist leader spent many years in Mussolini's prisons, where he completed much of his theoretical work, compiled as *The Prison Notebooks* (Gramsci, 1971)

In Gramsci's conception, the dominant class is not like a huge and impregnable machine that efficiently snuffs out all opposition. Instead, the hegemonic bloc is a collection of groups and individuals in loose alliance. What is more, it is a group that undergoes perpetual change; some of its members are in the ascendency and some are in decline. At times of crisis, the group may well evict some of its members and forge new alliances with others who have previously been members of subordinate groups. For example, at the time of writing a constitutional crisis is emerging as revelations about MP's expenses appear in the media every day. Recently, bonuses and pensions paid to senior figures in the City of London have also attracted a good deal of critical attention. In both cases, it seems likely that individuals will be 'made an example of', pilloried in the press and cast out of the corridors of power. They will be replaced by others, possibly others who have formally been seen as outsiders or 'not one of us' by the political and financial establishment. In this way, the ruling bloc is engaged in a constant process of renewal, forever engaged in a kind of ideological warfare with oppositional groups. As in a military war, there are advances and retreats, battles won and battles lost, alliances made and alliances broken. The objective of this struggle is hegemony, but it is a goal that is ultimately unachievable. Whilst the ruling bloc constantly seeks domination, there will always be opposition and struggle. From our point of view, the interesting aspect of this analysis is that much of this struggle takes place in the cultural sphere.

The concept of hegemony, then, gives us a useful tool in the understanding of cultural practices. Instead of seeing evidence for monolithic (i.e. massive and invulnerable) ruling class ideology at work, we can see culture as a site of struggle. The mass media, for example, simply do not suppress all views and opinions from subordinate groups, though it may be fair to say that such views receive less coverage than mainstream views. This is a theory that can help explain how battles over ideas can result in important social change, even though the underlying power structure of society remains intact. Examples of battles that have been won in spite of opposition from the ruling bloc include equal pay legislation, the minimum wage, the decline of racist and sexist stereotypes in the media and, in America, the President's renunciation of the use of torture by the CIA.

Bearing in mind that 'hegemonic struggle' does not always imply victory for the dominant and most powerful, we could also find evidence of such struggles in, for example, popular music and film, in social networking and supermarket developments.

ACTIVITY

Planning Disputes

Read the following extract from the *Colchester Gazette*:

Colchester: Delight at Tesco plans' defeat

9:20am Monday 27th October 2008

Comments (5) Have your say »

By Gareth Palmer »

RESIDENTS are claiming victory after plans for another Tesco Express in Colchester were rejected.

More than 700 signatures were collected on a petition opposing the proposed store on the site of Cherry Tree Garage in Mersea Road.

Residents had raised concerns about the extra traffic and antisocial behaviour the shop would generate.

Ward councillor Dave Harris (Lab, Berechurch) described the scheme's rejection by Colchester Council as 'superb news'.

'All the points raised by local people about this not being the right place for a supermarket were recognized and agreed with by the planning officers', he said.

The planning officers rejected the application because it went against policy.

Tesco had proposed building seven two-bed flats in a three-storey block and six two-bed houses alongside the shop.

A Tesco spokesman said: 'We are disappointed and will be reviewing our options.'

Source: http://www.gazette-news.co.uk/news/3792576.Colchester Delight_at_Tesco_plans_defeat/

- How helpful is hegemony theory in understanding this dispute.
- Using an Internet search, research more examples of planning disputes involving supermarkets. What are the underlying issues? How are they usually resolved?
- Can you think of other examples of 'hegemonic struggles' in areas of popular culture?

Marxism: Louis Althusser

Louis Althusser (1918–90) is another Marxist theorist who moved away from the idea that the economy is the 'bottom line' in all explanations of society and culture. According to Althusser, the mass media and other Ideological State Apparatuses play a key role in constituting individuals as subjects. The 'subjects' referred to here are all of us. We are 'brought into being' by ideology. In this sense, ideology is not just a type of information that is transmitted to us in various ways, it is everything that we do and say. We don't *receive* ideology, we do it, live it and breathe it.

In Althusser's view, the idea that we are free agents, capable of independent thought and decision-making, is simply an illusion. More accurately, we are the manifestations or 'effects' of ideology. We are brought into being by discourse (the ways in which we are addressed) in a process that Althusser describes as 'hailing' or interpellation. For example, we are constantly 'hailed' by advertisements that invite us to share the 'normality' of coveting objects that we are encouraged to buy, looking forward to the promises that they will fulfil.

We are addressed in different ways depending on, among other things, our class position, age, gender and ethnicity. In consequence, the 'subjects' that we become are not unified and whole but fragmented. The success of ideology lies in its invisibility; we are

Figure 2.10 'Hey. You!' Ideology constitutes us as subjects by 'hailing'

unaware of its very existence. Unfortunately, this raises the rather obvious question that, if ideology is so good at disguising its very existence, how would we get to know it is here? Unlike Gramsci, Althusser doesn't really deal with the possibility that subordinated or oppositional groups may be able to develop their own ideological positions.

Feminism

Moving from Marxism to feminism, it is worth reiterating our characterization of theoretical perspectives as 'ways of seeing', because it is clearly not the case that feminism is a profoundly alternative way of seeing to Marxism. Many feminists share at least some of the theoretical principles outlined in our account of Marxism and, like Marxists, most would see the purpose of theoretical analysis as a stepping stone towards social change.

As a political project that actively seeks social change, the objectives of feminism can be identified straightforwardly: equality between men and women in all walks of life and an end to injustices based on sexism. These aspirations are not confined to individuals or groups who have actively engaged in political struggles, such as the Suffragettes. Additionally, not all feminists have agreed on exactly what constitutes inequality and injustice or on the means of overcoming them, but in terms of a set of values and normative claims (i.e. claims about how society *should* be), equality is at the heart of feminist core beliefs.

As well as this normative aspect feminism is also deeply concerned with the description and analysis of women's disadvantage, both historically and in contemporary society. In other words, feminism as a theoretical perspective seeks to explain and illustrate inequality in order, ultimately, to liberate women from it.

PATRIARCHY: A social system in which men dominate. Women are systematically disadvantaged.

Sex and gender

In hierarchically ordered societies (and nearly all societies are hierarchically ordered) men are invariably more dominant, with power and status skewed in favour of males. Furthermore, this imbalance is supported by a set of assumptions about the supposedly natural roles of men and women. Feminism makes a crucial contribution to the study of culture by identifying and analysing these assumptions. Just what is meant by 'gender' in this context, and how is it different to sex? We could start by making a simple (or should that be *apparently* simple) distinction based on the difference between nature and culture. Sex is a matter of biological categorization based on chromosomes, hormones and the reproductive system. Gender, in contrast, is about the behaviour and attitudes that we learn to associate

Femininity	Masculinity
Caring	Tough
Nurturing	Providing
Emotional	Rational
Domestic, home-orientated	Public, work-orientated
Sensitive	Thick-skinned
Passive	Active
Gentle	Rough
Soft	Hard

Figure 2.11 Gender stereotypes

with biological males and biological females: masculinity and femininity. In other words, our sex (male or female) is determined at birth (or, more accurately, conception) but we still have to learn how to think and behave as a boy or girl according to the expectations of our culture. We are certainly interested in how these gender roles are communicated, how they change over time and how they differ between cultures and subcultures.

Primary socialization in the family and secondary socialization via education, the media and other institutions all contribute towards the moulding of gender identity. We are all familiar with the kind of gender stereotypes, often expressed as binary oppositions that mark out gendered identities. Figure 2.11 expresses just some of the contrasting stereotypes of masculinity and femininity.

ACTIVITY

Gender Roles

1. How are the properties of femininity and masculinity listed in Figure 2.11 reinforced? Can you think of examples from both primary and secondary socialization?
2. Looking at the same list, can you think of challenges or alternatives?
3. Can you add any more binary oppositions to this list?
4. Which cultures and subcultures are more accepting and which are less accepting of these stereotypical gender characteristics?

Figure 2.12 How much have gender stereotypes changed?

Although you may consider these characterizations of gender identity to be almost painfully old fashioned, your discussions in response to the activity will probably reveal that they are still familiar and widely circulated (though often challenged) by cultural practices and cultural products. Furthermore, it is easy to see how the contrasting gender characteristics identified here are linked to power. The list of masculine characteristics are also linked with influential roles, political or organizational leadership, higher status and well paid jobs. These are not just masculine attributes; they are often seen as the attributes of success in many types of work, especially those jobs that carry the highest pay and the highest status. In order to succeed, in these terms, many women have found themselves in situations where they feel that they must demonstrate attributes of masculinity in order to pursue careers, win promotions or succeed in job interviews. The stereotypically feminine qualities are similarly associated with certain occupational categories, but these are much more likely to be low status and poorly paid (or not paid at all); for example child care, nursing, teaching and domestic work.

Gender and the body

Your discussion in response to the activity above may well have concluded that many of the gender stereotypes listed in Figure 2.11 have been substantially eroded if not eradicated in recent years. If this is the case, it is largely due to the efforts of feminists battling against culturally ingrained inequalities. Some feminist writers, though, have suggested that the key site of struggle has moved away from the attribution of low-value qualities towards the visual presentation of the body. In an influential book, *The Beauty Myth*, Naomi Wolf wrote:

> **Beauty is a currency like the gold standard. Like any economy, it is determined by politics and in the modern age in the West, it is the last, best belief system that keeps male domination intact.**

(Wolf, 1991)

Wolf argues that contemporary cultural products are full of examples of a sustained patriarchal attack on women's bodies. Images of ultra-thin, 'size zero' models and the 'perfect bodies' glamorized by advertising, fashion and the cult of celebrity all contribute, she claims, to women's low self-esteem, mental and physical illness, starvation diets and eating disorders. Efrat Tseëlon in her work on the sociology of the body also reinforces this idea by analysing the 'no-win' situation in which dominant culture places women by imposing contradictory sets of expectations upon them. An example of this is the 'beauty paradox' wherein women signify beauty but do not embody body. In other words, a woman is supposed to represent timeless cultural fantasies of beauty, but is 'not more naturally attractive than a man. Her special beauty is at best a temporary state, and it takes hard work and concerted effort to maintain' (Tseëlon, 1995, p. 79).

The idea of the female body as an object to be presented for male pleasure was also explored by Laura Mulvey in a 1975 essay, 'Visual pleasure and narrative cinema' (Mulvey, 2003). She conceived the term 'male gaze' to communicate the idea that so many films assume that the spectator is male and/or construct reality from a masculine point of view. Her idea was that the darkened cinema offered the perfect opportunity for the male viewer to drool over the erotic exhibition of women's bodies on the screen. Because female characters are largely insignificant in narrative terms, female viewers also identify with the male protagonist, enjoying the spectacle of women through his eyes. (See Chapter 5 for further discussion of narrative.) This idea, that the products of popular culture encourage women to look critically at themselves, as if through the eyes of men, was also developed by Angela McRobbie in relation to girls' magazines. In a 1979 essay on *Jackie* magazine, McRobbie argued that the magazine helped to reinforce an obsession with romance:

> **The Jackie girl is alone in her quest for love; she refers back to her female peers for advice, comfort and reassurance only when she needs to do so or when she has nothing better to do. [. . .] To achieve self-respect, the girl has to escape the 'bitchy', 'catty' atmosphere of female company and find a boyfriend as quickly as possible. But in doing this she cannot slide into complacency. Her ruthlessly individualistic outlook must be retained in case she has to fight to keep him.**

(McRobbie, 1991, p. 131)

Figure 2.13 *Jackie* magazine (1964–93). In its heyday, *Jackie* sold over a million copies a week

ACTIVITY

Positioning Women in Popular Culture

Both Mulvey and McRobbie found good reasons to modify their views in more recent years, but do you agree with the basic premise that cultural products position women to see themselves through a 'male gaze'?

Do you think that men's bodies are just as likely as women's to be objectified in contemporary culture?

Carry out some of your own research on girls' comics and magazines (perhaps by interviewing people of your parents' generation). What significant changes have there been in the representations of gender?

Read the extract (below) from David Gauntlett's *Media, Gender and Identity*. Do you agree with his optimistic argument that the battle for equality in gender representation has, more or less, been won? Do you think that women needed to be shown 'how to be sexy at work'?

> Men and women are seen working side by side as equals, in the hospitals, schools and police stations of television land. Movie producers are wary of having women as screaming victims, and have realised that audiences will only laugh at images of the pretty housewife, and have reacted by showing women how to be sexy at work instead.

(Gauntlett, 2002, p. 57)

INFORMATION BOX – THE WAVES OF FEMINISM

First Wave

From the mid-nineteenth to early twentieth century feminist activism was focused on the fight for social and political equality. The struggle for women's suffrage was particularly hard fought. The right of all adult women in Britain to vote was won in 1928.

Second Wave

This movement of the 1960s and 1970s focused on the struggle for equal pay, equal rights at work and equal representation in political bodies as well as liberation from male oppression. Issues such as abortion, rape, domestic violence and child care were also important concerns of second wave feminists. The slogan 'The Personal is Political' aptly sums up the battles against sexism in the home and family as well as in the public sphere. The movement staged some spectacular protests at beauty contests, including Miss World, in order to draw attention to the objectification of women's bodies.

Third Wave

Feminists from the 1980s to the present have put less emphasis on battles for equality and more emphasis on the positive nature of ambiguity, difference and individualism. Key concerns of the movement include body image, reproductive control, sexual harassment, violence against women and the politics of transgender sexuality. Third wave feminists have also tackled some of the negative and derisory stereotypes attached to the label 'feminist', e.g. 'man-hating', 'bra-burning', 'joyless'.

The Riot Grrrl movement of the 1990s brought together the ideas of third wave feminism with punk values and anti-corporatism.

Postfeminism

This is the 'backlash to feminism' that began in reaction to second wave feminism and which attempted to redefine the women's movement. Postfeminism endorses consumerism and celebrates the idea of a powerful woman who no longer needs movements or collective action to establish her rights or her equality with men. As Alison Piepmeier puts it:

> While the third wave says, 'We've got a hell of a lot of work to do!' postfeminism says 'Go buy some Manolo Blahniks and stop whining.'
>
> (Piepmeier, 2006)

To acknowledge that many advances and improvements have been made in terms of equality is not necessarily to say that the battle is over. Recent debates within feminism have focused on the amount of progress that has been made and what still needs to be achieved. Some feminists, especially those with links to second wave feminism, have argued that many inequalities in work and pay still need to be overcome, and that representations of strong, assertive women are often little more than marketing ploys.

For example, independent, powerful and attractive female role models have become commonplace in car advertisements, but is this just to exploit a growing market of female consumers (see Kim Cattrall advertising as an example of this. Source: http://www.theage.com.au/ffximage/2006/03/22/MHfem.jpg)

Postfeminists, on the other hand, may well take a different position on representations such as these. What is wrong, they argue, with women expressing themselves in any number of different ways, whether buying cars, clothes, make-up or anything else? If men can have creative fun with the products of consumer capitalism and popular culture, then why can't women do the same thing without being accused of being the dupes of patriarchy? If women *know* that femininity is just a construct, then they can play with its signs, symbols and identities from a position of power. This is the territory of semiotic guerrilla warfare and postmodern irony, where the meanings attached to signifiers such as high heels, lipstick or designer handbags can be shifted from powerless to powerful.

Queer theory

In the introduction to Feminism we looked at the contrast between sex (biological differences) and gender (culturally learned difference). The premises on which this distinction is based are rejected by Queer Theory. Queer Theory offers the view that the ideas of 'male' and 'female' are just as much the product of representation as masculinity and femininity. Although the word queer has been deliberately appropriated in order to corrupt its negative connotations, Queer Theory does not concern itself exclusively with homosexuality; it is about all forms of identity, specially those linked to sexuality.

Like feminism, Queer Theory is a political and cultural project: one that wants to change the world as well as analyse it. Queer Theory is heavily influenced by Judith Butler's book *Gender Trouble* (1990), the title of which gives some indication of the theory's key objective: to break the link between the categories of 'sex' and 'gender' so that all forms of sexual identity can be accepted and celebrated. In order to do this Queer Theory attacks the binary oppositions that underlie many traditional ideas about sexuality, for example:

- Man : Woman
- Active : Passive
- Gay : Straight.

Butler rejects the idea that any of us has an innate sexual identity, one that is bestowed on us by our chromosomes. Instead she focuses on *performance* and in particular the normalizing effects of repeated performances and representations of heterosexuality that serve to create the illusion that heterosexuality is not only 'normal', but right. On the other hand, performances of alternatives to mainstream heterosexuality such as drag queens, 'butch' lesbians, 'camp' gays and macho gays have the capacity to denaturalize dominant heterosexual ideology.

Case Study
TRANSAMERICA (DIR. DUNCAN TUCKER, 2005)

Bree Osbourne (played by Felicity Hoffman of *Desperate Housewives* fame) is on the point of sex realignment surgery when she discovers that she has a 17-year-old son, Toby (Kevin Zegers). Bree (formerly Stanley) flies from Los Angeles to New York on order to bail Toby, who she finds is a small-time drug dealer and bisexual rent boy. Rather than reveal her true identity, Bree pretends to be a Christian missionary worker. The pair set off, by car, to Kentucky where Bree hopes to reunite Toby with his stepfather. This plan fails when it turns out that Toby has suffered sexual abuse as a child at the hands of his stepfather.

The pair head off for California together, their journey interrupted by Bree's traumatic reunion with her parents and Toby's discovery first, that Bree is a transsexual and second, that Bree (Stanley) is his father.

The film has all the features of a classic road movie with the added ingredients of Bree's (and Toby's) sexuality to complicate their journeys of self-discovery. The characters they encounter are variously open or close-minded about the many ambiguities of sexual identity. Those, like Bree's mother, who find it hardest to cope with anything outside their normal frame of reference are also shown to be highly unusual, if not eccentric, in other ways. Ultimately, the film's message is that there is no 'normal', just different performances of different identities. It's also very funny. (For a more detailed review see http://www.bfi.org.uk/sightandsound/review/3200)

Figure 2.14 Film poster for *Transamerica* (dir. Duncan Tucker, 2005)

The objective of Queer Theory is to challenge and undermine the labels and categories which dominant value systems use to 'pin down' identity, including sexual identity. Identity, Queer Theory suggests, is fluid, shifting and dynamic. None of us is completely 'man' or completely 'woman' and the same could be said of many other categories particularly in areas such as health and illness, ability and disability. So does Queer Theory have a useful role in the understanding of contemporary communication and culture? It certainly offers us some useful angles and lines of enquiry when we look at representation and identity in cultural practices and cultural products. You could argue that there is plenty of evidence of 'gender trouble' everywhere in the cultural landscape: gender-bending pop performers and youth subcultures, advertisements that toy with ideas of transgressive sexuality such as sadomasochism, celebrities who acknowledge their bisexuality and so on. The presence of a gay or lesbian character in television or film drama is no longer, necessarily, a plot device or an exercise in self-evident tokenism. (A 'token' character, in this context, would simply represent the liberal values of the programme-maker and little else.) The unambiguously 'all man' or 'all woman' celebrity persona is becoming the exception rather than the rule.

In spite of these examples, we should be cautious in drawing too many conclusions. As David Gauntlett notes, 'there remains a great deal of scope for the mass media to be much more challenging in these areas' (Gauntlett, 2002, p. 254). Queer Theory would suggest that the trends described above signify a move towards increasing tolerance of sexual diversity. But is this the case? Some have argued that representations such as these simply present titillating alternatives to the norm of heterosexuality, used for shock value not because of any desire to promote or celebrate diversity. This line of thinking suggests that alternatives to mainstream sexuality are represented only to show us where the line is; a line we should not cross. Proponents of this side of the argument might point to the ease with which drag and camp have been incorporated into mainstream culture, blunting any alternative 'edge' they may once have had. Does anyone think that the pantomime dame or the camp game show host on television does very much to subvert gender categories?

ACTIVITY

- Starting with your own analysis of the changing uses of the word 'gay' explore the ways in which popular cultural practices police the boundaries between gender categories.
- Draw up and discuss a list of celebrities whose sexual identity could be described as 'fluid' or unfixed.

Like most theories, Queer Theory doesn't provide all the answers but it does open up new ideas and, inevitably, new conflicts and debates.

Semiotics and structuralism

This section is a reminder, a consolidation and a development of one of the theoretical approaches that you encountered in AS Communication and Culture as a component of your Toolkits for the analysis of texts: semiotics. We would urge you not to ignore this section simply because neither semiotics nor structuralism appears in the specification in the list of Unit 3 theories. This is because an understanding of all of the critical theories that are listed relies, to a greater or lesser extent, on a familiarity with semiotics. What we shall attempt to do here is to refine your ability to use the semiotic toolkit and also to locate this analytical approach within the broader perspective of structuralism.

Semiotics deals with the production of meaning; an issue that is right at the heart of Communication and Culture. From day one of your AS course right through until your final A2 exam answer, you will be dealing with how texts create meanings. The text in question may be the tee shirt you're wearing, the latest James Bond movie or the Angel of the North but we are always interested in the same thing: *what does it mean*?

Language and codes

A perfectly sensible view of this tricky issue of meaning-making would go as follows. I am the writer of this sentence, therefore I put the meaning into it and you, the reader, take the meaning out of it. However, semiotics does not see things quite in this way. Texts (and here we must include all cultural products and cultural practices) are complex messages made up of *signs*. Semiotics is the science of understanding how signs work and how meaning emerges from the relationship between sender and receiver.

The person most usually cited as the founder of semiotics is the Swiss linguist Ferdinand de Saussure (1857–1913). Saussure showed that a language (like English or Spanish) is more than just a collection of words and sounds: it is a complex system in which all the components are defined by the way they relate to other components. In a simple example, the meaning of the word *tiny* can only be understood in relation to other words in the same area of meaning: not *big*, smaller than *small*, not quite as small as *minuscule*, and so on. Language, then, is a complicated structure; hence *structuralism*.

Semiotics may be based on the study of language, and it certainly derives many of its key concepts from de Saussure's ground-breaking work on language, but it is not *confined* to language. This is evident in the use of expressions like the 'the grammar of film' or 'the language of television'. Film, television, dress and appearance, ritual behaviour, spaces and places are all seen as meaning systems that work in very similar ways to language.

We are going to refer you back, now, to an important part of the AS that we covered in Chapter 2 of our *Essential Introduction*: Codes. (If you have the time, it would be useful to revisit the whole of the chapter at this stage.)

> **A code is a system of communication which requires three elements:**
>
> - **Signs. Anything that expresses a meaning, for example, a written word, a gesture or a cultural product such as an MP3 player.**
> - **Rules. Signs are nearly always used in combination with other signs to create complex meanings. However, they are not put together randomly but in accordance with underlying principles. For a language such as English we would call these rules a grammar.**
> - **Shared understanding. A code only works if a group of people share the knowledge and understanding of rules and signs. All cultures are based on the shared understanding of codes.**

(Bennett and Slater, 2008, p. 25)

Figure 2.15 Codes are based on shared understanding

Simply put, then, language is a code which consists of signs (words) and a set of rules (grammar). Semiotics applies the same model to all kinds of communication. For example, television includes signs such as:

- type of shot
- setting
- graphics
- camera movement
- music.

Television also draws upon a set of rules about how to assemble these signs into meaningful texts such as sequences, trailers, sitcoms or the tv news. In just the same way as we assimilate the codes of language as we grow up, we also assimilate the codes of television. We could say just the same of non-verbal communication. It too has its signs and its rules. As we grow up, we learn the non-verbal codes of our culture.

You should now refer to Chapter 4 of *The Essential Introduction to AS Communication and Culture* and re-familiarize yourself with the semiotic toolkit. Make sure that you are confident in the use and application of the following before going on:

- Signifier/Signified
- Denotation and Connotation
- Myth
- Ideology (as an order of signification)
- Paradigm and Syntagm
- Anchorage and Relay
- Motivation
- Icon/Index/Symbol

Refreshed and invigorated after plunging back into the world of semiotics, you are ready for your next challenge: structuralism.

Structuralism

As noted above, this approach owes a good deal to de Saussure's work on language. We have seen how language and other systems of communication rely on a shared understanding of a set of rules; even though the users of these systems may not be consciously aware of the existence of these rules. Because of this 'unawareness', linguists have had to find other methods for finding out how the rules work instead of just asking language users. The principal method has been the very close observation and recording of what people actually say. This is referred to as the *surface structure* of speech. Having collected enough evidence of surface structures, linguists are able to work out the underlying rules that are being applied (albeit unconsciously) by native speakers. These are the *deep structures*.

Structuralists take the same approach to other forms of communication. By looking very closely at, say, a film genre or young people dancing in a night club, structuralists would claim to be able to work out the deep structures: the under-lying principles guiding the production of meaning. Exactly as the case would be with language, it would come as no surprise to find that none of the participants (i.e. film makers, film viewers, dancers) were particularly aware of these deep structures.

It seems perfectly sensible to argue that language is a wholly cultural phenomenon. Why else would kids in France grow up to speak French and kids in Portugal grow up to speak Portuguese? We would expect a similar pattern for other codes of communication, so that only those who grow up with the full repertoire of, say, non-verbal behaviour in southern Italy or Bollywood films in India, will ever fully understand these complex codes. This view, sometimes referred to as *cultural relativism*, is not entirely shared by structuralists. The American linguist Noam Chomsky argues that all children have an innate capacity to learn language. He calls this a Language Acquisition Device. It is as if all humans are hard-wired like a new computer, ready to accept the software of the particular language that they are exposed to as they grow up. This has led structuralist linguists to search for the *universals* of language: deep structure features that are common to all human languages.

Figure 2.16 Just like an iceberg, the surface structures of language are supported by an awful lot of deep structures

In a similar sort of endeavour, the anthropologist Claude Lévi-Strauss (born Belgium, 1908) searched for principles held in common by all cultures and myths. A myth, you will recall, is a chain of connotations; a component in a culture's belief system. The idea of myth is dealt with in more detail in Chapter 5, Fictions. It is definitely a concept with which you should be familiar even if you do not choose Fictions as one of your specialist study areas for COMM3. Following Lévi-Strauss, structuralists have searched for the deep structures in narratives and stories, using versions of the binary opposition. Examples of binary opposites include:

Culture : Nature

Man : Woman

Interior : Exterior

Good : Evil

A structuralist analysis of a cultural product or cultural practice would examine the ways in which tensions between these (and other) oppositions are introduced, developed and resolved in cultural texts.

Structuralism was highly influential in the in the 1960s and 1970s and became closely associated with some variants of Marxism such as those developed by Louis Althusser (see above) and with the semiotic tradition developed from Saussure's work on language. More recently, though, the search for deep structures that are universal to all cultures has stimulated less interest than more relativist perspectives (see Information Box) such as poststructuralism.

INFORMATION BOX – CULTURAL RELATIVISM　*i*

This is the idea that all of our perceptions of the world are filtered through our culture. As cultures are different, so our perceptions are different. However, relativists make no value judgements about culture: none is superior or inferior to any other. This means that no way of seeing the world is any better or any worse than another, just different. For relativists, there are no absolute truths or certainties, only the taken for granted assumptions of each different culture.

Opponents of cultural relativism are likely to criticize this approach because they say that there *are* absolute, fundamental and incontrovertible truths, whether in science (e.g. water always boils at 100 degrees) or in politics; for example the idea of universal human rights.

A problem for relativists is that when they say, 'There are no truths, all things are relative', their critics reply, 'Really? It sounds as though you have just asserted an absolute truth, even though you say such things don't exist.' Don't think about it for too long!

Poststructuralism

Poststructuralists, as we have noted, are not at all interested in finding the underlying principles that the structuralists seek to discover in all acts of communication. They do not accept the basic idea of deep structures or of universals that are common to all cultures. The search for any fixed and coherent meaning in a text is pointless, they argue, because meaning just cannot be pinned down in this way. As Rob Pope puts it:

> **Whereas a structuralist approach would tend to treat a sign-system as a complete, finished, knowable whole with a notional centre, a *post*structuralist approach would tend to treat a sign-system as an incomplete, unfinished and ultimately unknowable fragment with many potential centres or no centres at all.**

(Pope, 1998, p. 124)

How can we begin to apply anything resembling a poststructuralist analysis in our approaches to texts? We must give up the idea that any text has a stable meaning. Rather, we must cope with the notion that the text is generating multiple meanings and, to make things even more difficult, these meanings are both temporary and in a constant state of flux. It's a bit like trying to catch fish with your bare hands; the very act of grasping for a meaning makes that meaning even more slippery and more likely to slide out of your clutch. Within a poststructuralist analysis, the focus is shifted away from the underlying meaning of a text towards the many possible interpretations of the text.

The analytical technique used by poststructuralists is called *deconstruction*, but texts are not deconstructed or 'taken apart' in order to find the 'real' meaning. The purpose of deconstruction is to explore the assumptions made by the text: 'How does this text think I may interpret it?' In this form of analysis, the intentions of the creator of the text count for very little (hence the expression 'death of the author'). In the classic (structuralist) formulation of semiotics, the Sign comprises the Signifier (the physical form of the sign, like the words printed on the page of this book) and the Signified (the mental construct or the ideas in your head that are triggered by these signifiers). The signifier and signified have been likened to the two sides of the same coin; you can't have one without the other. Poststructuralists do not see the connection between sign, signifier and signified in quite the same way at all. Jacques Derrida (1930–2004), one of the principal theorists of poststructuralism, refers to the 'freeplay' of signifiers in which signifiers are never firmly attached to a signified, but keep pointing to more signifiers. In a similar vein, poststructuralists observe that almost any referent or any signified can be temporarily attached to a signifier, leading to the concept of 'floating signifier'; a sign that has a physical form but no identifiable or fixed meaning.

Figure 2.17 Deconstruction for Beginners is the title of a mission in GTA4. It has nothing to do with deconstruction in the poststructuralists' sense, except that we have used it in this chapter, therefore temporarily assigning a new signified to this signifier

A deconstructive approach involves a consideration of what is absent from a text. This means that in the deconstruction of a text, whether it's a shopping centre or a television advertisement, we should be thinking about the missing elements; the *possible* components that have been left out. This can certainly be useful in looking at images containing groups of people, for example, as it prompts us to ask who has been excluded as well as who has been included.

Another technique of deconstruction is called foregrounding. This means moving the apparently trivial or insignificant components of the text from the background to the centre of the stage. This helps to establish what may have been taken for granted by a text as our attention is drawn away from the carefully constructed foreground and towards the more unconsidered detail that is almost (but not quite) hidden from view. These absences, gaps, silences and marginal elements can help to reveal who or what is being privileged by the text. For example, West may be privileged over East, man over woman, science over nature, language over pictures or writing over speech. At its best, poststructuralism can offer powerful insights into imperialist or patriarchal discourses. At its worst, it can seem like a futile hunt for elusive meanings.

Many poststructuralist ideas are remote and difficult to grasp. Derrida, for example, argued that words are inadequate because they are so difficult to pin down. His published works include many examples of words that have been crossed out or struck through to show this frailty and indeterminacy of meaning. Derrida certainly had his critics, some of whom, like Michel Foucault and Noam Chomsky, suggested that he deliberately expressed his ideas in as obscure a form as possible. However, for us as students of communication and culture, the idea that meaning can be shifting, uncertain and contingent upon different cultures is a useful one in some circumstances. It is an idea that certainly has implications for the sense of self or identity that is an important aspect of our studies. If we define ourselves by the language we use, the cultural products we consume and the cultural practices in which we participate, then our identities, too, must be as shifting and uncertain as the signifiers of our culture. Much as we might search for reliable signposts and solid landmarks to tell us where we are and who we are, we find only unreliable signifiers that tell us, 'You could be anywhere. You could be anyone'. Only if we are prepared to suspend disbelief in our culture can we regain the reassurance of (apparently) fixed meanings about the world, or lives and ourselves. It's a bit like having to forget that what you are watching is only a film if you want to enjoy the film.

Postmodernism

One of the attractions of postmodernism to many students is that it celebrates the fact that it is not so much a theory as an anti-theory; an approach that dismisses all other approaches as irrelevant. According to postmodernists (who, it should be said, share some common territory with poststructuralists) any theory that makes claims about universal or underlying truths is just missing the point. For them, the point is that modern culture is so fragmented, so diverse, so full of differences that no unified theory could possibly explain such a melting pot. Postmodernists are prone to describe other perspectives as metanarratives: all encompassing theories that can be applied in any situation at any time. Jean-François Lyotard (1924–98), in his 1979 book *The Postmodern Condition*, identified 'a crisis in the status of knowledge in western societies. This is expressed

Figure 2.18 Jean-François Lyotard, possibly rejecting a passing metanarrative

as "incredulity towards metanarratives" [. . .] This refers to the supposed contemporary rejection of all overarching and totalizing thought: Marxism, liberalism, Christianity, for example, that tell universalist stories' (Storey, 1997, p. 174).

And it isn't just the metanarrative that postmodernists have in their sights; they also tend to reject the idea of cultural value. You will, no doubt, remember all those discussions you had in the AS course about the 'popular culture debate', about which cultural products and practices are 'worthy of study' according to the likes of Matthew Arnold, the Leavises and T.S. Eliot, amongst others. The idea that some cultural products are, in any sense, *better* than others, is simply dismissed by postmodernists. Popular culture is no longer seen as the poor relation to high culture, but simply as another form of expression; rap music stands on a par with Shakespeare's sonnets. Bricolage (literally, French for 'do it yourself') is just as creative as any other art form and plundering the canon of 'great works' for ideas and inspiration is just playfully subversive.

We can see evidence everywhere of this bricolage and the recycling of ideas from the past: pop songs with sample riffs and licks from the 'classics' of popular and serious music, the instant nostalgia of television programmes like *Ashes to Ashes* and advertising's endless appropriation of visual and musical icons. Exactly the same sort of thing is at work in postmodern architecture where contemporary buildings may 'mix'n'match' various architectural styles from different periods (see Chapter 4, Spaces and Places).

Figure 2.19 In postmodern culture, images as familiar and famous as Edvard Munch's *The Scream* (1893) are appropriated for use in all sorts of situations, from entertainment to advertising

ACTIVITY

Postmodern Appropriation

Compile your own selection of examples of the postmodern sampling of music, visual art, film and architecture.

Using Internet image searches, see how many examples you can find of the sampling or appropriation of the following.

The Mona Lisa (Leonardo da Vinci)

Campbell's Tomato Soup Can (Andy Warhol)

The Laughing Cavalier (Frans Hals)

The Thinker (Auguste Rodin)

Sgt Pepper's Lonely Hearts Club Band (Album cover, Peter Blake)

The Austin Mini (Alec Issigonis, see Figure 2.20)

Figure 2.20 The Mini, a 'Design Classic'

Of course, the meanings attached to these samplings and borrowings from the past can be accepted, rejected or manipulated, often in the name of 'postmodern irony'. Lads' magazines, stand-up comedians, schlock films and homophobic rap artistes have all deflected criticism that they are being offensive and tasteless by claiming that their work should be interpreted in the spirit it is intended: a kind of 'postmodern chic'. This doesn't always cut much ice!

Concepts in postmodernism: style over substance

Postmodernism concerns itself primarily with surfaces rather than the 'hidden depths' of structuralism or psychoanalytical theory. Much of contemporary culture communicates this idea of *depthlessness*, like a film set that may appear to be three-dimensional but isn't. Often, a cultural product can *look as if* it is heavily weighted down with meaningful signifiers, but this is an impression given by the form rather than the content of the artefact. For example, it would be fairly easy to make a video in the style of, say, a German expressionist film, but without any meaningful content. The text looks very significant, but that is as far as it goes. For some analysts, the idea of 'style without content' would be a pretty damning criticism, but not for postmodernists. From their point of view, a mismatch between surface appearance and underlying reality doesn't matter in the slightest, because there is no underlying reality; the surface is all that matters. If you are asking the question 'What does it mean?', you have already missed the point because, as the saying has it, 'what you see is what you get'.

This 'style over substance' idea can also be applied to the postmodern identity. In this view, a person's surface appearance (their clothing, make-up, hairstyle, personal possessions and body adornments) neither mask or transmit that person's true identity because they *are* the true identity. Personal identity becomes a matter of surface appearance and therefore infinitely variable and changeable.

Concepts in postmodernism: hyperreality

One of the key figures in postmodern theory, Jean Baudrillard (1929–2007), suggested three principles for understanding contemporary reality:

- simulation
- implosion
- hyperreality.

For Baudrillard, we live in an era of *media saturation* in which we are bombarded with information and signs. So much of our experience is in the form of media texts rather than first-hand direct experience that mediated signs become 'more real than reality itself'. This is *simulation*: the part of our lives that is dominated by computer games, television, social networking on the Internet, magazines and all

Figure 2.21 A trip to Paris: reality or hyperreality?

other forms of media experience. For many of us, this is a very big part of our lives; maybe the biggest and most important. Consequently, Baudrillard argues, the distinction between reality and simulation breaks down altogether: we make no distinction between the direct reality that we experience first hand and the simulated experience offered by media. This is *implosion*. Finally, we may get to the stage where the difference between reality and mediated experience hasn't just got blurred, the 'image' part has got the upper hand; this is *hyperreality*.

Here is an example that may help to explain the rather baffling concept of hyperreality. Let's imagine that I have never visited Paris. In spite of this I have a huge fund of impressions based on simulations of Paris that I have seen in films or television, usually to the accompaniment of accordion music. I have looked at magazines, travel brochures and my friends' holiday snaps. I have read about the food, the entertainment and the nightlife. This simulated Paris that I know so well is a lively, exciting and sophisticated place. One day, I decide to visit Paris – the real Paris – for the first time. When I get there it is cold and raining, my hotel room is cramped and dirty, nobody is very friendly and I get ripped off in a restaurant. Now I have a fund of rather negative 'real' experiences to add to my very positive simulated experiences. Which of these will win out in my overall perception of Paris? If Baudrillard is right, the two sets of impressions will merge together; they will implode. However, the set of perceptions based on my earlier simulated experience will be just a bit more powerful than my later direct experience. My Paris is hyperreal.

Concepts in postmodernism: playfulness

Taking ideas, styles and designs and playing around with them is one of the hallmarks of postmodernism, particularly in such disciplines as architecture where postmodern buildings are recognizable for their witty designs. Similarly, postmodern novels and films deal extensively with parody and pastiche and certainly like to play around with audience expectations of narrative (for example, by confusing us with sequences out of conventional time order) and genre (for example by mixing several genre categories together, otherwise known as *hybridity*).

An example of the first technique is *Pulp Fiction* (dir. Quentin Tarantino, 1994), whilst *Shaun of the Dead* (dir. Edgar Wright, 2004) is a hybrid, described on its release as a RomComZom.

Optimistic and pessimistic postmodernism

This can be a useful distinction in discussions of postmodernism. Optimistic postmodernism embraces the enormous range of diversity in contemporary culture without finding the need to analyse and explain. It celebrates pleasure and playfulness and the debunking of traditional 'rules' about how we should behave or what we should like. Optimistic postmodernists will approvingly recognize a 'postmodern turn' in arts and culture, so that postmodern film and postmodern architecture, for example, are recognizable and distinctive styles.

Pessimistic postmodernists, on the other hand, are more likely to see postmodernism as a way of characterizing contemporary society and culture as a whole. They focus on the breakdown of meaning and the domination of simulation. Critics of postmodernism are scornful of the ways in which postmodernists seem to sidestep or ignore issues of material inequality, poverty and deprivation.

Post-colonialism

Though the term post-colonialism embraces a wide range of theoretical and practical approaches, all of these are linked by an understanding of the continuing impact of the colonial experience on contemporary culture. Colonialism itself is a product of imperialism, so we shall start our exploration of this area with a brief consideration of imperialism.

Most European countries, including Britain, have a history of military imperialism. They attempted to build their empires by the conquest of less developed countries across the globe and imposed their rule upon them, usually to ensure a supply of cheap raw materials to help support the development of European economies. A most notorious aspect of imperialism was the slave trade. Africans were forcibly shipped to the Americas to be sold to plantation owners; a practice which was not abolished until the early part of the nineteenth century. The wealth of many British cities, including London, Liverpool, Bristol and Glasgow, was built on the 'triangular trade' in which slaves were bartered for sugar, tobacco and cotton. The legacy of this wealth is still visible today in many of the opulent buildings of these cities, but it is an aspect of British history that was unacknowledged for many years. This is no longer the case as cities such as Liverpool now play an important role in representing the history of slavery, for example in the International Slavery Museum. Source: (http://www.liverpoolmuseums.org.uk/ism/)

The demise of the Atlantic slave trade did not, of course, signal the end of imperialism. In fact, the major conquests of European imperialism only began as the slave trade came to an end. Britain's empire reached its peak, in terms of territory, in 1924 when it amounted to nearly a third of the world's territory. This was the empire on which 'the sun never set', including India, Jamaica, South Africa, Egypt, Ireland and Australia. It held a powerful grip on the British national consciousness, particularly the upper classes, who convinced themselves that the interests of Britain, the Empire and God amounted to more or less the same thing. The empire began to fall apart in the period after the Second World War as most of the colonies successfully fought for independence, kicked out the British rulers and set up their own governments. The same process, often painful, occurred in the colonies of other European powers including France, Portugal, Holland and Belgium. However, the influence of the former colonial powers, including Britain, still lingers on in the cultures of the former colonies. A most obvious example is the English language, but there are many other legacies of imperialism in politics, migration, sport, architecture, music and other forms of entertainment. In addition, the time of direct political rule may be over, but the former colonial powers have maintained and even strengthened their economic hold over countries that once were colonized. Although we could interpret postcolonialism as simply a label for 'the period that came after colonialism', Simon Featherstone warns that this would be a misleading approach:

> **Embedded in this 'post' is a notion of colonialism coming to an end and being superseded by another set of political and cultural practices. The implicitly neat break between the colonial and the postcolonial consequently threatens to elide both the often lengthy transitional periods of change and struggle between colony and 'independence' – actually, the most intense moments of physical risk, ideological debate and cultural redefinition – and the persistence of colonialism in other economic, cultural and political forms after the formal end of its military or governmental presence.**

(Featherstone, 2005, p. 4)

Notice that Featherstone has put the word 'independence' in inverted commas to suggest that the moment of independence (for example, 15 August 1947, India's Independence Day) was not necessarily the end of dependence or the end of the colonial experience.

This, then, is the territory covered by post-colonialism. As students of contemporary communication and culture we need to know something of this colonial history simply because it continues to have such a profound effect on the culture of both the former colonized and the former colonizers. The empire wasn't just a collection of countries ruled by Britain, it was a complex set of ideas; a way of envisaging the world including many assumptions about right and wrong including, it must be said, many implicitly racist attitudes. Post-colonialism seeks to analyse and explain this 'set of ideas' whilst also giving expression to those many ideas, opinions and voices that were suppressed by the colonial experience.

The 'family of nations'

As a brief case study, let's look at just one component of this 'set of ideas' which became so deeply embedded during the period of empire: ideas about the family and paternalism. The British empire was often portrayed as a 'family of nations'; an idea that still persists in the Commonwealth. The indigenous populations of colonies (i.e. the people who were there before the British turned up) were frequently represented in books, paintings, magazines, newspapers and songs as having child-like qualities. Some of these qualities were more positive, such as innocence and naturalness, but others were more negative, such as immaturity and the need for a 'controlling hand'. The idea of the white, male ruler as a benign father figure was widely circulated well into the twentieth century and is still, perhaps, quite potent in some quarters today.

Similarly, gender stereotypes have also been inflected by the colonial/imperialist experience. Colonialists, of course, retained the right to name countries, territories, settlements and even geographical features and many of these were feminine: Virginia, Victoria Falls, Elizabethville. Women of colonized countries were often depicted as colluding in the imperialist project; deferential figures juxtaposed with the manly, upright white Europeans. Women of the colonizing powers, on the other hand, were represented in imperialist mythology as chaste, virtuous and steadfast. One of the most powerful of imperialist narratives is the metaphor of the ravaged white woman: a symbol of the ultimate act of defiance to the imperial power.

ACTIVITY

A Day With the R.M.

Examine the extract from the *Empire Youth Annual for 1951*. It comes from an article by W.H. Halford Thompson in which he describes his experience as an R.M. (Resident Magistrate) in the Territory of Papua in the island of New Guinea.

How would you describe the tone or *mode of address* with which Halford Thompson addresses his readers?

How does Halford Thompson envisage his relationship with the Papuans?

Books like the *Empire Youth Annual* were very popular in the 1950s. How do you account for this popularity?

continued

To what extent are the stereotypes of colonialism still found in today's cultural products?

How has the fight to reject these stereotypes been fought in cultural practices and products?

EMPIRE YOUTH ANNUAL

commits a murder or a burglary will, as often as not, rush off to his Village Constable, report the matter and then hold out his arm for the Government "mark" to be attached to it. This "mark" takes the form of a pair of handcuffs which are affixed to one wrist only. Once he has these on, the "criminal" feels that he belongs to the Government and therefore no one should dare to touch him. Even then he may still be somewhat anxious about his own personal safety, so to make assurance doubly sure, he makes a dash for the nearest Government Station. The Village Constable collects the witnesses and follows on leisurely behind. So the R.M. may be roused at night by a gentle murderer come to confess to his own crime and thereafter begging to be locked up with all speed since the victim's relatives are after him in no uncertain manner.

TWO or three times a year there is great excitement on the Station when the Administrator is expected on one of his periodical visits of inspection. With him will come the Judge who will hold a sitting of the Supreme Court to which the Magistrate has committed any indictable cases that have come up since the previous "official" visit. For days the police scour the district for witnesses and the Police Sergeant drills his detachment for the Guard of Honour. This will be an anxious day for the R.M., for not only has he to attend to the Administrator and his party, but at the same time he must be responsible for the cases being presented properly in Court—Interpreters, Witnesses, Exhibits and the Accused all being present at the right time. But when it is all over he will watch the departure of the "Royal" yacht with no misgivings as all will have gone well thanks to the loyal co-operation of his staff, both white and brown.

The R.M. does not spend *all* his days on the Station, far from it. He is often away touring his District on patrols that sometimes last for weeks on end. These patrols are of two kinds. One involves such matters as the periodical inspection of villages and roads, collecting the head-tax and visits to the copra and rubber plantations where indentured labour is employed. The other is occasioned by a sudden call to a disturbed area where, for instance, one mountain tribe has just carried out a murderous raid on another and a wanted man whom it may take months to catch is still at large. One patrol after another is sent until the wrongdoer is lodged in gaol, for the Royal Papuan Constabulary always get their men in the end.

THERE are only two police forces in the entire British Commonwealth and Empire which are entitled to use the proud prefix "Royal"—the Royal Canadian Mounted Police and the Royal Papuan Constabulary. Until the war with Japan in 1941 there were only about 500 members of the R.P.C. to maintain law and order amongst 300,000 of their compatriots. This they succeeded in doing in a quiet and remarkably efficient manner. The men of the force are most loyal to their white officers and are as smart on parade as they are competent on bush patrols. Indeed, without their trustworthy and unstinting assistance it would have been impossible to pacify Papua. Once a magistrate or a patrol officer wins their confidence, they will never let him down. The force is entirely composed of full-blooded Papuan N.C.O.s and constables—a notably high tribute to our brown friends the "Fuzzy-Wuzzies", as they are termed in Australia.

Assisting the R.P.C. are village constables of which there is one to each village of any size—he is usually the Chief or his son. Except in cases of emergency these V.C.s only act in their own village. This is a good idea since there is far less likelihood of trouble when a man is arrested by his own chief, rather than by an outsider. This V.C. organization, which was constituted by the late Sir William MacGregor during his tenure of office as Governor of Papua about forty years ago, has proved a great success. The V.C.s are not

106

... you will have an adventurous ride in a native double-canoe

107

Figure 2.22 From the *Empire Youth Annual for 1951* (Halford Thompson, 1951)

'Otherness'

The Palestinian-American Scholar Edward Said (1935–2003) is one of the most important contributors to post-colonialist thought and theory. His book *Orientalism* (Said, 1978) is certainly a key text. He argues that the Western colonizers of the Orient (the East) had little interest in exploring or understanding the cultures they encountered. Instead, they were more interested in reinforcing a set of misguided assumptions that said more about the west than the east. McLeod summarizes Said's view of the colonizers as follows:

> ... they recorded their observations based upon commonly-held assumptions about 'the Orient' as a mythic place of exoticism, moral laxity, sexual degen-

The Orient, then, became an idea that benefited the West by holding up a mirror-image of dominant western values and beliefs. It stood for all that was regarded as alien and inferior: the West's 'other'. Crucially, the economic and military power of the imperialists was matched by their cultural power; they were able to convert this set of 'commonly-held assumptions', beneficial to themselves, into the 'truth' through their enormous capacity to produce and circulate representations. This idea of 'the other' has been extended beyond Said's immediate terms of reference to many other colonial-type relationships. The creation of myths of 'the other' require a rejection of history in the making of essentialized 'types'; a process in which people and their cultures are reduced to a few characteristics held to be 'natural, absolute, invariable' (Pickering, 2001, p. 48). The consequence of this is that 'the other', whether oriental, African or whatever, never changes. It is a view that cannot be overcome by rational argument and evidence because it is one that is based on deeply held prejudices. Complex and sophisticated cultures are reduced to a few simple components whose sole function is to serve the interests of the dominant culture.

Examples of 'othering' are still very prevalent in contemporary culture. For example, advertisers may offer consumers 'a taste of the East' or the 'mysteries of the Orient' whilst film producers scour the globe for locations (and attendant extras) to serve as a tastefully exotic background to the latest action adventure film. Similarly, architects and designers may incorporate hints of mystery, difference or 'otherness' in their work by utilizing symbols such as a palm tree or a pagoda shape.

On the other hand, there are many cultural products that criticize, problematize or contradict the assumptions of 'the other'. A few London-based examples include:

- *Brick Lane* (Ali, 2004) Monica Ali's novel has also been filmed (dir. Sarah Gavron, 2007)
- *Bend It Like Beckham* (dir. Gurinder Chadha, 2002)
- *Small Island* by Andrea Levy (Levy, 2004)
- *White Teeth* by Zadie Smith (Smith, 2000)
- *Dirty Pretty Things* (dir. Stephen Frears, 2002)
- Also, the work of poets Benjamin Zephaniah and Linton Kwesi Johnson. For the latter, try *Bass Culture* (Island Records, 1980).

As a final exercise, try the activity on African footballers, using the webpage article as a basis for discussion.

ACTIVITY

African Footballers

Read the BBC Sport article Scouting for African Talent online.

What do African footballers contribute to the English Premier League?

Is there evidence of a 'colonialist legacy' in representations of African footballers?

Steve Rand comments that African footballers are motivated 'because they come from a difficult and poor background'. What are the implications of this statement?

Source: http://news.bbc.co.uk/sport1/hi/ football/africa/7198078.stm

Conclusion

This chapter has done no more than introduce you to the perspectives identified in the A2 specification and suggested some applications in the field of Communication and Culture. Almost certainly, you will need more depth and detail for at least one of them, particularly when you get going with your coursework Case Study and Presentation. The references below are a starting point for further study and you are certain to find David Gauntlett's theory.org.uk site useful. And a last thought on theory:

> **Whenever a theory appears to you as the only possible one, take this as a sign that you have neither understood the theory nor the problem that it was intended to solve.**

Karl Popper

References and further reading

Ali, M. (2004) *Brick Lane*, London: Black Swan.

Bennett, P. and Slater, J. (2008) *AS Communication and Culture; The Essential Introduction*, Abingdon: Routledge.

Butler, J. (1990) *Gender Trouble: Feminism and the Subversion of Identity*, Abingdon: Routledge.

Featherstone, S. (2005) *Postcolonial Cultures*, Edinburgh: Edinburgh University Press.

Freedland, J. (3 December 2008) *In this recession, we want comfort culture to go with our comfort food*. Retrieved 22 May 2009, from Guardian.co.uk: http://www.guardian.co.uk/commentisfree/2008/dec/03/comment-credit-crunch-food-culture

Gauntlett, D. (2002) *Media, Gender and Identity; An Introduction*, Abingdon: Routledge.

Gramsci, A. (1971) *Selections from the Prison Notebooks*, Q. Hoare and G. Nowell Smith (eds) London: Lawrence and Wishart.

Halford Thompson, W. (1951) A Day With the R.M, in R. Fawcett (ed.) *Empire Youth Annual for 1951*, London: P.R. Gawthorn.

Lash, S. and Lury, C. (2007) *Global Culture Industry*, Cambridge: Polity Press.

Levy, A. (2004) *Small Island*, London: Review Headline.

Longhurst, B., Smith, G., Gaynor, B., Crawford, G. and Ogborn, M. (2008) *Introducing Cultural Studies* (2nd edn), Harlow: Pearson Longman.

McLeod, J. (2000) *Beginning Postcolonialism*, Manchester: Manchester University Press.

McRobbie, A. (1991) *Feminism and Youth Culture: From Jackie to Just 17*, Basingstoke: Macmillan.

Mulvey, L. (2003) Visual Pleasure and Narrative Cinema, in W. Brooker and D. Jermyn (eds), *The Audience Studies Reader*, Abingdon: Routledge.

Oswell, D. (2006) *Culture and Society; An Introduction to Cultural Studies*, London: Sage.

Pickering, M. (2001) *Stereotyping; The Politics of Representation*, Basingstoke: Palgrave.

Piepmeier, A. (17 March 2006) *Postfeminism vs. the Third Wave*. Retrieved 1 May 2009, from Electronic Book Review: http://www.electronicbookreview.com/thread/writingpostfeminism/reconfiguredrip2

Pope, R. (1998) *The English Studies Book*, Abingdon: Routledge.

Said, E. (1978) *Orientalism*, London: Pantheon Books.

Senior, J. (May 2009) *Recession Culture*. Retrieved 22 May 2009, from New York Magazine: http://nymag.com/news/features/56623/

Smith, Z. (2000) *White Teeth*, London: Penguin.

Storey, J. (1997) *An Introduction to Cultural Theory and Popular Culture* (2nd edn), Hemel Hempstead: Prentice Hall.

Storey, J. (1998) *Cultural Theory and Popular Culture; A Reader* (2nd edn), London: Prentice Hall.

Strinati, D. (1995) *An Introduction to Theories of Popular Culture*, London: Routledge.

Tseëlon, E. (1995), *The Masque of Femininity: The Presentation of Women in Everyday Life*, London: Sage.

Wolf, N. (1991) *The Beauty Myth; How Images of Beauty Are Used Against Women*, London: Vintage.

3 KEY CONCEPTS

This chapter deals, briefly, with each of the A2 key concepts. The AS key concepts are:

- Context
- Representation
- Value

- Identity
- Power
- Code

as well, of course, as Communication and Culture. These were dealt with in our AS text book and they continue to feature prominently in A2. The A2 programme adds the following:

- Ideology
- Mode of Address
- Discourse

- Narrative
- Technology.

What are the key concepts for?

The specification includes key concepts to help ensure that the components and units of the course are well-integrated. There are many different ways of interpreting the specification and there are also a number of choices to make; for example, you may not choose to study all three Cultural Sites (Spaces and Places, Fictions, Objects of Desire) or all of the prescribed coursework topics. This is all perfectly legitimate and we would hope that this flexibility is a strength of the specification. Whichever routes you (and your teachers) choose to follow, the key concepts should be ever-present as points of reference and guidance, helping to link the various elements together. They will crop up again and again, as they do in this book, so that be the end of the course you will be thoroughly well immersed in these concepts.

Not least, the key concepts are important because they indicate areas of contrast and comparison between the theoretical approaches discussed in the last chapter.

They also play a synoptic role in pulling together diverse elements of the course. This is reflected in the coursework and in the COMM3 exam, where you will certainly encounter explicit references to the key concepts. For this reason, you should certainly focus on the list of concepts at the head of this chapter when the time comes for revision and exam preparation.

Ideology

In common with quite a few of the specialist terms we use in Communication and Culture, ideology presents us with some problems because it is used in so many different ways by different writers. To make matters even worse, the same writer will often use 'ideology' in different senses in the same paragraph. This makes it impossible for us to offer a simple all-purpose definition. Instead, we have to consider several different meanings, although we can agree that ideology is 'concerned with how we as individuals understand the world in which we live'. In spite of this, it doesn't really make much sense to talk about an individual or personal ideology ('my ideology') because ideology involves the *relationship* between the individual and broader social or cultural structures. Just how this relationship works is a major area of debate.

As we saw in the last chapter, the traditional Marxist formulation of ideology is fairly straightforward. For Marx, ideology equates to the lies and distortions propagated by the rulers in order to perpetuate unfair and unequal systems such as slave-owning, feudal or capitalist societies. Marx summed this up in one of his most frequently quoted sentences;

> **The ideas of the ruling class are in every epoch the ruling ideas, i.e. the class which is the ruling material force is at the same time its ruling intellectual force.**

(Longhurst, Smith, Gaynor, Crawford and Ogborn, 2008, p. 36)

The consequence of this view is that those who are ruled have a view of the world that is permanently skewed against their real or material interests. Whether via religion or the mass media, people are blind to the reality of their own exploitation, seeing only a naturalness or inevitability about the way things are ordered. This is the sense in which ideology has been likened to a pair of glasses that distorts the colours and shapes of the real world, though the person wearing them doesn't even realize they are there. This is ideology as illusion; once anyone becomes conscious of the presence of an ideological effect, it ceases to work: it is no longer ideology.

This, then, is the traditional or classic Marxist position: the ruling class quite deliberately brainwashes subordinate classes into a false consciousness. Consequently, they fail to recognize the unfairness and inefficiency of capitalism and would not dream of trying to overthrow the system. This view is also known as the dominant ideology thesis and can easily be applied by other perspectives that would prefer to put the emphasis on gender (feminism) or ethnicity (post-colonialism). Some feminists certainly regard patriarchal ideology in very much the same way. Men, the argument goes, use their power to perpetuate a set of sexist values and beliefs that make women complicit in their own exploitation.

Critics of the dominant ideology thesis see things rather differently. First, they are more likely to acknowledge the existence of competing sets of beliefs and different ways of seeing the world, for example, those held by feminists or class-conscious workers. Second, they are likely to see ideology arising spontaneously from people's experience of the world. Since that experience, for most of us, is based on capitalist relations, it is not surprising that we see the world in these terms, and that applies to bosses, workers, men, women and people of all ethnic groups. In this view, ideology is not so much a conspiracy cooked up by those in power but more a structural property of relations of production. Or, to put it another way, an inevitable consequence of a capitalist economy is that the people within it see the world in capitalist terms.

Another aspect of the traditional Marxist position on ideology is that it relies on a distinction between reality and perceived reality. This implies that ideology distorts or disguises the real world (material reality) and that therefore there must be a real world to distort or disguise. Not all theoretical perspectives share this view of an underlying reality which we would all see clearly if we were able to throw off the veil of false consciousness. Poststructuralism and postmodernism tend to approach reality rather differently and hence take a different approach to postmodernism (see Information Box on Cultural Relativism, p.61)

We have described the dominant ideology thesis as a 'traditional', Marxist approach, but some Marxists have taken a rather different line on ideology as we saw in Chapter 2. For example, Gramsci's concept of hegemony offers a more sophisticated view of ideological contests in which 'ruling ideas' are continually struggling with the competing world views of other interest groups in society. In order to perpetuate the capitalist system, ruling class ideology cannot be inflexible. It must accommodate change in order to make alliances, conduct tactical 'wars of manoeuvre' and make compromises. Gramsci's version is much more likely to focus on the 'ideological struggles' involved in hegemony, rather than seeing ideology as a giant monolith that simply crushes all opposition.

Figure 3.1
Louis Althusser

Althusser's version of ideology has also been influential, but he shifted the focus away from ideology as a set of beliefs towards the idea of ideology as structure. In Althusser's view, ideology is everywhere: in society's institutions (such as the family, the education system and the mass media) in the environment and in language. We have already seen how Althusser envisages the impact of ideology on the individual by 'hailing' or calling us into being. From our point of view as students of communication and culture, Althusser's idea that ideology is to be found in

practices is a useful and interesting one. This means that ideology isn't just a matter of what we *think*, it is just as much about what we *do*: eating dinner, going to a concert, walking through the park are all manifestations of ideology.

A pluralist (or market liberal) version of ideology would be more likely to define ideology as 'a coherent set of beliefs'. In this sense, Marxism, feminism and liberalism could all be termed ideologies. Michael Freeden suggests that we need to add a few more provisions to this definition, as follows:

> **A political ideology is a set of ideas, beliefs opinions and values that**
>
> 1. **Exhibit a recurring pattern**
> 2. **Are held by significant groups**
> 3. **Compete over providing and controlling plans for public policy**
> 4. **Do so with the aim of justifying, contesting or changing the social and political arrangements and processes of a political community.**

(Freeden, 2003, p. 32)

At this stage, though, we are beginning to move towards definitions of ideology that have something in common with the programmes of political parties. This is fine and we should certainly be aware of this usage and, in particular, the habit of many politicians to use the term ideology simply to mean 'a set of ideas or policies with which I disagree'. From our point of view, those definitions that dwell on the 'normalizing' potential of ideology are probably the most useful. Throughout this book you will find many examples of the analysis of cultural products and cultural practices in which, explicitly or implicitly, ideology plays a key role. As Cormack put it, in warning against too wide and vague an interpretation of ideology:

> **As a general rule, the wider the application of a concept, the less analytically useful it becomes . . . Its analytical force, however, can be preserved by emphasising ideology's role as an unconscious stabilizer and justifier of the status quo. It can be used to make clear the distinction between 'natural', 'commonsense', and 'obvious' views and the class-weighted, socially produced beliefs and practices which we all, to some extent, have and need.**

(Cormack, 1992, p. 16)

Discourse

As with ideology, you will find the term 'discourse' used in a number of contrasting ways in different contexts. Here, we shall identify three interpretations of particular use in the context of communication and culture, but it is the third of these that is probably of most value. The first two relate principally, though not exclusively, to language and can be dealt with quite straightforwardly.

1. A piece of language or 'language event' that is longer than a sentence, such as a conversation, a poem, the lyric of a song or a paragraph in a newspaper report. Unlike the linguistic analysis of sentences, the analysis of discourse in this sense is not confined to language alone, as Guy Cook observes:

> **It also examines the context of communication: who is communicating with whom and why; in what kind of society and situation: through what medium; how different types and acts of communication evolved, and their relationship to each other.**

(Cook, 1992, p. 1)

The very close analysis of language in context is often highly productive in revealing the latent or hidden meanings that lurk beneath the surface.

2. A type of language used in a particular context or by a particular group. For example, this could be the language typically used by lawyers or doctors or a subcultural group. The concepts of Emo discourse or football fan discourse certainly make sense and we can extend the idea from language to other communicative codes, e.g. dress and appearance, cultural rituals and so forth in order to build up a picture of a 'discourse community'. This could be put into practice by, for example, examining an Internet message board or discussion group in order to work out the defining features of this discourse community.

3. The third meaning of 'discourse' makes a lot more sense if you are reasonably familiar with the concept of ideology. This is discourse as a way of constructing reality or a form of knowledge. This approach is associated with the French cultural theorist Michel Foucault (1926–84).

Foucault explored the ways in which discourses are used as methods of control in areas such as sexuality, mental illness and criminality. He argued that the power to observe, categorize and normalize created new forms of knowledge and control. He showed how the exercise of power in modern societies takes much more subtle and hidden forms than in the pre-modern era. For example, his work on prisons and punishment shows how the emphasis changes from the 'spectacular punishment' such as public executions to methods of examination and surveillance that mould the body of the prisoner towards conformity. This method of ensuring conformity is not confined to the prison system; Foucault generalizes this approach to the whole of contemporary society. The education system, with its emphasis on classification and examination, is a case in point.

> **Disciplinary power [. . .] is exercised through its invisibility; at the same time it imposes on those whom it subjects a principle of compulsory visibility. In discipline, it is the subjects who have to be seen. [. . .] (T)he examination is the technique by which power, instead of emitting the signs of its potency, instead of imposing its mark on its subjects, holds them in a mechanism of objectification. In this space of domination, disciplinary power manifests its potency, essentially, by arranging objects. The examination is, as it were, the ceremony of this objectification.**

(Foucault, 1977, p. 187)

The examination provides an interesting case study of Foucault's approach to discourse and power. The exam is a discursive practice that doesn't seem, either to the examiner or the examinee, as a particularly potent method of exercising control. But in Foucault's terms, this is exactly how power works: not by wielding a big stick but by watching, placing into categories, assigning grades and 'arranging objects'. It is certainly something to ponder when you are taking your A2 exams!

A key point about a discourse (or, as a larger body of knowledge is known, a discursive formation) is that it sets boundaries: it places limits on what may or may not be said, what can be done and what cannot be done and, by implication, what can be thought and what cannot be thought. As power works softly and stealthily, the boundaries are not enforced by tough policing but by gentle admonishments like, 'That behaviour isn't really appropriate, is it?'

We noted in our discussion of ideology as a key concept (above) that there are some theorists who reject the idea of an 'underlying truth'; Foucault is certainly one who falls into this camp. Discourses produce knowledge; 'truths' may hold for a particular time and place but there are no fixed, immutable truths. As societies evolve, power changes and the relationship between power and knowledge is such that when one changes, so does the other.

So how can we use this Foucauldian concept of discourse in our analyses of texts, products and practices? One way is to formulate a set of questions which reflect these ideas. For example, in approaching say, a town centre shopping complex or mall, we could ask:

- How are spaces and people organized and categorized?
- By whom?
- Who is being watched and who is watching?
- Which activities are encouraged and which are discouraged?
- How?
- What kinds of knowledge are needed to negotiate this environment?
- How is this knowledge circulated?

Mode of address

It is a fundamental principle of Communication and Culture that all texts have the capacity to communicate. As we investigate cultural practices and cultural products we are searching for their meanings or, more precisely, the ways in which meanings are generated. We know that the simple process model (Sender – Message – Receiver) has its limitations because it is not really adequate in conceptualizing the *relationship* between text (message) and receiver. This is where Mode of Address comes in. We start with the question:

Who does this text think I am?

In other words, what assumptions are made about me and how am I expected to read the text? If you walk into a High Street bank, how are you addressed by the décor, the carpet, the fixtures and fittings, the signage, the lighting, the uniforms of the staff and the way they use language? All of these constitute a mode of address, the underlying message of which is probably something like, ' You are very welcome here as long as you want to deposit money, borrow money or otherwise contribute to the profitability of the organization.' But it may be that you don't feel welcome: you feel intimidated, patronized and out of place. In both cases, the mode of address has contributed to your *subjectivity*; it has formed you as a person in much the same way as Althusser describes the process of interpellation or 'hailing' (see Ideology, above).

Marxists are likely to find evidence in the modes of address of almost every text that confirms a view of a class-divided society in which workers are exploited by capitalists. Feminists will find evidence in modes of address of the sets of assumptions that create gendered subjectivities.

However, without denying the validity of these perspectives, it is surely the case that texts offer a range of different and sometimes contradictory subjectivities. For example, some advertisements address us as rebels and some invite us to fit in and be one of the crowd. Texts are often multifaceted and, intentionally or not, allow us the possibility of many readings (otherwise known as *polysemy*). As with the bank example above, we all recognize from time to time that a text is trying to manipulate us; to ease us into a subjectivity that we'd rather not have, thank you very much. As soon as we 'see through' the ideological effect of a mode of address, it becomes counter-productive and is likely to have the opposite effect

Figure 3.2 Inside Whitney Bank, New Orleans – how are you addressed by this décor?

to the one intended. To use the example of advertising again, adverts from the 1960s and 1970s now seem so unsophisticated and blatant in their attempts to manoeuvre consumers into a particular subjectivity, that they are usually only shown today for their comedy effect.

Even in this case, though, resistance is more likely to occur at the level of content rather than code. The specific idea that, say, a cigarette can be linked to a form of rugged, outdoor manliness (as in Marlboro Man) may seem a bit daft to most of us today. Yet the underlying convention of the encoded mode of address is still acceptable, i.e. we still expect consumer products to be linked to desirable gender identities.

Two useful terms associated with mode of address are *positioning* and *register*. The idea that a text or message can position the receiver should be familiar to you from your study of Eric Berne's Transactional Analysis (Bennett and Slater, 2008, pp. 83–7). If your friend addresses you from their Controlling Parent ego state by giving you orders in a loud voice accompanied by a wagging finger and a steady stare, then you are being positioned as an Adapted Child. Of course, you may choose to reject this subject position, but to do so is to place yourself in conflict with your friend because he or she will have to change subject position if you respond from your Adult ego state. Perhaps it is more obviously the case in a face-to-face interaction such as this, but we can see how all relationships with texts, cultural products and cultural practices position us in one way or another. As with the TA example, it usually requires an effort of will to reject the invitation to a certain position and we are often tempted to just 'go with the flow'.

Register involves modifications to codes of communication, usually to fit in with the requirements of a particular group or a particular situation. For example, the mode of address of that bank we visited a few paragraphs ago may adopt a formal register or an informal register, a serious register or a light-hearted register.

Narrative

Narrative refers to the ways in which meanings are structured as stories. These stories may or may not be true: narrative certainly isn't confined to the world of fiction. To avoid confusion, narrative also needs to be distinguished from narration. Narration is the 'telling of the tale'; an activity carried out, of course, by the narrator.

Narrative in the context of Fictions (as a Cultural Site) is dealt with at some length in Chapter 5 and it may be worth turning, briefly, to the section on Narrative, Story and Plot (p. 139) just to establish the distinctions between these three linked concepts.

Some have argued that it is our propensity to narrativize as much as our capacity for language that distinguishes human beings from other species. Certainly, narrative is at the core of any culture, simply because cultures must be able to reproduce themselves in the next generation or they will be wiped out. A culture's narratives could be seen as the way it encodes itself in order to be passed on from generation to generation. All of us are powerfully motivated by a desire to formulate and detect narratives. Presented with a set of signifiers, the human mind looks for meaningful order, for sequences and for causality. We find it very hard to accept the possibility of things being entirely random or meaningless, so the narrative always tempts us.

We cannot entirely separate the concepts of narrative and ideology, for the way in which our culture frames narrative is essentially ideological: we have a 'common sense' set of expectations about what should happen next. For example, Schirato and Yell describe the 'framing expectation' of narrative in the field of romance as follows:

> Narratives are used as ways of interpreting and structuring everyday life, and can take on a very powerful function in validating the events in people's lives. An example of the validating power of narratives is the way in which the heterosexual romance myth is used within some cultural groups as a measure of a woman's

'success' in life; those women whose lives don't match this narrative may be judged, or even judge themselves (in some sense) 'failures'. 🙶

(Schirato and Yell, 1996, p. 95)

Although rather brutal, this example serves to remind us that narrative is not a concept whose usefulness is restricted to clearly identifiable genres of the novel, bed-time story or feature film; it is a crucial link between the individual and wider culture. Just as the filmmaker deploys the conventions of a genre to unite story, plot and narrative, so we as individuals utilize the narrative codes of our culture to project our identities to others. We weave together stories about ourselves that invite others to place us within familiar narratives with familiar characters and familiar chains of events. As with any storytelling, the skill of narration lies in striking a balance between the familiar and the unpredictable.

Organizations, too, rely on the utilization of narratives to project institutional iden-tities. We are accustomed to the idea that corporations are 'going somewhere', that they are 'on the move' or that they expect us to 'come aboard'. This relates to one of the most deeply rooted of narrative structures: the story as a journey or a quest. Needless to say, the preferred narrative journey of most organizations is one of constant improvement, progress and expansion. Individuals have to be socialized into the corporate style of the organization as employees, clients, customers or students and this can be accomplished, in part, by mythologizing the organization. The mission statement, the annual report, the round of social functions and the company website can all contribute to an 'official narrative'. In the same way, cities, regions and countries work on their narratives in order to accentuate the positive aspects and marginalize the negative.

Technology

To some extent, technology is a bit of an odd one out amongst these A2 key con-cepts in that it is slightly misleading to label technology as a concept. After all, we all know what technology is, so why make things more complex than they need to be? On the other hand, there is no escaping the obvious fact that technology plays an absolutely crucial role in contemporary communication and culture; in some senses modern culture is *defined* by its relationship with technology – it has even been dubbed a *techno*culture. A few snapshots in support of this contention:

Barack Obama made extensive use of the Internet and social media in his victorious 2008 Presidential election campaign. Blogs, video-sharing sites such as YouTube and message services like Twitter were all used to mobilize his supporters, raise money and to get his message across.

Street protests against the Iranian elections in 2009 were communicated via social network sites, video uploads and mobile phone images in spite of the government's attempts to suppress this information. As Bobbie Johnson posted to the Guardian technology blog:

> The internet is a brilliant machine for spreading information. Data shoots across the network at the speed of light, passing from one node to another. It's unmotivated by fear or repression or greed, and can shine a torch into the darkest corners to help bring what was hidden to the world.
>
> The uprising in Iran has been a perfect case in point – despite state censorship, the suppression of journalists and the shutdown of communications – the story has been covered from almost every angle: and the internet [. . .] has played a vital part in getting the information out.
>
> (Johnson, 2009)

A Price Waterhouse Cooper report in June 2009 assessed the American video gaming industry as follows:

> The report says the video game industry – without hardware – in North America will bring in $17.2 billion in sales this year, growing to $21.6 billion in 2013. By then, the game industry will be three times larger than the recorded music industry, which is expected to sink 4.4% annually to $7.2 billion in 2013.
>
> (Bond, 2009)

These examples are here to illustrate two important aspects of technology. First, the thorough integration of technology into almost every aspect of contemporary culture; second, the dynamism, rapidity and (often) total unpredictability of technocultural change.

How, then, do we theorize this relationship between technology and culture, beyond merely noting that it is a very close relationship? How do we explain the impact of technoculture on the meanings and practices of everyday life. One

Figure 3.3 In 1965 Gordon Moore stated that the processing power of silicon chips (and hence of computers) would double every 18 months. What are the cultural implications of 'Moore's Law'?

approach which we discussed in the AS book is called technological determinism. 'This is the view that technological developments are a primary cause of social change and cultural perceptions. It is the underlying principle for historians who link technological inventions to specific timeframes to give us, for example, the Railway Age, the Nuclear Age, the Computer Age and so on' (Bennett and Slater, 2008, pp. 264–5). The view that new developments in technology drive forward social change is certainly a very widely held belief, and for this reason alone we should take it seriously. However, if we look at some of the effects that have been linked with technological change, then some of the problems with this approach become evident:

- Unemployment
- Greater job opportunities
- Loss of attention span
- Decline of family life
- End of High Street shopping
- Laziness
- Death of cinema
- Decline in interpersonal communication skills

- Paperless Office
- Death of newspapers
- Decline of commuting as everybody works at home.

All of the above have been linked to technological developments or devices and cited as effects. But is it really so simple? We'll leave you to speculate about the specific examples of technology held to be responsible for these effects, but suffice to say that the 'cause and effect' relationship is somewhat undermined by a discussion that starts with the supposed effects and works backwards to the causes. This is not to say that these phenomena have nothing to do with technology in any circumstances, more to say that the link is more complex and subtle than the one suggested by technological determinists.

A further problem with technological determinism is that it 'leaves us feeling passive about technology' (Mackay, 2001, p. 30). As some of our 'snapshot' examples above clearly show, people can be highly active in appropriating the potential of technology for their own ends – including the use of technology to oppose or resist dominant forces or dominant values. Furthermore, technological determinism fails to deal with the *causes of* technology as opposed to the social phenomena that may be caused by technology; it doesn't deal with the external factors that drive technological development, such as commercial or military requirements.

An alternative view stresses the social shaping of technology in its inception, development and application. This approach, sometimes referred to as SCOT, the Social Construction of Technology, puts the emphasis on cultural practice. As Brett Farmer puts it:

> **For cultural studies, technology is not something that simply engages scientists or industrial designers, nor is it merely an element of the hardware, a piece of machinery or electronic circuitry. *Instead it is an integral part of how we live in a society and it functions as a vital site of cultural production and negotiation wherein meanings and identities are constructed, exchanged, struggled over and reformed.***

(Farmer, 2003, p. 177)

In *Doing Cultural Studies; The Story of the Sony Walkman*, DuGay et al. (1997). identify five cultural processes that form the basis of their analysis (Figure. 3.4).

They argue that 'to study the Walkman culturally one should at least explore how it is represented, what social identities are associated with it, how it is produced and consumed and what mechanisms regulate its distribution and use' (du Gay, Hall, Janes, Mackay and Negus, 1997, p. 3). Although the cassette Walkman that

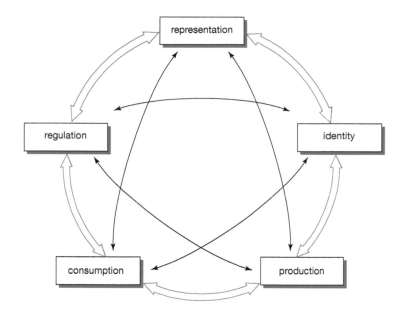

Figure 3.4 The circuit of culture

is analysed in this study looks distinctly out of date now, the mode of analysis is still highly relevant and suitable for the consideration of any technology or technological product.

The Circuit of Culture is a useful model and it is certainly not restricted to *communication* technology. Without understating the significance of information and communication technology, it is worth remembering that technoculture embraces many other fields of technology from transport to healthcare to construction to those labour-saving domestic devices that have, supposedly, transformed housework from drudgery to pleasure. All have implications worthy for study and discussion as we consider the relationship between culture and technology. Joe Moran's *Queuing for Beginners* (a highly readable and indispensable companion for students of the meanings and practices of everyday life) charts the relationship between numerous cultural products and changing cultural practices. Here, he considers the fate of that great factory institution, the tea break:

> In the 1960s the fixed tea break began to be abolished and 'free' or flexible breaks introduced instead. The key catalyst for this change was the hot drinks vending machine, which arrived from America in the 1950s. After a tea strike at Ford's Dagenham plant in 1962, Primapax's general manager wrote to Ford, pointing out his vending machines could help avoid future industrial strife. Vending machines could be placed throughout

workplaces, dispensing with the mass trek to the canteen or the long wait for the tea trolley, and workers could refill according to their own unique 'fatigue curve'. [. . .] Break times now had to be staggered because vending machines could not cope with a rush on their services in fixed breaks. The machines also helped to develop the public's taste for instant coffee: stewed vending machine tea was virtually undrinkable.

"

(Moran, 2008, p. 51)

Another idea which can help us to understand the development of technology and technoculture is *convergence*. This involves the bringing together of previously distinct industries, for example, computing, telecommunications and television; the merging of media, e.g. Internet radio, streaming video on your mobile phone; and the convergence of content such as music, digital images and games on the iPod (Mackay, 2001, p. 8). However, Henry Jenkins warns us not to see the convergence phenomenon too much in terms of content, what he calls the 'black box fallacy': the idea that we shall all, eventually, carry around one little black box that does absolutely everything. For most of us, he points out, we are actually collecting more and more 'black boxes' whether in the form of mobile devices or the pile of equipment that constitutes a home entertainment system. The real convergence, adds Jenkins, 'alters the relationship between existing technologies, industries, markets, genres and audiences [. . .] convergence refers to a process, not an endpoint' (Jenkins, 2006, pp. 15–16). And, of course, it is a profoundly *cultural* process as the title of Jenkins' book – *Convergence Culture* – suggests.

References and further reading

Bennett, P. and Slater, J. (2008) *AS Communication and Culture; The Essential Introduction*, Abingdon: Routledge.

Bond, P. (16 June 2009). *Recession? Not for video games*. Retrieved 22 June 2009, from Hollywood Reporter.com: http://www.hollywoodreporter.com/hr/content_display/news/e3i4031fc1b18a4c6b4ea56d2b196dc2c9a

Cook, G. (1992) *The Discourse of Advertising*, London: Routledge.

Cormack, M. (1992) *Ideology*, London: Batsford.

du Gay, P., Hall, S., Janes, L., Mackay, H. and Negus, K. (1997) *Doing Cultural Studies; The Story of the Sony Walkman*, London: Sage/Open University.

Farmer, B. (2003) Everyday Technology, in F. Martin, *Interpreting Everyday Culture*, London: Edward Arnold, pp. 173–87.

Foucault, M. (1977) *Discipline and Punish; The Birth of the Prison* (A. Sheridan, Trans.), London: Penguin.

Freeden, M. (2003) *Ideology: A Very Short Introduction*, Oxford: Oxford University Press.

Jenkins, H. (2006) *Convergence Culture; Where Old and New Media Collide*, New York: New York University Press.

Johnson, B. (17 June 2009,). *Net Response to Iran Shows We're All Newsmakers Now.* Retrieved 19 June 2009, from Guardian.co.uk: www.guardian.co.uk/ technology/blog/2009/jun/17/twitter-socialnetworking

Longhurst, B., Smith, G., Gaynor, B., Crawford, G. and Ogborn, M. (2008) *Introducing Cultural Studies* (2nd edn), Harlow: Pearson Longman.

Mackay, H. (2001) *Investigating the Information Society,* London: Routledge/ Open University.

Moran, J. (2008) *Queuing for Beginners; The Story of Daily Life from Breakfast to Bedtime,* London: Profile.

Schirato, T. and Yell, S. (1996) *Communication and Cultural Literacy; An Introduction,* St Leonard's, NSW, Australia: Allen and Unwin.

4 SPACES AND PLACES

This chapter deals with the constructed environment: the places we observe and move about in, places we have visited or we would like to visit, spaces that we know and love as well as those that we really don't like at all. Most of these places are real and tangible, yet the boundaries between 'real' places, imagined places and virtual places are not always clear cut. As we shall see, the ways in which we think about places and spaces is not always determined by their physical qualities.

In referring to the 'constructed environment' we are using the term 'constructed' in two distinctly different but linked senses. The first use of 'constructed' relates to the artificiality of the environment – the degree to which the environment has been physically and deliberately fashioned by humans. In this sense buildings, towns and cities are all made but so too are fields, forests and national parks. In the second sense of the word we are dealing with the construction of meanings. Having got this far into a course in Communication and Culture you will be very familiar with the idea that meanings are negotiated and contested. In this view, a particular place may have many different meanings to different people at different times.

Even at this early stage in the chapter, you will probably feel the need for some reassurance. The territory covered by Spaces and Places seems intimidating in its size, scope and range of connections to areas as diverse as Architecture, Geography, Interior Design, Urban Planning, Civil Engineering, Tourism, Landscaping and Environmental Studies . . . to name just a few! You can't possibly expect to become an expert in all of these subjects, but you will need to cultivate the skill of 'dipping in' to a wide variety of material from many different sources in order to serve your own needs. With such a diverse and potentially bewildering range of influences and connections, a few handholds in the form of key questions will be helpful. Much of your investigation into spaces and places will take the form of case studies. If your analyses and discussions are rooted in the following questions, you will always have a firm foundation:

Who created this space/place, and why?

What are the intended (preferred) meanings?

What are the alternative meanings?

Who uses, inhabits or observes this space/place and how are meanings communicated to them?

Have meanings changed over time?

With these questions in mind we can start with a very straightforward exercise: an account of the very place you are located at the moment, using these key questions. This is my account of my location as I write.

Case study
THE SPACE I OCCUPY

I am sitting at a desk in the library of a sixth form college in Essex. The library is on the first floor of the college's 'old building' (Figure 4.1). This building was originally a technical school but has gone through many modifications and refurbishments since its Edwardian origins. It is a

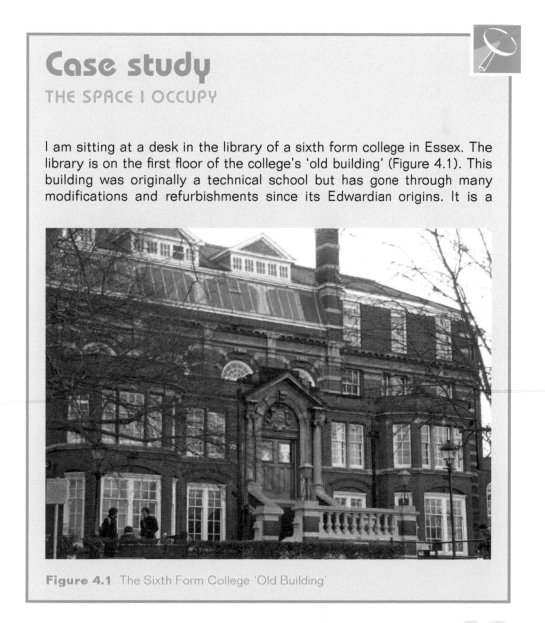

Figure 4.1 The Sixth Form College 'Old Building'

predominantly redbrick building with decorative features including a stone balustrade, dormers, bay windows, a pediment, a coat of arms and fanlights above the windows. As the photographs show, the exterior has a rather gothic appearance and the interior has many high-ceilinged rooms with ornate features such as plaster mouldings and casts. Figure 4.2 shows the library with the large joists supporting a mezzanine floor. During the course of redevelopment, many of the rooms have had their ceilings lowered to create extra usable space.

Figure 4.2 College Library

The style of the old building, in keeping with the period, reflected the idea that educational buildings should be uplifting and inspirational with deliberate references to the classical architecture of ancient Greece and Rome. Just as cathedrals and churches enclose huge interior spaces to lift the spirits of worshippers, many Victorian and Edwardian schools were designed to enrich the experience of pupils. Perhaps they were also intended to inspire a certain amount of awe in the educational system and respect for the teachers who worked in them. To modern eyes, buildings such as these probably look rather elaborate and fussy with too much attention to unnecessary detail. Large, light and airy spaces are impractical, not least because they are difficult and expensive to clean and to heat.

The college's new buildings (Figure 4.3) communicate rather different messages about education as well as contemporary tastes and design trends. Their clean-cut lines suggest a more functional and business-like approach. There are few, if any, direct references to historical architectural styles though aspects of the design and construction do suggest a concern for the environment and thermal efficiency. The disparate styles of the buildings are linked by unifying colour schemes and some design features such as the use of redbrick that provide echoes of the old building in the appearance of the new.

Figure 4.3 New and old college buildings. Different messages about education?

Overall, the preferred reading of the modern building and modernized interiors of the old building is to project the image of an efficient and effective provider of educational opportunity. The older parts of the building, though, still communicate an idea of education that seems rather outdated and irrelevant today. In common with many public buildings of its era, the old building communicates a self-assured pride, confidence and sense of historical continuity; qualities that were swept away by the First World War a few short years after its construction. For the many thousands who have passed through its corridors there are, no doubt, many contrasting personal meanings. For some, the building would have symbolized all that is dark and oppressive about the education system whilst others will have affectionate memories of the best years of their lives. What is without doubt is that there are a great many competing meanings, memories and perceptions attached to the bricks and mortar of this place and the spaces within it.

Without, as yet, engaging with theoretical concepts and perspectives, this introductory case study addresses our key questions and refers to the relationship between the physical properties of a space or place and the meanings that we assign to these properties. You will have noticed an explicit reference to 'architectural style' and the use of some architectural terms such as *pediment* and *mezzanine*. In describing and analysing the physical properties of places and spaces, it is difficult to avoid the occasional use of technical terms as a preferred alternative to such vague generalizations as 'old looking' or 'funny shaped'. It seems that a brief foray into architecture is unavoidable.

Architecture

We need to set out our distinctively Communication and Culture approach to Architecture as a formal professional discipline. Here it is dealt with in a linguistically pragmatic way as a set of cultural codes, as a series of statements with varying force and effect. We are not particularly interested in architectural theory or architectural movements. We are not really concerned with the means of construction, though the 'how' will inevitably feature in some aspects of the communicative text. However the implicit conversation that we are having with (often anonymous) architects, designers and planners must be acknowledged. England's most famous architect, Sir Christopher Wren is buried within his greatest creation: St Paul's cathedral. Above his tomb a plaque declares: *Reader, if you seek his memorial – look around you*. For us (as well as for Wren) this is a rather suitable maxim. As this topic requires a lot of looking around, we can expect to be 'registering' a good many monuments. Whatever manifestos inform them, buildings always make statements, and it is our job (as readers) to analyse, decode and contest these statements. Many of these statements are aesthetic:

statements relating to notions of taste and beauty. As the great modern architect Le Corbusier wrote:

> **ARCHITECTURE is a thing of art, a phenomenon of the emotions, lying outside questions of construction and beyond them. The purpose of construction is TO MAKE THINGS HOLD TOGETHER; of architecture TO MOVE US [. . .] Architecture is a matter of 'harmonies' it is 'a pure creation of the spirit'.**
>
> (Corbusier, 1986, p. 19)

We may immediately think how much easier it is to be moved by the sight of St Paul's or even a monumental modernist monument like the Centre Point Tower in London than the often mundane range of buildings we encounter on our way to college or work. If so we perhaps need to remind ourselves how comparatively rarely we encounter these set-piece 'marvels' and remember the variously more subtle ways we are regularly moved by our immediate landscapes and dwellings. Here 'the phenomenon of the emotions' relates not to the 'artist' but more significantly to the spectator. This spectator, in fact is not really a spectator at all, since few of us would regard our daily lives as a spectator sport. We are more accurately described as participants, inhabitants and interpreters of these spaces and their meanings.

You are already familiar with the idea of 'reading the text', and with using such terms as connotation and denotation, myth and ideology. It will not be such a great leap to apply these concepts in the analysis of buildings, just as you have applied them to printed texts and other cultural products. We should be wary in such analyses of allowing too high a priority to the stated intentions of architects or those who commission them. Connotations cannot be disallowed by an insistence on the denotative meanings of a text; in fact they are stimulated by such a contention. Buildings in this respect are like many other texts, including us human texts; they occupy 'space' and make implicit and explicit statements about themselves (the most important being 'I am here'). Equally, though relatively adaptable, they are, by virtue of their existence, open to interpretation and liable to be denied their preferred reading. Moreover as they continue to exist and be inhabited and interpreted they are subjected to the preferred readings of others; connotations morphing into myths. These 'myths' like the buildings themselves have their foundations hidden (historically, politically, socially and, always, culturally).

It is another facet of this work that we are forever grappling with a language of 'architecture' which is also a language of our everyday lives and our attempts to understand them. We often talk of *building theories on sound foundations*, of *constructing arguments*, of *inhabiting positions*. We also talk about the 'faces' of buildings as '*façades*'. This is very reminiscent of interpersonal communication, in particular Goffman's approach to the masks that we wear in different contexts. It seems there are powerful metaphorical links between the building and the human body: between the ways in which buildings communicate and the ways in which people communicate. We are addressed by buildings and we in turn address them. Any recording of Channel Four's *Grand Designs* will reinforce this idea, as Kevin McCloud frequently reminds his viewers that buildings 'speak in many voices' or 'write their own stories' or, even, 'compose many narratives'.

Buildings that make statements

As our example here we shall take the International Style, a movement in architecture that gained prominence in the mid-twentieth century. In its early days the International Style, represented by Le Corbusier, Mies van der Rohe and Walter Gropius, was characterized by a simplicity of form and absence of decorative features. The architects working in this new tradition favoured modern materials including steel, reinforced concrete and plate glass. Their idea was that any building that was 'true' to its functions and its materials would naturally attain an aesthetic appeal. Le Corbusier famously designated houses as 'machines for living' and his ideal was to create a modern dwelling perfectly matched to the needs of a modern family using the best of modern materials. These principles were embodied in the design and construction of Villa Savoye (see Figure 4.4)

Figure 4.4 Le Corbusier's Villa Savoye completed in 1929

By the 1950s the International Style was firmly established in the United States and became the 'house style' of large corporations, many of which vyed with one another to commission increasingly large and impressive buildings to symbolize their prestige. Two famous examples are Lever House in New York (originally the headquarters of the detergent company, Lever Brothers) and Sears Tower in Chicago. The latter was built to signify the pre-eminent position of Sears Roebuck and Company as the world's largest retailer (Avery, 2003, p. 127).

Figure 4.5 Lever House, New York, completed 1952

Figure 4.6 Sears Tower (formerly The Sears Building) Chicago, completed 1974

The International Style began to fall out of favour in the 1970s, not least because it began to be associated with elitism, corporate greed and excess – all of these in stark contrast to the ideals of Le Corbusier. New thinking in architecture saw the re-emergence of decoration and adornment and a renewed interest in previous architectural traditions. The clean-lined box-like simplicity of modernism and the International Style was gradually usurped by a style that soon became known as postmodernism.

You are already familiar with the tenets of postmodernism as a theoretical perspective (Chapter 2), so you will not be too surprised by the characteristics of postmodernism as a movement in architecture. Although there is no single defining feature of a postmodern building, most are easily recognized as they all possess at least one of the following qualities:

- Juxtaposition of styles from different historical periods
- Simulation and reproduction
- A sense of humour
- Surprise or wonderment
- Deliberate flouting of the 'rule book'
- Defamiliarization; making the ordinary seem strange

Some of these features can be seen in Figures 4.7–4.9.

Figure 4.7 Les Espaces d' Abraxas (architect Ricardo Bofill) Marne-la-Vallée, 1982

Figure 4.8 Charing Cross Station 1990

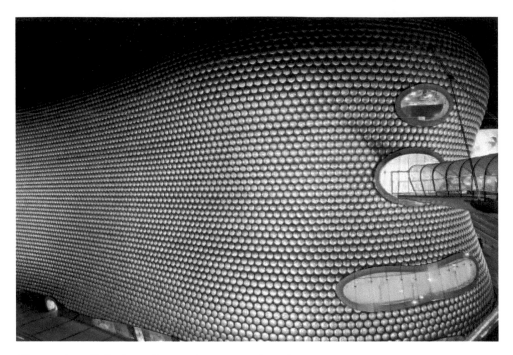

Figure 4.9 Selfridges, Birmingham opened in 2003

ACTIVITY

Look for examples of modernist and postmodern buildings in your own area, collecting images for discussion. Analyse these buildings using the questions on p. 92 as your starting point.

These buildings do not have to be on a grand scale. This canal-side warehouse in Milton Keynes isn't a real warehouse, nor is the canal or even the narrowboat real; it's a fairly recently built pub hotel designed with a sense of postmodern fun.

Figure 4.10 Not quite what it seems; canal-side pub, Milton Keynes

From home to school

As we noted above, the distinction between the building and the human body is not always straightforward, especially when it comes to the making and interpretation of meanings. Like faces and bodies we have expectations of what features to expect in a building – especially a domestic house (doors, windows, a roof) – and we are profoundly affected when these expectations are not met.

For people of a particular age the set of expectations for the simplest dwelling, the house, was defined by the BBC's children's programme *Play School* which began with Brian Cant's distinctive voice anchoring the accompanying drawing in this way.

Here's a house,
Here's a door,

Windows, one, two,
three four,

Ready to knock?

Turn the lock
It's *Play School*.

Figure 4.11 *Play School*

For literally millions of people this house, consciously symmetrical and face-like, was 'home': the essence, a convention. Moreover it was a special house whose familiarity, far from breeding contempt, uniquely captured the simplicity of early childhood (*Play School* was for pre-schoolers and ran for 24 years; a quick search of YouTube will soon find some examples). In the process the simple line drawing was able to generate something akin to what we feel when our own well-established house (or flat or maisonette) becomes a home. This is like the moment when the particular arrangement of features (nose, mouth, eyes) which make a human face become combined in the recognition that merits the title 'friend'. In both cases the affection must be bestowed: it cannot be assumed.

Milder forms of this recognition come in the form of acquaintances such as classmates or work colleagues and correspondingly in our responses to those places we regularly visit for work or play. Sometimes, even infrequent visits can produce strongly positive responses, for example to the regular (albeit annual) visits to the locations of family holidays. There is something comforting about the idea that we can come to 'know' a place in the same way that we know our friends and acquaintances. For work or school, this familiarity may not reach the warm glow until after we've left. Schools and colleges are places that are often 'explored' gradually as a matter of maturation (or, perhaps, merely surviving). All of us form some sort of relationship with our schools, whether as somewhere we would prefer to forget (if only we could!) or somewhere for which we have the fondest sentimental memories. Most will recall the stresses of leaving a junior or infants school to head for 'big school' – a vast, forbidding and undiscovered country. Not only are you once again the smallest but also you face a new territory without 'muscle memory', that autopilot that gets you around familiar locations.

It's not that you have no clues, though as you traverse the landscape of the school. 'Educational buildings' are part of a well-established genre so it's not the elements but the order that is unknown. It may be that you've moved out of the 'school' sub-genre into the 'college' sub-genre, with an attendant re-negotiation of the mode of address. On the other hand staying on in the sixth form is also a rite of passage of sorts. As a sixth former you usually 'inherit' a special place which (like diplomatic immunity) operates in a slightly different way to the rest of the school. As a result of this special context you are also then transformed in all the other parts of the school, where hitherto you have just been an unprivileged and uniformed grunt.

This next activity builds (yes, we're 'building' again) on your first attempt at analysing 'my space' in order to consider places of education more closely

ACTIVITY

Schools and colleges: Reading the Constructed Environment.

This is effectively a Case Study which can be attempted at differing levels of detail. It asks you to consider your school or college as a 'place' and as an 'organized space'.

- How many sites are there?
- How are these sites laid out? (Around a quad, in four blocks, around a central reception, etc.)
- What are the messages in this division? (Management of institution, vocational/academic, subject/faculty divisions)
- Where do the important people 'live'? (and how do you know?)
- How are visitors addressed by the reception area and how is this area differentiated from other parts of the site?
- Identify some of the anchors that help to assign meaning. (Signs, colour schemes, furniture, fixture and fittings)
- Classify the different kinds of spaces and places that constitute the institution.
- What do the spaces assigned to the following subjects tell you about the expectations of the experience:

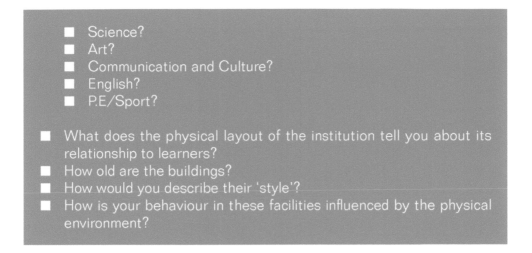

The final question in this activity is the real key to understanding 'Places and Spaces' since it identifies the inferred third element: 'People'. Thinking about 'Places, (People) and Spaces' reminds us that while context is often vital, it too is subject to negotiation, that 'knowing where you are' is rarely a simple matter. This is to say that places are defined by our practices in and around them, physically, psychologically and intellectually. In semiotic terms what is denoted might most often be an explicit function like 'school' or even 'Physics lab' but that is not the end of the conversation. Umberto Eco sees these as the primary and secondary functions of 'architectures'. In an essay entitled 'Function and Sign: the Semiotics of Architecture' he addresses the necessary tension between the functional and the symbolic or expressive elements concluding that architects and designers need to accept that the 'readers' of their work are beyond their control. All they can hope to do is to allow for 'variable primary functions and open secondary functions' (Leach, 1997, p. 173).

The point here is that even the designations 'primary' and 'secondary' are properly dynamic and potentially problematic. Even if we take a simple interior text like 'the classroom' we almost inevitably run into a series of unforeseen issues. Given we spend large parts of our young lives in these generic locations, which come in different flavours but invariably taste the same, we ought to be in a good position to 'decode' them. However no sooner do we begin than we realize how inseparable places are from the things we do in them. These cultural products unsurprisingly take their various meanings from our cultural responses in, around and in response to them. Thus, while the primary function of a classroom (its literal, denotative meaning) might be to 'contain' learners for the purpose of learning, even this is hedged by what Stuart Hall would call hegemony. Classrooms, for others, are containers of different sorts: restrainers of the human spirit or merely daytime detention centres. In other words a classroom becomes symbolic of education, a hotly disputed form of socialization/enculturation. Moreover, the meaning of 'classroom' will vary depending on whether you are one of the many (learners) or

one of the few (teachers) and whether you are, as a result of either of these, empowered within this context. Particular classrooms will also have particular resonances. They may be places where you first met Jenny or Jim or had your life changed by Keats or the delights of double-entry book-keeping. By this point it's becoming very clear how little can be seen as literal, as denotative, that generic places function semiotically as *myths*; sets of collective connotations and carriers of ideology.

Inside classrooms there is a dynamic relationship between people and things in the context of space. This relationship is to some extent compromised by furniture and other equipment and by expectations of how lessons are to be structured. For example, most classrooms have a point of attention set by the orientation of the chairs and the fixed position of the whiteboard or projection screen. Conventionally these are not rooms to move around in, nor are they particularly places that are geared to collaboration. Implicitly they are about instruction, a particular kind of teaching which focuses on knowledge, the whiteboard and the teacher. It's an approach that implies that everyone learns, or should learn, in the same way: largely by listening. The conventional classroom layout also communicates the authority of the teacher; a role enshrined by the teacher's desk, the altar on which the learners make worship. None of these elements can find any particular validation in theories of learning but that's not the point. The 'classroom' is an image in the mind's eye, both individual and collective and if in the future you visit the schools of your own children you will possibly feel relieved that in spite of a few hi-tech gadgets, the essence remains the same. However there is much to say about the values associated with these images. Such values are most evident perhaps when they are implicitly challenged by very different versions of the 'learning space' deployed in a subject like Art. In the art (class)room a more significant democracy has clearly broken out which again has to do with an arrangement of people and objects in space.

Beyond the school gate

Having looked in some detail at the implications of space and place in the context of education, it is time to broaden our horizons with some activities and case studies drawn from the wider world.

ACTIVITY

Portable 'class' rooms: the meaning of First Class on the railway

Something similar is going on if we move our attention to the ways in which our responses to first class accommodation on a train are addressed. Again the ultimate negotiation is of and with space.

Consider the two photographs below:

Figure 4.13 Train interiors; First Class and Standard Class

continued

What are the principal differences between the two scenes?

How is space used in each case and what is signified by this 'use'?

Who is the intended audience for each of these experiences?

What part does anchorage play in this process?

Case study

THE MILLENNIUM DOME: SUFFOCATED BY THE OXYGEN OF PUBLICITY.

In modern parlance 'first class', as in the train compartments we have just discussed, has connotations of being the best: the 'bee's knees', the dog's unmentionables. In the 1990s, something was needed to welcome in the third millennium; something even better than first class, in fact, something

Figure 4.14 The Millennium Dome (now the O2). Architect Richard Rogers, completed 1999

'world class'; a project that would catch people's imagination around the globe. What we got was the Millennium Dome. Well before its completion, its critics had written it off as a spectacular folly, a massively over-priced white elephant. But were they right? If one of its jobs was to attract attention and create a landmark recognizable to all, it must surely be counted as a great success. However, its many meanings as a significant contemporary London site (place and space) make for a fascinating case study. At one stage, the Dome seemed to unite almost everyone against it: politicians, journalists and the public. In spite of the negative publicity, it soon became one of Britain's most visited tourist attractions and an instantly recognizable symbol of London.

We can identify some of the Dome's initial functions as follows:

- To stage the Millennium night party
- To house the 'Millennium Experience' exhibitions for one calendar year
- To create a positive impression on visitors (the awe factor)

Figure 4.15 The Dome as a James Bond location; *The World Is Not Enough* (1999 dir. Michael Apted)

However it seems clear it was also intended to:

- Represent the state of the nation at the beginning of the third millennium
- Be a source of national pride
- Be a symbol of national optimism
- Be emblematic of the New Labour project.

In fact, as you can see in the article below, far from winning support for the government of the day, the Dome rather put the New Labour project in some jeopardy. It did though provide us with one new cultural practice, Dome-bashing. This was so widespread that Wonderbra ran an advertising campaign with the slogan 'Not all domes lack public support'.

A typical article on the Dome

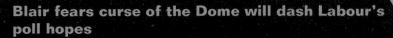

Blair fears curse of the Dome will dash Labour's poll hopes

Sunday, 9 January 2000

By Jo Dillon, Political Correspondent

Tony Blair fears the Millennium Dome could become a humiliating white elephant, generating continued bad publicity in the run-up to a possible spring general election next year.

The Prime Minister has ordered his press secretary Alastair Campbell to go on a 'charm offensive' as delays and difficulties at the £758m venue prompt a barrage of criticism.

It is understood that Mr Campbell met Jennie Page, chief executive of the New Millennium Experience Company, at the end of last week to agree a strategy on how Downing Street could help prop up the Dome's flagging image.

He promptly contacted national newspapers in an attempt to close down the post-new year run of negative publicity.

The Prime Minister's official spokesman blamed the critical coverage on the fact that 'a lot of editors were inconvenienced at Stratford', where queues held up revellers for hours on Millennium Eve.

'Nobody is denying there was a problem. People who should not have been inconvenienced were inconvenienced. But the way this has coloured the coverage of the Dome is totally out of proportion to what happened,' he said. 'There is a major ivory tower problem going on. The vast majority more than enjoyed it and really did have a good time.'

The co-ordinated offensive to put the positive case for the beleaguered Dome comes in the context of a fast-approaching general election in which Labour hopes to win a second term.

The Dome is already being used by opposition parties as a political football and, having pinned much on its success, the Government is now beginning to show signs of panic.

The Liberal Democrat Dome spokesman, Norman Baker, said: 'New Labour's dream is turning into New Labour's nightmare and the Millennium Dome is unravelling at a rate of knots.'

The shadow culture secretary, Peter Ainsworth, said the Dome would face financial crisis before the end of the year.

'Ministers are reported to be looking for scapegoats. It would be wrong for chief executive Jennie Page to face the axe,' he said. 'I believe she did her best to fend off the persistent meddling of Government ministers. It is they who should carry the can for the growing crisis surrounding the Dome.'

But Mr Blair's spokesman paid tribute to Ms Page and her team, adding: 'Not for one minute does he regret the decision the Cabinet took to go ahead with it.'

Source: http://www.independent.co.uk/news/uk/this-britain/blair-fears-curse-of-the-dome-will-dash-labours-poll-hopes-728420.html

Other articles can be found at:

http://edition.cnn.com/2000/STYLE/design/09/08/charles.dome.reut/index.html

and

http://edition.cnn.com/2000/WORLD/europe/UK/12/15/milleniu m.dome/

Clearly, the meanings of this particular place were appropriated by those who wanted to manipulate it as a sign. In the case of the Dome it was widely argued that its fate was sealed on its opening night at the Millennium party. Poor organization meant that luminaries and invited guests, including a full set of newspaper editors, were left queuing for hours in the cold. From that moment on, reviews of the Dome experience in the popular press were scathing and vindictive. This may have been one of the last great examples of the influence of a declining tabloid press, leading Prime Minister Tony Blair to comment darkly, 'Those who should not have been inconvenienced, were inconvenienced'.

It is interesting to note that the Queen's decision to open Buckingham Palace to the public in the same period sparked no such controversy, perhaps because it was a more comfortable symbol of Britishness (however elite and remote). Historically any thoughts of recreating the optimistic mood which inspired the 1951 Festival of Britain and its attendant 'landmark' (The Royal Festival Hall) were probably unlikely to succeed. The Festival of Britain was a conscious response to a recently finished world war and a growing feeling that winning the peace would be harder than expected. By comparison, the millennium was a more abstract project brought into alignment with that even more abstract project, 'Britishness'. The Dome became, as public places and spaces often do, the fault line in this debate and its inevitable symbol. Nobody doubted its visual impact or its engineering; the debate was about its content, its substance, its meaning. The Dome was never going to win this one, despite the enormous cost. There were suggestions that it should be demolished at the end of the year or left empty as a draughty reminder of the implications of overweening ambition. Interestingly, the incoming Conservative government in 1953 cleared the original Festival of Britain site, leaving only the Festival Hall.

In the event the Dome was, of course, re-cast, renamed and in the blink of an eye rehabilitated. Going to the Dome was in 2000 akin to going to the dogs. However, by 2007 when Led Zeppelin (aka 'the greatest rock band the world has ever known') reformed for a one-off tribute to the founder of Atlantic Records, there was only one place to go.

Tempting though it is to talk of the patient being given oxygen, the truth is that the resuscitation was performed with no such significant intervention. Put simply, a spectacular architectural 'event' was merely presented with a more realistic set of commercial functions:

- Be a spectacular venue for musical events
- Provide space and cover for support services (restaurants, cafés, outlets, etc.).

This is a very different project to that of containing 'the hopes and fears of all the years'. Unburdened of being Britain in a nutshell (despite offending millions by merely being located in London) the O2 arena can now find a more sympathetic place in the affections of the public. The O2 website now confidently describes the arena experience in glowing terms:

> The arena at The O2 truly creates a new benchmark in what both fan and performer can and should expect from a rock or pop concert in the UK. You will only see the world's hottest and most sought after acts on this stage; Bon Jovi, Justin Timberlake, Scissor Sisters, Prince, The Rolling Stones, Elton John, Take That. . . and what a way to enjoy them. With perfect sight-lines from every angle, crystal clear acoustics, obscenely comfy seating, wide concourses between aisles and a huge variety of snack and drink options to enjoy throughout the show. We've even put paid to that excruciatingly painful and frustrating tradition of the 'fifty minute queue for the loo' by fitting 548 toilets.

Sports

> The O2 arena can be transformed from a concert venue into a breathtaking world class sporting arena within hours and will proudly host major events throughout the year. The O2 are dedicated to promoting and supporting British sport, and as an official partner of London's successful bid to host the 2012 Olympic Games we will be hosting both the gymnastics and basketball finals.

Source: http://www.theo2.co.uk/inside/the-o2-arena.html

ACTIVITY

Re-issue, repackage, rebrand

Consider the re-branding of the Millennium Dome in the following ways

- What is your impression of the O2 arena?
- What are the sources of this impression?
- When you think O2 arena, do you also think 'Millennium Dome'?
- Consider specifically the advantages of the name change (O2 Arena versus Millennium Dome)

continued

If we needed to choose places/buildings/monuments to represent Britain now, what would they be? Choose a set of five and save images that can be shared and discussed.

What is it that these places represent to you?

Do you share the version of Britishness that they represent?

From landmarks to landscape: in the streets where we live

The debates that circulate around significant public landmarks are a very explicit manifestation of the process of negotiation that is going on all the time between people and their environments. Seeing your local cinema, or the supermarket or even your own modest semi as a text is largely unproblematic. As set-pieces they are susceptible to analysis in the usual way but equally, they are too easily divorced from their dynamic contexts as products can be divorced from practices. When Barthes famously declared that 'the city is a writing' he was talking about more than a collection of discrete texts. The immediate context of his essay 'Semiology and the Urban' deserves further analysis:

> **He who moves about the city, e.g. the user of the city (what we all are) is a kind of reader who, following his obligations and his movements, appropriates fragments of the utterance in order to actualise them in secret.**

(Leach, 1997, p. 170)

'Appropriation' is a key concept in this respect since it links national debates over the Dome to the local political acts of residents reclaiming their own neighbourhoods. It is also key to Henri Lefebvre's arguments about the way space is produced (i.e. identified and controlled) in a world dominated by imbalances of power (and the attendant ideology). Lefebvre sees the abstract spaces produced by a largely undecorated modernist architecture as potential sites of appropriation; in their apparent openness and easy democracy he sees the potential for action. For the Marxist Lefebvre we are classically alienated from this public 'dead' space and we are challenged to change this. This may be much more like the kind of active reading of the city that Barthes is suggesting. Barthes writes of a reader who follows his 'obligations and his movements' to appropriate parts of the experience which he can then 'actualise . . . in secret'. Here is a process of active negotiation and the 'tactics' of semiotic resistance.

For Michel de Certeau, who was significantly influenced by Lefebvre, this resistance is central to the practice of everyday life. The 'appropriation' of experience is a mode of resistance to the dominant practices of capitalism, since it is the equivalent of an oppositional reading of a text. This notion is clarified in the introduction to de Certeau's influential work *The Practice of Everyday Life*:

> **Many everyday practices (talking, reading, moving about, shopping, cooking) are tactical in character. And so are more generally, many 'ways of operating': Victories of the weak over the strong (whether the strength be that of powerful people or the violence of things or of an imposed order, etc.) clever tricks, knowing how to get away with things, 'hunter's cunning'. . . from the depths of the oceans to the streets of modern metropolises, there is a creativity and permanence in these tactics.**

(de Certeau, 2002, p. xix)

De Certeau sees the habitation of spaces as an act of creative reading, in fact almost an act of rewriting. He sees our interactions with social space (and its attendant human relationships) as a kind of improvisation.

> **This mutation makes the text habitable, like a rented apartment. It transforms another person's property into a space borrowed for the moment by a transient. Renters make comparable change in an apartment they furnish with their acts and memories; as do speakers in the language into which they insert both the messages of their native tongue and, through their accent, through their own 'turns of phrase,' etc., their own history; as do pedestrians, in the streets they fill with the forests of their desires and goals.**

(de Certeau, 2002, p. xxi)

In many ways, this is an attractive and liberating idea. Architects, planners and developers may be able to mould the *form* of our streets and cities, but they cannot determine the ways in which we actually *use* them. On the other hand, most pedestrians would probably be surprised to know that they were 'filling the streets with the forests of their desires' as they hurried to the bus stop or tube station and we should note that de Certeau's detractors have been rather dubious about his characterization of everyday life as 'resistant'. However, he certainly leads towards a further consideration of 'the street' and its many meanings.

In *Leisure and Tourism Landscapes* Cara Aitchison and her co-authors note that geographies of the street 'have shifted from viewing the street as a place of residence or business to a place of leisure, consumption, identity formation, fashion, spectacle and performance' (Aitchison, MacLeod and Shaw, 2000, p. 21). This accords with de Certeau's idea that it is the people who use a street who transform it into their own space. This 'production of space' is also a central theme of Lefebvre's theories and is a helpful idea in tackling the next activity.

ACTIVITY

Meanings of the street

Use the following binary pairs to discuss and explore the meanings of the street in your own experience

Leisure	Work
Freedom	Inhibition
Subordination	Domination
Enjoyment	Anxiety
Surveillance	Anonymity
Ours	Theirs

Are there places in your neighbourhood which have been transformed into spaces for performing your own cultural identity; where you can 'be yourself'?

Figure 4.16 The urban landscape is a powerful metaphor, widely used in music, art and literature

How have meanings of 'the street' been influenced by musicians, writers and performers?

For many years, the concrete caverns below the Queen Elizabeth Hall on London's South Bank provided a major, if unofficial, venue for the city's skateboarders and graffiti artists. This space, close to the popular riverside walk, became famous as a place to show off your board skills or to mark out the territory with spray paint; all in front of the clacking cameras of tourists from all over the world. At the time of writing, Skate City has been 'saved' following closure threats, though the graffiti has been replaced by artist Robin Rhode's 'optical illusory landscape'.

Figure 4.17 The South Bank Undercroft: a venue for skateboarders and graffiti artists

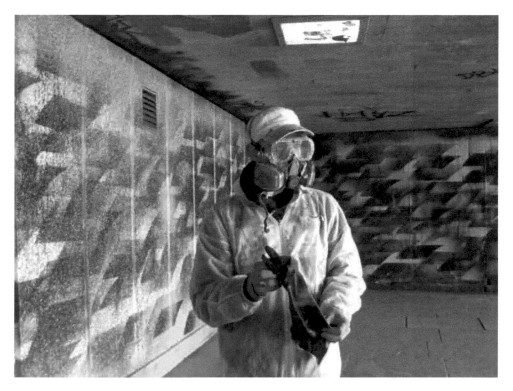

Figure 4.18 Robin Rhode creating his (officially sanctioned) work of optical illusion in Skate City, October 2008

In many towns and villages such 'invasions' of space are seen as gratuitous acts of vandalism and certainly a threat to the status quo. Here the appropriation of public places and their transformation into constructive and constructed spaces is not seen as either creative or empowering. Groups of teenagers often find themselves being moved on from their meeting places by security guards or the police. Interventions like this are frequently supported by street surveillance cameras and, more recently, by the Mosquito, a 'teenage deterrent system' (see Figure 4.19). Here social encounters are always political, since they're always concerned with power.

Mosquito Products

The Mosquito™ Anti-Vandal System is the solution to the eternal problem of unwanted gatherings of youths and teenagers in shopping malls, around shops and anywhere else they are causing problems. The presence of these teenagers discourages genuine shoppers and customers from coming into your shop, affecting your turnover and profits. Anti social behaviour has become the biggest threat to private property over the last decade and there has been no effective deterrent until now.

Acclaimed by the Police forces of many areas of the United Kingdom, the Mosquito Anti-Vandal System has been described as 'the most effective tool in our fight against anti social behaviour'. Shop keepers around the world have purchased the device to move along unwanted gatherings of teenagers and anti social youths. Railway companies have placed the device to discourage youths from spraying graffiti on their trains and the walls of stations.

Figure 4.19 The Mosquito™ Anti-Vandal System: from the website of the Mosquito's makers http://www.compoundsecurity.co.uk/

For Lefebvre and de Certeau, these acts of resistance should not only be recognized, but also celebrated. Lefebvre sees the social production of urban space (in other words the classification of it and the subjecting of it to rules and conventions) as essential to the reproduction of a capitalist society. When Lefebvre refers to 'struggles', he is not particularly thinking of physical confrontation over a piece of territory, but the more subtle contestation over the cultural meaning of a space. He suggests that we all have the capacity to resist 'official' determinations of a space by developing our own notions of 'lived space'; a meaning that is kept alive in our imaginations. As Rob Shields explains, this is the fullest and richest version of 'space':

> **Although suppressed in the abstract space of capitalist societies it remains in art, literature and fantasy. Lefebvre cites Dada, the work of the surrealists and, particularly the work of René Magritte as examples challenging taken-for-granted understandings and practices of space. Also included in this aspect are clandestine and underground spatial practices that suggest and prompt revolutionary restructurings of institutionalized discourses of space and new modes of spatial praxis, such as that of squatters, illegal aliens and Third World slum dwellers, who fashion a spatial presence and practice outside of the norms of the prevailing (enforced) social spatialization.**

(Shields, 2004, p. 210)

In gathering around the village war memorial or in the 1970s open shopping centre young people are, only partly consciously, challenging a hegemony that in turn imposes itself in more or less subtle ways. These challenging behaviours are not explicitly criminalized (at least not at first) or brutally suppressed ('if you are too violent' wrote the philosopher Michel Foucault 'you risk providing revolts. . .') rather they are 'outlawed' by a disapproving common sense which is value-laden despite seeming otherwise. Foucault talks about the 'observing gaze' which subjects everything to the effect of this disabling conformity:

> **There is no need for arms, physical violence, material constraints. Just a gaze. An inspecting gaze, a gaze which each individual under its weight will end by interiorising to the point that he is his own overseer, each individual thus exercising this surveillance over, and against, himself. A superb formula: power exercised continuously and for what turns out to be a minimal cost.**

(Foucault, 1980, p. 155)

In simple terms Foucault is by implication asking whether the restraints applied to us when we are out in the world which condition our behaviour are a matter of self-discipline or self-handicapping. We are sold a set of common sense values which are clearly touched by power in the sense that they vary according to the most significant demographic determiners: gender, age and ethnicity. Even in the wilds of the countryside we may seem inclined not to raise our voices, even when there's no one there to hear or see:

> **The observing gaze refrains from intervening: it is silent and gestureless. Observation leaves things: as they are; there is nothing hidden to it in what is given. The correlative of observation is never the invisible, but always the immediately visible, once one has removed the obstacles erected to reason by theories and to the senses by the imagination.**

(Foucault, 2003, p. 131)

Thus the fact that city centres are not seen as appropriate places for young women to get roaring drunk in, is clear and not a matter for debate. And what of theory and imagination? They'll only stop you from seeing this, so they must be avoided. The gaze tries to imply a singularity of meaning in a set of essentially polysemic texts. In fact it is merely a dominant way of seeing that attempts to suppress other views. It is through these ways of seeing, according to Bender, that people 'differently engaged and differently empowered, appropriate and contest their landscapes' (Aitchison, MacLeod and Shaw, 2000, p. 22).

The city is full of contested landscapes and appropriated spaces so any mover in it had better be a 'reader'. The human geographer Edward Soja coined the term 'spatiality' to reinforce the negotiated nature of all places and spaces, rural and urban. Their meanings are negotiated in the context of power relations which are informed by socio-cultural constructs such as gender, age and (dis)ability. 'No go areas' work both ways as messages from texts to readers with an exclusivity that can be seen in the smartest gallery and the hardest estate. Both the up-market shopping gallery and the tough housing estate are susceptible to appropriation, but it is an appropriation that may take place at the level of perception rather than by physically occupying and changing the shape of the places.

Sometimes, patterns of behaviour in a particular place become formalized into conventions or rules that are preserved by the punishment of transgressors, even if the punishment only amounts to a dirty look. Not knowing the social 'rules' of behaviour in public spaces is a frequent cause of tension between people of different cultural groups, leading to accusations that one group or other are ill-mannered or lack respect. Differences of age, social class and ethnicity often contribute to the tensions that arise in 'shared spaces'. Perhaps this is because public spaces are most importantly the arena for our most significant communication need, self-presentation: the performance of our social and cultural identities. In the public sphere we learn how to be who we are with all of the attendant difficulties. In learning the rules we learn about power and just how much power we have in any given circumstance. Can I enforce *my* rules in a particular space, or must I conform to someone else's rules?

It has been argued that in the past 150 years or so our lives have become more complex partly because we have abandoned an explicit sense of hierarchy. In the nineteenth century everyone knew their place because this was enshrined in public

A2 COMMUNICATION AND CULTURE

life: where they sat in their local church, in the schools they did or didn't attend, in the level of control they had over their own lives. Interestingly it is in traditional social and cultural institutions like organized religions and education that these still most explicitly survive; for example where males and females sit in the temple or synagogue, at weddings and funerals, where the 13 year old is allowed to sit at school dinners. As far as 'good' schools are concerned, particularly those you pay to go to, part of the experience seems almost to be the creation of something historical, where behaviour is as consciously traditional as the physical sur- roundings.

In addition to the allure of being part of the few rather than the many, private schools offer an image of themselves as citadels of old-fashioned order in the face of new-fangled disorder; in Arnold's terms strongholds of culture in the badlands of Anarchy. As for the rest of us, perhaps we are expected to put up with appar- ently deteriorating standards of public behaviour as if there were no alternative. Yet could anyone seriously argue that, for example, London in 2009 is more disorderly than London in 1909 or 1809? One difference is the level of expectation. What was expected of the urban poor a hundred years ago was conditioned by their relative unimportance as a largely disenfranchised underclass: crime, and general brutishness was all their supposed 'betters' expected.

In more enlightened and democratic times we sometimes don't seem to do much better, though we feel more inclined to address our concerns (which range between horror and guilt). Often we simply ask the wrong questions and therefore unsurprisingly get the wrong answers. Often, symbolic solutions are preferred to practical policies. The idea that parts of the country are 'out of control' is fre- quently taken up as a cause by the popular press. 'Who owns the streets of our cities?' we are asked on such occasions. Clearly, the expected answer is that ownership of the streets should be in the hands of those who respect law, order and sobriety. Here again, Arnold's view of Culture and Anarchy rears its head: in Britain it is sometimes too easy to see a line being drawn between the 'good folks and the bad'. How is this line drawn? Often, all too visibly in the form of gated communities, ASBOs, exclusion orders and 'zero tolerance' policing.

We can certainly see this process at work in what Lefebvre labelled 'abstract space': the characterless concrete piazzas, the soulless underpasses and over- passes of so many twentieth-century city developments. It seems neither paradoxical nor surprising that what in Britain was derided as the 'New Brutalism' should condition the experiences of a growing underclass whose city centre hous- ing had been swept away to enable concrete to dominate. These are landscapes made for squalor and 'ultraviolence'. The opening of Stanley Kubrick's 1971 film version of Anthony Burgess's A Clockwork Orange was a fitting indictment of the relationship between a degraded environment and a degraded morality.

Kubrick has Alex walking home towards a Brutalist suburban housing development, somewhere that might once have been England. We travel with him through the barely lit and desolate landscape. There is design here but it has been overtaken by negligent usage. There is even a mural in the foyer of his tower block home,

Figure 4.20 Violent acts in violent places: *A Clockwork Orange*

modelling a sort of socialist realist ideal but disfigured by unsightly smears and obscenities. The figures now bear enormous male sex organs together with instructions on how to use them: 'Suck it and see'.

There are at least two issues here. One is the model of designing environments without reference to the people who are to live in them, which we in Britain have only recently (and only partially) cured ourselves of. A cluster of recently demolished high rise blocks in the Black Country bore this condescension in their names: Chaucer House, Shakespeare House, Milton House. In her account of a life spent living in high rise council estates, including the Wood estate in Chelmsley Wood, Lynsey Hanley describes the mind set of estate life as 'the wall in the head'.

> **Walls in the head are insurmountable because they are invisible to the naked eye. It makes it easier for those who don't possess them to pretend that they don't exist at all. Brick walls are easy to climb, if you're agile; mental ones less so, when your mind is bruised by 'the hidden injuries of class'. That's the nature of housing people according to their social group, in places where other people don't have to live or work. Those other people are far luckier because, according to the jolly-**

(Hanley, 2007, p. 180)

The second issue is the disturbing but necessary empathy that we might learn from Kubrick for the perspectives of those who are otherwise labelled 'social problems'. Kubrick's dual focus, first and third person, partly represents this dichotomy: the inside and outside view. All social and cultural practices are comprehensible and coherent to the practitioners and civic disorder is nothing if not a cultural practice. The problem is that we only look for contexts when they suit us. British film is full of representations of decent working class folk dealing bravely with their social circumstances and these representations clearly contextualize the behaviour of Alex and that of his 'droogs' (friends). Kubrick (and Burgess) ask us to consider whether the droogs' amoral thrill seeking may just be a product of the environment in which they find themselves.

In exploring the relationship between behaviour and the built environment, a detailed history of domestic housing and urban planning would certainly be useful, but it is rather beyond the scope of this chapter. With respect to the history of social housing since the 1960s, Lynsey Hanley's book is certainly a good starting point. Hanley frequently reinforces the point that a history of housing is also a political, social, economic and cultural history. She charts the chequered saga of utopian good intentions, slum clearances, tower blocks, mass-scale housing, the 'right to buy' and the widespread demolitions of the late 1980s and 1990s. and concludes that:

❝ **No person in this country should have to feel that they**
live in a second-class home, which translates into a
belief that they are a second-class citizen with no stake
in a society dominated by property owners. ❞

(Hanley, 2007, p. 218)

This may be contrasted with Conservative Prime Minister Margaret Thatcher, who cogently expressed her views in a 1987 interview:

❝ **I think we've been through a period where too many**
people have been given to understand that if they have
a problem, it's the government's job to cope with it. 'I
have a problem, I'll get a grant.' 'I'm homeless, the gov-
ernment must house me.' They're casting their problem
on society. And, you know, *there is no such thing as*

society. **There are individual men and women, and there are families. And no government can do anything except through people, and people must look to themselves first.** 🙶

Just as telling as Hanley's vivid personal account of life on the council estate is the fictional world *of Only Fools and Horses*. In developments like the Docklands project in east London the sites of working class 'slums' were bulldozed to make way for what that comic parody of 1980s man Del Trotter would have called 'posh gaffs'. In a poignant episode of the sitcom, former merchant seaman (Uncle) Albert Trotter returns to his dockland home only to find a soulless concrete marina fronted by expensive apartments. Overwhelmed, he speaks for all those who might think that there is such a thing as society. Del, on the other hand, expresses a more Thatcherite view:

DEL, RODNEY and ALBERT stand on a jetty looking into the heart of darkness that is the Docklands Development

UNCLE ALBERT:

There were tugs nudging freighters into position, cranes lifting timber from Canada, bananas from Jamaica. The pubs and the cafes they were filled with sailors from a hundred countries. By the time I was seven I could swear in ten different languages

DEL and RODNEY laugh

There used to be streets all around here: loads of two up 'n two down houses, 'Dockers' mansions' they called 'em. Ragamuffins kicking foot-balls up against the walls. Women used to come and chase us away with their brooms. They were rough people but they was good people.

During the blitz some of the men painted a sign on the roof of a ware-house so that Luftwaffe pilots could see it. It said 'Dear Adolf: you can break our windows but not our hearts!' Look at what they done to it now.

Camera cuts to a view of the Dockland development

DEL:

Yeh, it's terrific, int it?

RODNEY:

Terrific?

DEL:

Yeh. I mean do you know how much some of these drums are worth Rodney? Well I'll tell you what they're worth, they're worth an arm and a leg. You know Lord Linley's got one of these and Michael Caine. Oh yeh, makes you proud to be British dunnit. I could do with a bit of this. . . .

Compare the vista of the Docklands marina described above to this description of 'abstract space' that comes from K. Michael Hays' introduction to the work of Lefebvre. One of the key implications here is that one of the functions of abstract space is to 'dissolve all differences' (to project a kind of default equality) and that this is bound to be provocative in a context in which 'difference' (especially inequality) so obviously exists and thrives.

> **Abstract space is at once fragmented and homogeneous: capitalism compartmentalises and routinises all activity . . . such contradictions cause differences to exert themselves even as abstract space tends to dissolve all difference. And it is precisely the instability of abstract space that produces the potential to resist its domination, to produce an 'other' space, by what Lefebvre calls the 'appropriation' of space from its alienation to capitalism – 'the "real" appropriation of space, which is incompatible with abstract signs of appropriation serving merely to mask domination'.**

(Hays, 1998, p. 175)

Partly this is about understanding that the implicit function of 'abstract space' (open areas with no explicit function) is to entice us into approved and to some extent prescribed activities. These are places of social gathering, meeting places, sitting and thinking places: places of productive social activity. If we 'enter' them in this way we are not really appropriating them we are merely conforming to social and cultural expectations, allowing our social relations to be 'routinized' and 'compartmentalized'. We are, as it were, ignoring the instability of open texts, choosing instead to agree that they are closed.

Landscape

If the comments above are true of the urban environment, then surely the notion of 'abstract space' is just as applicable to the project 'nature' and its attendant landscapes. The 'country walk' with its co-relative 'natural beauty' is a routine like any other, a cultural practice hemmed in with ideological expectations. And with landscape in Britain so tied up with ownership and thus social class, Cosgrove is surely right when he says:

> **Landscape, I shall argue, is an ideological concept. It represents a way in which certain classes of people have signified themselves and their world through their imagined relationships with nature, and through which they have underlined and communicated their own social role and that of others with respect to external nature.**

(Cosgrove, 1998, p. 15)

The truth is that for many the responsible country walk occurs within some controlled environment and takes organized trails from dedicated bench to dedicated bench. These memorials to those who have enjoyed 'spectacular views' are also indications of the partially programmed nature of the 'natural' experience (if not natural world itself). And those of us who routinize their walks enough to largely take in the same sites (and sights) every time we go: woe betide anyone who has appropriated 'our' bench or dares to share our favourite view!

ACTIVITY

Landscapes of the mind

Your task here is to think about how 'landscape', 'nature' and 'the countryside' are constituted as powerful myths. Much as we like to think of the rural environment as a natural, untouched alternative to the heavy-handed artificiality of the town, we probably know we are kidding ourselves. The British countryside is every bit as constructed, managed and commoditized as the city.

What is your first impression of this image?

What does it mean to you?

Figure 4.21 Wiltshire countryside

What do you feel?

What do you see? (think denotatively)

What are the significant myths at work here?

Look back to the activity 'Meanings of the street'. How well can the same set of binary pairs be used in an analysis of the countryside?

Use the web to investigate the work of organizations that are largely concerned with the countryside, e.g. The Campaign to Protect Rural England, The National Trust, English Heritage, National Parks, The Conservation Foundation. There are numerous groups associated with conservation and the environment, some national some local. Try to establish what it is that such groups want to protect and conserve, using your own set of images.

Our notions of countryside derive, of course, at least as much from images of the rural environment as from our direct experience of getting our boots muddy. A significant contribution to these myths has been made by landscape art. At first glance, landscape paintings appear to be a kind of extravagant form of still life but on closer inspection they are so much more. For a painter like John Constable, reproductions of whose classic English landscapes politely adorn many a sitting room wall and place mat, landscape art was about an open emotional confrontation. At a time when composition of paintings was thought to be a matter for the imagination he pioneered painting in oils on location in the open air. His skies are particularly expressive, and justifiably famous since he thought the sky 'the key note, the standard of scale, and the chief organ of sentiment' in a landscape. His 'Weymouth Bay' pictured below offers in every sense an 'aspect' of the scene: both a view of it and an interpretation of it that is equally realistic and symbolic.

Figure 4.22
Weymouth Bay

Despite the fixed frame and the motionless motion of sea, sky and land this landscape is in a real sense both unknowable and uncontrollable, slipping always beyond our frames of reference. Such it must be with all our places and spaces since we may only grasp them tenuously and intermittently. As Bender quite rightly says:

> **Landscapes are thus polysemic, and not so much artefact as in process of construction and reconstruction. The landscape is never inert, people engage with it, rework it, appropriate and contest it. It is part of the way in which identities are created and disputed, whether as individual, group or nation-state.**

(Aitchison, MacLeod and Shaw, 2000, p. 22)

Like music, places such as Clent Hills contain memories of when you were there before and one of the functions of the conservation of the countryside is to ensure that it, unlike us, 'does not grow old'. For the poet William Butler Yeats this was the abiding experience of returning to Coole Park in Dublin to see the swans, a sight he first experienced as a child. He is shocked to find them unchanged; in fact they are so only as metaphor:

The Wild Swans at Coole

The trees are in their autumn beauty,
The woodland paths are dry,
Under the October twilight the water
Mirrors a still sky;
Upon the brimming water among the stones
Are nine and fifty swans.

The nineteenth Autumn has come upon me
Since I first made my count;
I saw, before I had well finished,
All suddenly mount
And scatter wheeling in great broken rings
Upon their clamorous wings.

> I have looked upon those brilliant creatures,
> And now my heart is sore.
> All's changed since I, hearing at twilight,
> The first time on this shore,
> The bell-beat of their wings above my head,
> Trod with a lighter tread.
>
> Unwearied still, lover by lover,
> They paddle in the cold,
> Companionable streams or climb the air;
> Their hearts have not grown old;
> Passion or conquest, wander where they will,
> Attend upon them still.
>
> But now they drift on the still water
> Mysterious, beautiful;
> Among what rushes will they build,
> By what lake's edge or pool
> Delight men's eyes, when I awake some day
> To find they have flown away?

Yeats' musing on age and mortality begins in a simple description of a simple land-scape, albeit a consciously artistic one. Some would argue that 'far from being a "natural" relationship, the affinity that humans have for landscape is predominantly a (by-)product of the imagination, shaped by a variety of social and cultural con-structs' (Aitchison, MacLeod and Shaw, 2000, p. 77).

Music, space and place

When images and music come together a sense of place can be powerfully evoked. There are, for example, many songs that capture a sense of place, from *Massachusetts* (a big hit for the Bee Gees in the 1960s) to *Stanley Road* (Paul Weller's album-length tribute to the street where he lived). Though many of these contain snatches of narrative they are more importantly about the essence of a place at a moment in time, they are discourses on the meanings of places. Take Duffy's 2008 hit *Warwick Avenue*, named not after her childhood home in Nefyn, North Wales but after a North London thoroughfare. In this song the explicit place gives a focus for a strong personal feeling, that of regret and the imminent termi-nation of a relationship. She begins:

> When I get to Warwick Avenue
> Meet me by the entrance of the Tube
> We can talk things over a little time
> Promise me you won't step out of line.

This is the pressure of the song embodied in the banality of the terminal point, which could be anywhere but has to be somewhere. Warwick Avenue is any street yet also explicitly only one. The truth of the matter is very simple:

> When I get to Warwick Avenue
> I'll tell you baby, that we're through.

However, and as ever, it's dealing with the complex emotions that underlie the simple words, that is the problem. To travel hopefully they say is better than to arrive, perhaps even in this case and the ending is inconclusive. The train may have departed but as the song fades it is unclear whether Warwick Avenue has actually been reached.

An altogether more hopeful and wistful mood is evident in Ray Davies' masterful evocation of the 1960s twilight in the Kinks' *Waterloo Sunset*. Whether or not Terry and Julie are 1960s superstar actors Terrence Stamp and Julie Christie or as Davies suggested in 2004 'real people', is not significant. It merely confirms the mythical impact of the song. In fact, *Waterloo Sunset* does just what it suggests: it presents a place, a time of day and a reflection on the moods associated with this time and place. This landscape is full of people, though only Terry and Julie are named, and this is an essential part of its wisdom. It gives a feeling of being grounded, based in reality as a prerequisite to being content and as a result free. Its wistfulness and poignancy remind us, like Yeats' *Wild Swans at Coole*, of the curious relationship between a place and a time. The language is descriptive rather than figurative to embody this idea:

> Dirty old river, must you keep rolling
> Flowing into the night
> People so busy, makes me feel dizzy
> Taxi light shines so bright
> But I don't need no friends
> As long as I gaze on Waterloo Sunset
> I am in paradise.
>
> Every day I look at the world from my window
> But chilly, chilly is the evening time
> Waterloo Sunset's fine
>
> Terry meets Julie, Waterloo station
> Every Friday night
> But I am so lazy, don't want to wander
> I stay at home at night
> But I don't feel afraid
> As long as I gaze on Waterloo Sunset
> I am in paradise.

Every day I look at the world from my window
But chilly, chilly is the evening time
Waterloo Sunset's fine

Millions of people swarming like flies round Waterloo underground
But Terry and Julie cross over the river
Where they feel safe and sound
And they don't need no friends
As long as they gaze on Waterloo sunset
They are in paradise

(Ray Davis 1967)

At the outset of this chapter we acknowledged the intimidating scope of 'spaces and places' as a topic area. We cannot hope to do full justice to all the possible approaches to the topic here, but we do hope that we have given you the confidence to launch your own explorations.

References and further reading

Aitchison, C., MacLeod, N. E. and Shaw, S. J. (2000) *Leisure and Tourism Landscapes: Social and Cultural Geographies*, Abingdon: Routledge.

Avery, D. (2003) *Modern Architecture*, London: Chaucer Press.

Bennett, P., Hickman, A. and Wall, P. (2006) *Film Studies: The Essential Resource*, Abingdon: Routledge.

Corbusier, L (1986) *Towards a New Architecture*, Mineola, New York: Dover.

Cosgrove, D. E. (1998) *Social Formation and Symbolic Landscape*, Madison: University of Wisconsin Press.

Davies, R. (Composer) (1967) *Waterloo Sunset*.

de Certeau, M. (2002) *The Practice of Everyday Life* (S. Rendell, Trans.), Berkeley: University of California Press.

Foucault, M. (1980s) *Power/Knowledge: Selected Interviews and Other Writings 1972–1977* (C. Gordon, Trans.), New York: Pantheon.

Foucault, M. (2003) *The Birth of the Clinic: An Archeology of Medical Perception* (A. Sheridan, Trans.), Abingdon: Routledge.

Hanley, L. (2007) *Estates, An Intimate History*, London: Granta.

Hays, K. M. (1998) *Architectural Theory Since 1968*, Cambridge MA: MIT Press.

Leach, N. (1997) *Rethinking Architecture*, Abingdon: Routledge.

Shields, R. (2004) Henri Lefebvre, in P. Hubbard and R. V. Kitchen (eds), *Key Thinkers on Space and Place*, London: Sage, pp. 208–13.

Tinniswood, A. (1998) *Visions of Power; Ambition and Architecture from Ancient Times to the Present*, New York: Stewart, Tabori and Chang.

5 FICTIONS

Let us start by being very clear about just what we mean by 'fictions' in the context of *A2 Communication and Culture*. Fictions are *stories*; imagined or invented series of events that are organized in some way in order to be communicated. Such stories range from the wildest flights of fantasy to the recounting of real events. The form of communication may be the bedtime story, the novel, the feature film or the museum exhibition. In the last chapter we saw how buildings, places and spaces may be seen as texts that have the capacity to communicate a range of meanings. In just the same way, this chapter examines the ways in which cultural products and cultural practices communicate as fictions.

You may well find yourself questioning the use of the term 'fictions' on the grounds that fiction, surely, implies a falsehood, an untruth – at the very least something that has been 'made up'. On occasions, this may well be the case, but what we have in mind here is a use of the term that lies closer to the idea of *myth*: a way of explaining, simplifying and organizing our perceptions of the world – making our shared understanding seem natural or taken for granted. As you will recall from your AS studies, this 'shared understanding' is a crucial concept. For a culture (or subculture) to have any relevance, its members must have in common a core of more or less taken for granted assumptions about how to interpret the world around them. In his book, *Mythologies*, Roland Barthes set out to analyse those assumptions that just 'go without saying' in a culture. (For example, Barthes sees in a wrestling match representations of good and evil, justice and heroism as the opponents enact the 'great legendary themes' of popular mythology.) This is also our intention in the exploration of Fictions. Some of the stories that reinforce these assumptions may make no claims to truth at all (for example the fairy story), whilst others may make strong truth claims (for example a celebrity's autobiography). However, our task here is not to assess the presence or absence of 'truth' in our fictions, it is to understand the role that they play in defining our culture. Our underlying questions are: What are the stories we tell (and, more significantly, *re-tell*) and what are they for?

This chapter, then, concerns stories both explicitly and implicitly; it is about the ways in which fictions are embedded in our cultural experiences and into the processes of enculturation. We are certainly interested in **narrative** forms, how stories are put together, and in **genres**, the different categories of stories, but it is worth stressing that our field of enquiry is much wider than just those texts, such as the novel or television play, which are traditionally associated with 'fiction'. In this way, a concept such as the Quest Narrative (see Information Box) may be applied to a theme park or a retail store just as easily as *The Lord of the Rings* or *Apocalypse Now*.

INFORMATION BOX – THE QUEST NARRATIVE *i*

The quest is a type of story in which a hero sets off on a mission to retrieve some object of value or solve a great mystery. The mission involves many obstacles and difficulties which must be overcome to achieve an ultimate goal. Standing between the hero and this goal is the villain. The villain (and any villainous allies) must be vanquished before the hero can accomplish the objectives of the mission before triumphantly returning home to claim a well-earned reward.

The Russian narrative theorist, Vladimir Propp, identified a set of 'character types' typically found in the quest:

The Hero	The protagonist and main agent of change
The Villain	Places obstacles in the path of the hero. Must be defeated in order that the hero can carry off the prize. Often assisted by henchmen who oppose the hero before the climactic confrontation.
Donor	Provides the hero with a 'gift'. This could be a magical power, a piece of valuable information or a talisman.
Helper	The hero's trusted sidekick(s). Often a dangerous role in quests as helpers are quite likely to find themselves sacrificed to the cause – helpfully providing or strengthening the hero's revenge motive.
Dispatcher	Sends the hero off. May also act as the hero's mentor.
Sought for Person	Or 'Princess' – may be the object of the hero's mission and/or the reward for succeeding in the quest
False Hero	Often mistaken for the real hero by other characters (including the Princess's Father – who may be tempted

to bestow the reward on the False Hero instead of the Real Hero).

Whilst Propp originally detected the role types and narrative stages in folk and fairy tales, they can also be found in many of the fictions of contemporary culture. For example, in TV makeover programmes such as *How To Look Good Naked* the hero's mission is to improve their looks and self-confidence with the aid of the show's presenter (the 'helper'). Various experts ('donors') give tips or practical help whilst a doubting family member ('villain') may tempt the hero away from the goal. The hero's reward is a new sense of self-worth and the accolades of friends and family.

Before going on to illustrate Fictions as a cultural site, we need to draw an important distinction between two related but distinct cultural roles played by fictions:

1. Fictions communicate cultural norms and values to us. In this sense fictions are a significant part of the enculturation process; they help to define, reinforce, reproduce and, sometimes, challenge culture.
2. Fictions provide us with structural devices that enable us to 'enact' our culture. For example, I may plan or choose a holiday that provides a framework for me to live out a story of my own devising. This same framework gives me a *way of telling* the events of my holiday, so I can recount the events to others.

In order to illustrate and further explore these two roles, we shall use some variants of the story of Christmas.

ACTIVITY

Read the story and attempt the questions below.

> Father Christmas is a jolly old man with a long white beard and a bright red coat, hat and trousers. He lives at the North Pole. On the night before Christmas he sets out on his sleigh, loaded with presents and pulled through the night sky by reindeer. At each destination he fills his sack with presents and descends the chimney to leave gifts

continued

under a decorated tree or in children's stockings. Children may be able to meet Father Christmas in the weeks before Christmas – often in a large department store. They are able to make requests for special presents, but Father Christmas will always ask, 'Have you been good?' because presents are for good children.

What are the cultural functions of this story?

Can you think of alternative fictions that challenge the assumptions of the Father Christmas story?

How is the story circulated in contemporary culture?

Is the story culturally inclusive, i.e. does it embrace a wide range of different cultures, or is it culturally exclusive, i.e. does it reinforce the values of one culture in opposition to those of other cultures?

Figure 5.1 Father Christmas

The first activity relates principally to the first set of roles assigned to fictions. In answering the questions, you may have considered the normative value of a story that stresses the view that presents are a reward for good behaviour. You could, perhaps, have drawn on some of the theoretical perspectives discussed in Chapter 2 in order to link the story to capitalism or the implications of Father Christmas as a patriarchal character. The story is circulated by numerous means, including word of mouth, but it has particularly strong links with advertising campaigns. The Coca-Cola company has associated its products with the Father Christmas (or Santa Claus) story since the 1930s, to such an extent that it is widely, though mistakenly, believed that Coca Cola 'invented' Santa Claus.

The next activity relates more to the second set of cultural roles played by fictions; how we devise and insert ourselves into stories. Once again we shall use 'Christmas story' as a starting point. For some of us, an early experience of 'inhabiting our own story' could be gained from the personalized books available from mail order catalogues for children. Your parents would supply a few details about you; the name of your best friend or favourite toy, perhaps, and back would come an apparently personalized tale with you as the main character. Now, of course, the Internet provides us with a similar though much more rapid service.

ACTIVITY

Interactive Stories

Make your own Christmas story using

http://blackdog.net/cgi-bin/story/xmas.cgi

Analyse Pete's Christmas Story (below). What are the cultural functions of this story?

Investigate more personalized story sites e.g

www.penwizard.co.uk

www.cleverbooks.co.uk

What sorts of stories are chosen for personalization?

What is the appeal of the personalized story to its audience?

PETE'S CHRISTMAS STORY

It was a Christmas Eve Pete and Jerry will never forget. Jerry was visiting Pete for the holidays. They had just finished a grand Christmas dinner with lots of sticky toffee pudding, Pete's favorite. The grown-ups were in the kitchen cleaning up. Jerry and Pete were playing in the living room when all of a sudden they heard singing outside. Pete and Jerry ran to the door, and there standing in the lightly falling snow were Christmas carolers singing Frosty the Snowman. It was so cold you could see the singers' breath rising in the air like puffs of smoke.

The carolers called for Jerry and Pete to join them. It was late, but Pete asked if they could go for a little while. Yes! So, Pete and Jerry grabbed their coats and hats and gloves and went out to sing with the carolers. It was great fun!

continued

As Pete and Jerry headed home, the snow stopped, the stars started twinkling and the moon was so bright, they could see through the darkness. Just as they arrived at Pete's door, Jerry stopped. 'Listen Pete, did you hear that? It sounds like bells!'

'I hear it, too!' Pete said hurrying toward Jerry. 'Look up there,' Jerry pointed. 'Are you thinking what I'm thinking?' Pete asked. 'Yes! It's Santa! It has to be!' Jerry gasped excitedly. 'Listen, I think I can hear him calling out "Ho, Ho, Ho."'

'Yes!' Pete said, 'I hear it too! It looks like he's over Aileen's house. We better get inside and put out the milk and cookies! We need to get to bed ourselves.'

'Let's run,' Jerry said.

The grownups were just finishing the dishes when Jerry and Pete slid across the kitchen floor. 'We saw Santa!' Pete huffed. 'He was flying over Aileen's house. We've got to hurry and put out Santa's snack. If we're not in bed Santa won't stop here!'

Quickly, Jerry and Pete poured Santa's milk in a glass and put five chocolate chip cookies on a plate. They placed the snack on the hearth near the fireplace so Santa would be sure to see it. As they climbed into bed, they heard the grownups downstairs chuckling. 'That must have been one big shooting star those kids saw,' one said. Jerry and Pete just smiled at each other as they drifted off to sleep. They knew what they saw was not a shooting star. Shooting stars don't ring bells and they don't sing out, 'Merry Christmas to all and to all a goodnight!'

Variants of the Christmas Stories

You may need to refresh your memory of the analytical terms and techniques used in semiotics including

Denotation	Arbitrary Signs	Symbol
Connotation	Iconic Signs	Index
Paradigm	Redundancy	Myth
Syntagm	Entropy	

My Christmas Story is explicitly a fiction and, despite a level of incompetence that exposes the means of its construction, largely a traditional narrative. However, whatever the level of impact and engagement, My Christmas story is still dealing with meanings and values in a cultural context. Its 'fiction' is operating within other fictions. This is partly, perhaps largely, how it relates to its audience (though the limited interactivity is also a more potent force than we can probably give credit for). What is denoted by the combinations of words and images is not chiefly the issue here; pragmatically what is 'referenced' is merely a surface, scarcely more entropic than a traditional Christmas card design. The key concepts here are connotation and ultimately myth.

In a semiotic sense a myth is little more than a set of related connotations triggered by some aspect of the text, a confirmation but also a negation of personal response. The iconic signs which denote an old bearded man in a red suit or the written signifier 'Santa Claus' offer very little room for interpretation. The first order sign has been 'drained' of meaning at the second order and myth is the result. In some ways this is very useful if the job of 'fictions' is, in the end, to engage an audience. Myths deliver familiar meanings and more importantly prompt particular emotional responses. With Santa, in every sense, there are no ambiguities because we know what he is, what his story is and how we are expected to respond (even if we choose not to respond in this way). This is not only true with the consciously fictive it is a procedure by which all of the activities of man in society might be understood. Hawkes sums up Barthes' understanding of myth in a social context as 'the complex system of images and beliefs which a society constructs in order to sustain and authenticate its sense of its own being: i.e. the very fabric of its system of meaning' (Hawkes, 1977, p. 131). Society, then, delivers its 'system of meaning' through its fictions, both consciously and unconsciously, actively and passively.

Narrative, story and plot

As we have said, fictions are essentially the *stories* that enable culture to reproduce itself from one generation to the next; stories that, in their telling and re-telling, allow us to *enact* our culture. Whilst our focus is broadly on fiction in the sense of 'made up', we have acknowledged that fiction also embraces areas such as news, current affairs and the everyday relating of factual events. It is no surprise that journalists routinely refer to the raw material of news as 'stories', just as any one of us may 'tell the story' of a holiday or last weekend's party. We have also introduced the concepts of myth and narrative. At this stage, before exploring further examples and case studies, it is helpful to offer further definitions and make some distinctions between some of the terms and concepts widely used in discussion of fictions in Communication and Culture.

Narrative is a series of events. 'I am cold' is not a narrative, but 'I am cold because the evil Tesks of Orthorn have imprisoned me in an ice cavern' is a narrative. As the film theorists Bordwell and Thompson put it, a narrative is 'a chain of events in a cause–effect relationship occurring in time and space' (1990, p. 56). This is a very useful definition from our Communication and Culture point of view because it places emphasis on the three key components of narrative:

- **Causality** or why things happen, ('. . . because the Tesks imprisoned me.')
- **Time** or when things happen ('. . . I was imprisoned in an ice cavern, *then* I got cold.')
- **Space** or where things happen ('. . . the ice caverns of Orthorn.')

Clearly, though, these elements can be assembled in many different ways. The storyteller may very well withhold certain key pieces of information or may choose to relate events in non-chronological order. This leads us to make a distinction between two components of narrative: the *story itself* and the *way that the story is told*, the narrative discourse. All children are avid and enthusiastic consumers of stories, often delighting in the same story being told many times over. However as anyone who has regularly read books to children or told bedtime tales will know, their listeners are highly insistent that stories should not simply be told, they must be 'told properly'. Children certainly regard narrative discourse as being every bit as important as the story itself.

The term **plot** is often used to describe the fashioning of a story before it is told – it involves the planning of narrative discourse as well as the organization of story events. If we take the example of a film, the plot includes all of the information that is sequentially presented to the viewer. This includes theme music, titles, camera shots and angles, dialogue and sound effects (for example) as well as the events themselves. (See Information Box on Diegesis, p. 150.) From all of this information we (as viewers of the film) piece together the story through a process of inference. We make informed guesses about causal relationships between events and about the nature and functions of the characters we encounter. Imagine a scene in which we are introduced to two adult sisters in which it is made very clear that they have a jealous and resentful relationship. Most of us will *infer* that the cause of this unhappy state of affairs lies in their childhood experiences, even though we have been given no direct evidence that this is the case. In this way, we are building a story in our imaginations that occupies a much longer timescale than the events presented to us in the film; the story time is longer than plot time.

It is as if we are being given pieces of a puzzle one by one. At first, they make little sense but gradually the overall picture becomes clearer as we assemble the story from the evidence available. Often, of course, the plot feeds us deliberately misleading or inconsequential pieces of information. Frustrating as this can be, it gives us all the more pleasure as we finally put all the pieces together in the right order. We could say that the film-maker (or any story maker) turns the story into a plot whilst the audience converts the plot into a story. To put it another way, you can tell a story but you can't tell a plot.

A useful development of the plot idea is H. Porter Abbot's concept of the master-plot. These are the stories that recur in numerous forms, connecting to our deepest cultural values as well as our hopes and fears, Cinderella, Romeo and Juliet, 'things that go bump in the night', 'rags to riches' are all examples of masterplots, or:

> **Recurent skeletal stories, belonging to cultures and individuals that play a powerful role in questions of identity, values and the understanding of life. Masterplots can also exert influence on the way we take in new information, causing us to overread or underread narratives in an often unconscious effort to bring them into conformity with a masterplot.**

(Abbott, 2008, p. 236)

As we shall see, the masterplot is similar in many ways to Barthes' myth. The process of inference described above draws on our underlying knowledge of a wide range of masterplots. This fund of knowledge enables us to make *informed* guesses as we convert the plot into a story.

ACTIVITY

Masterplots

Look back at the two examples of Christmas Stories. What are the masterplots at work here?

Identify and discuss the masterplots referenced by an animated feature film such as *Shrek* or *Wall-E*.

Lessons in school or college often conform to narrative structures. Can you identify any of Abbott's masterplots in your classes?

Think of examples of narratives that draw upon the 'rags to riches' masterplot.

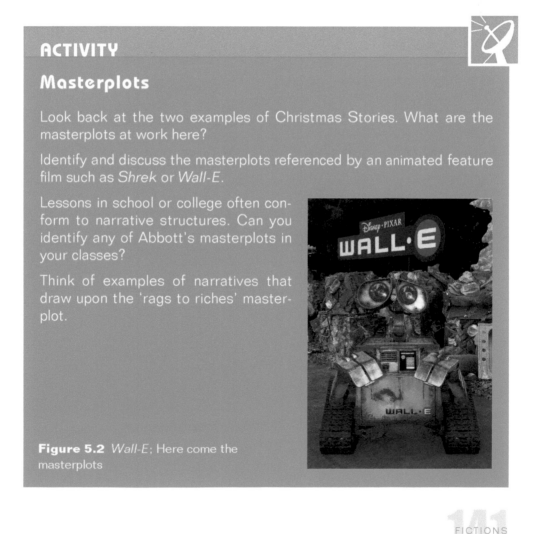

Figure 5.2 *Wall-E*; Here come the masterplots

Myth

ACTIVITY

Look at the two visual sequences in Figures 5.3 and 5.4.

In the case of Figure 5.3 Skittles, arrange the images to form a coherent narrative with your own captions

Identify the mythic elements in both cases

What are the differences between the two sequences?

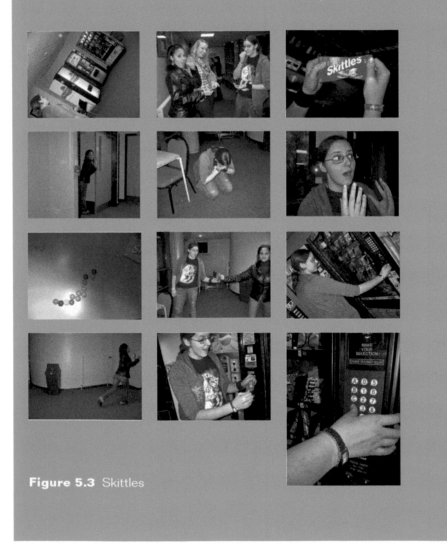

Figure 5.3 Skittles

Figure 5.4 Twelfth Night photostory. Created by Oxted School, Surrey for a BBC competition in 2005

Source:http://www.bbc.co.uk/drama/shakespear e/60secondshakespeare/writing_photostory_twelf thnight.shtml

The challenge of Fictions as a topic is represented by the two sets of images above. Robert Stam defines narrative as 'the recounting of two or more events . . . that are logically connected, occur over time and are linked by a consistent subject into a whole' (Stam and Flitterman-Lewis, 1992, p. 70). The key word here is 'recounting': it is in the act of communication that 'storying' takes place, that reality becomes realism. As the film-maker Alexander Kluge provocatively pointed out 'we must be able to render reality as the historical fiction that it is' (Bennett, Hickman and Wall, 2007, p. 203). In rendering our own realities we are essentially creating our own fictions: In telling our own stories we are giving structure to our own lives. This adds a new depth to Wittgenstein's famous dictum that 'the limits of my language are the limits of my world'. This world is not only 'referential' (reached out to by words) but also mythic (given symbolic value). As the structuralist anthropologist Lévi-Strauss pointed out: 'Myth is language functioning on an especially high level' (1963, p. 210).

What this means in practice is that these fictions, these stories are both structuring devices in which cultural meanings are constructed and at the same time perceptual frames, through which these meanings are interpreted and understood. Graeme Turner describes narrative as a 'major mechanism through which culture produces and reproduces social meanings' (Turner, 1999, p. 59). However these narratives might just as easily guide us around a heritage site or shopping mall as dissect for us the problematic relationships between step-children and step-parents (think *Hamlet* or *The Lion King* as you prefer). Hawkes attempts an overarching summary of all of these issues when he writes:

> **The definitive shape of that universal 'human mind' which locates itself in 'savage' as well as in 'civilised' carriers, and is borne indiscriminately by all of us, regardless of time, place or history, emerges clearly in its fictive acts, in its stories, its myths and it follows, in their 'civilised' counterparts: novels, plays and poems. However apparently firmly rooted in a particular and concrete 'present' and an individual response to it each of these may be, they betray beyond that immediate present and beyond that individual response, the trans-historical and trans-personal imprint that marks them as human constructs.**

(Hawkes, 1977, p. 58)

To 'novels, plays and poems' we might easily add 'films, television programmes and computer games' but this is not really our focus. The key for us lies in the phrase *in our fictive acts* since it potentially offers a scope well beyond formal narrative artefacts, be they civilized or otherwise. Hawkes is suggesting that a consideration of all of our 'fictions' will reveal something essential about us as human beings and about the cultures we create and maintain. The passage above comes at the end of a chapter entitled 'Linguistics and Anthropology' in which Hawkes chiefly focuses on the work of Claude Lévi-Strauss and particularly on his treatment of myth, which Lévi-Strauss sees as the key to a whole culture. Lévi-Strauss says that his aim is not to show how men think in myths, but rather 'how myths think in men, unbeknown to them'. Here is an argument for the central importance of 'fictive acts' that stems from Lévi-Strauss' study of so-called 'primitive' (i.e. pre-literate) societies. Hawkes quotes two long passages in which Lévi-Strauss is contrasting a tribal shamen's (witch doctor's) approach to 'curing the sick' with that of modern medicine. The shamen's cure, Hawkes explains, 'rests upon his ability to relate the disease to the world of myth and monsters in which the sick person genuinely believes'. He then decisively quotes Lévi-Strauss: 'The shamen provides the sick woman with a *language* by means of which unexpressed, and otherwise inexpressible, psychic states can be meaningfully expressed' (Hawkes, 1977, p. 26). There is much here for us as Communication and Culture students and we will go further with Lévi-Strauss later in this section.

Certainly there is a crossover here with the concept of '*bardic function*' proposed by Fiske and Hartley in their book *Reading Television* (Fiske and Hartley, 1978). Written in the 1970s, in some ways the heyday of terrestrial television when massive audiences for a single show were commonplace, *Reading Television* argued for a central and powerful place for television within modern culture. Fiske and Hartley compared television's role to that of the ancient bard or tribal storyteller. Very much in the way that Lévi-Strauss was suggesting, the bardic function of television provides us with a language to talk about contemporary reality. In doing so it also reassures us of our place in the scheme of things, looking after both a sense of identity and of community. Moreover it implies that the whole world of mass media entertainment is potentially a mythic world since it meets Roger Silverstone's definition of the mythic world as a world 'of feeling, participation and transformation' (Silverstone, 1981, p. 57). Here, the suggestion is that the fictional world of television encroaches on our own world to such an extent that it provides a framework for our emotional responses and actions.

ACTIVITY

Feel, participate, transform.

If the world of myth is a world of feeling, participation and transformation where is this evident in the contemporary media. Choose THREE significant texts and simply ask the following questions:

- What feelings are provoked?
- How is participation enabled and controlled?
- What transformations are proposed?

Example: *Crimewatch UK* – Long-running crime-stopper programme.

- What feelings? : **some apprehension and fear but also self-righteous outrage and moral superiority**.
- How participate?: **we 'can' technically phone in but more importantly sit looking on as justice is done in our name**.
- What transformations? **We clean up the streets together, gently**.

These examples of the mythic functions of television are not just examples of the 'language of the tribe'. Inevitably, they also represent the values of the tribe, that is to say our values, the values of our culture. In a world in which the influence of the traditional nuclear family is, arguably, in decline, the socializing influence of the mass media is all the more powerful. Few of our spaces are beyond the reach of the media; we are united by their fictions.

Case study

THE BLOODY CHAMBER

Many writers (not to mention TV programme makers, film makers and so on) have explored the nature of myth, narrative and the role of the story in contemporary culture. A notable example is Angela Carter's much acclaimed set of re-written fairy tales collected under the title *The Bloody Chamber* (Carter, 1998). Across seven, often gory, tales Carter exposes the nature of the mythic narrative along with its particular functions and uses. Carter reserves particular contempt for the 'Little Red Riding Hood' story, of which she makes two versions (*The Werewolf* and *The Company of Wolves*) and through which she extends her message to storytellers as well as stories.

In *The Werewolf* for instance she addresses the moral and ideological dubiousness of a story that tells girls to keep to the right path and teaches them to be fearful. These are stories told to them stereotypically 'on Grandma's knee', in circumstances in which, Carter tentatively proposes, sisters are doing it to themselves. Thereafter she unleashes in only thirteen hundred words, an attack on the unwitting but explicit role played by those mouthpieces of a dominant culture – the storytellers. In Carter's version a familiar story is rendered unfamiliar by a couple of spectacular twists. So 'go and visit grandmother, who has been sick' sets the scene and everything is OK until the attack of the wolf, 'a huge one with red eyes. . .' This is the cue for twist one: 'It went for her throat, as wolves do, but she made a great swipe at it with her father's knife and slashed off its right forepaw'.

Finding a little girl with 'kick-ass moves' in a fairy tale leaves us as surprised as the wolf: 'The wolf let out a gulp, almost a sob, when it saw what had happened to it.' Next we trek to Grandma's house to face twist two. Grandma is ill, feverish and in moments the truth is out: 'There was a bloody stump where her right hand should have been, festering already.' In taking her revenge, this particular little girl is taking symbolic revenge for all the stories told to little girls to keep them passive and fearful. As a result her prospects improve:

'Now the child lived in her grandmother's house; she prospered.'

Carter is concerned to expose the ideological forces at work in seemingly innocuous children's stories. Partly these are issues of representation to which we are all subjected through the process of ideological 'hailing', as Althusser had it. Carter is at her most economic and most brutal with *The Snow Child*.

The Snow Child

Midwinter – invincible, immaculate. The Count and his wife go riding, he on a grey mare and she on a black one, she wrapped in the glittering pelts of black foxes; and she wore high, black, shining boots with scarlet heels and spurs. Fresh snow fell on snow already fallen; when it ceased, the whole world was white. 'I wish I had a girl as white as snow,' says the Count. They ride on. They come to a hole in the snow; this hole is filled with blood. He says: 'I wish I had a girl as red as blood.' So they ride on again; here is a raven, perched on a bare bough. 'I wish I had a girl as black as that bird's feather.'

As soon as he had completed her description, there she stood, beside the road, white skin, red mouth, black hair and stark naked; she was the child of his desire and the Countess hated her. The Count lifted her up and sat her in front of him on his saddle but the Countess had only one thought: how shall I be rid of her?

The Countess dropped her glove in the snow and told the girl to get down to look for it; she meant to gallop off and leave her there but the Count said: 'I'll buy you new gloves.'

At that, the furs sprang off the Countess's shoulders and twined round the naked girl. Then the Countess threw her diamond brooch through the ice of a frozen pond: 'Dive in and fetch it for me,' she said; she thought the girl would drown. But the Count said: 'Is she a fish to swim in such cold weather?' Then her boots leapt off the Countess's feet and on to the girl's legs. Now the Countess was bare as a bone and the girl furred and booted; the Count felt sorry for his wife. They came to a bush of roses, all in flower. 'Pick me one,' said the Countess to the girl. 'I can't deny you that,' said the Count.

So the girl picks a rose; pricks her finger on the thorn; bleeds; screams; falls.

Weeping, the Count got off his horse, unfastened his breeches and thrust his virile member into the dead girl. The Countess reined in her stamping mare and watched him narrowly; he was soon finished.

Then the girl began to melt. Soon there was nothing left of her but a feather a bird might have dropped; a bloodstain, like the trace of a fox's kill on the snow; and the rose she had pulled off the bush. Now the Countess had all her clothes on again. With her long hand, she stroked her furs. The Count picked up the rose, bowed and handed it to his wife; when she touched it, she dropped it.

'It bites!' she said.

ACTIVITY

The Snow Child

Consider in detail the representations in the story of

- the Count
- the Countess
- the Girl

What is the impact of the setting for the story?

How does Carter challenge our expectations of the 'fairy story'?

Explore the symbolism of the rose in the story.

In the story 'The Snow Child' Angela Carter appears to be making points about the roles of women in mythic narratives. The brutality of the story, which deliberately shocks us, is there to make us sit up and take notice. We could go on to ask to what extent her 'model' of the relationship between women and 'romance' in stories is relevant to an understanding of the role played by women in contemporary Hollywood films. Similarly, to what extend might A List female stars find themselves agreeing with the Countess that, despite the money and the fame, 'it bites'?

What Carter is enabling us to do (or perhaps insisting that we do) is to appreciate the elements of the story, of the myth-making, which potentially give it meaning. At this stage, we can return to the anthropologist Lévi-Strauss, who gave us some useful tools for the analysis of myth.

As a structuralist, Lévi-Strauss was intent on finding the underlying 'rules' of myth: the structures common to all myths in all cultures. Structuralists working in language have sought to identify the basic units of language (for example, phonemes and morphemes) and the rules that enable us to generate meaningful sentences. Lévi-Strauss applied exactly the same approach to myth. He identified the basic irreducible element, the smallest part, of any myth as a *mytheme.*

Lévi-Strauss collected stories from all over the world from all sorts of diverse cultures and noted that they had many themes and features in common. Of course, these stories illustrated all sorts of difference and diversity in terms of their characters and events, but Lévi-Strauss was more interested in the underlying similarities of structure. Furthermore, because a myth has to be *told* in order to be brought into existence, Lévi-Strauss contended that myth *is* a language. The basic units – mythemes – form relations with each other based on binary oppositions. These binary oppositions are the building blocks of myth.

This is where Lévi-Strauss's ideas become really useful to us as students of Communication and Culture working with fictions. A culture needs its myths to provide explanations, to resolve contradictions and to impose order on a chaotic world. For this reason, myths set up tensions between a pair of opposing ideas and then negotiate an outcome that favours one or the other. Here's an example that should help to explain the process. None of us can simultaneously believe in both absolute self-interest and devoted attention to the needs of others. Selfishness and Altruism are binary opposites. Some stories deal with this opposition by reinforcing the values of enlightened self-interest: tales of overcoming great odds to make it to the top, for example. These stories would be prevalent in a culture with a strong emphasis on individualism and competitiveness. On the other hand, stories could deal with the same opposition by lauding a hero who is prepared to make sacrifices – maybe even the ultimate sacrifice of life – in the interests of wider society. We would expect to find these stories predominant in a culture with a predominantly collective or co-operative value system.

A culture's myths are unlikely to provide a uniformly powerful reinforcement of a single set of values; this is why we have used words like 'prevalent' and 'predominant' in the paragraph above. Most cultures accommodate competing myths, suggesting a much more subtle interplay of values and beliefs, but with an underlying pattern of dominant and subordinate morality.

ACTIVITY

Binary Opposition

Here are a few more sets of binary oppositions.

- Good vs Evil
- Masculinity vs Femininity
- Rural vs Urban
- Aggressive vs Passive
- Wealth vs Poverty
- Past vs Present

Which of each pair does your culture favour?

Are there stories that go against the grain?

How do the *Bloody Chamber* stories discussed above deal with these oppositions? With other oppositions?

Our exploration of myth takes us back to a basic semiotic grasp of selections and sets, or more formally, syntagms and paradigms. As a story progresses in time (syntagmatically), putting one sign in front of the other, it also draws down and emits information which enhances the impact of the progress; this energy emerges from the activation of sign sets (paradigms). Barthes addressed this process theoretically in his model of five narrative codes: two of which move the story forward (syntagmatically) and three of which connect it to everything else (paradigmatically). Barthes proposes two ways of addressing the issue of moving a story on: through action (via the *prioretic code*) and through suspense (via the *hermeneutic code*). In other words the momentum of a story derives from what is given in terms of actions and what is withheld as a kind of suspense.

INFORMATION BOX – DIEGESIS

i

This is the world of the characters in the story. In a film there is information that is only available to the audience, for example captions, theme music or the celebrity persona of an actor. This is non-diegetic information. In terms of the distinction we made earlier, non-diegetic information is part of the plot but not part of the story.

However Barthes was much more interested in those codes of narrative which govern the ways in which the world of narrative (the diegesis) is represented. These three codes concern:

- the connotations of signs within a narrative: a descriptive code (the *semic code*)
- the relationship of signs to the wider world outside: a code of realism (the *referential code*)
- the meanings of elements within the narrative: a representational code (the *symbolic code*)

These codes work cumulatively to constitute the texture of the narrative, to negotiate the mode of address and mode of reception, to challenge or confirm the reader's expectation. The openings of texts are good places to emphasize the usefulness of this approach: the place where texts and readers first meet. Consider for example the famous opening of Sergio Leone's Western *Once Upon a Time in the West*, where three gunmen wait for the train at a station somewhere and nowhere 'Out West'.

In this sequence few words are spoken and the three men occupy themselves in rituals of waiting: one of them ominously chasing a fly around his face with the barrel of his gun while another deals with a water drip that is irritatingly dropping

Figure 5.5 Tension mounts. The opening sequence of *Once Upon a Time in the West* (dir. Leone, 1968)

on his head. Here is the semic code, the code of connotations, describing a world to us in a way that gives weight to the film's forward movement into an uncertainty that gives way ultimately (because sustained) to doubt and dread (the hermeneutic code). The attention to detail both historically and psychologically also adds its own 'referential' contribution connecting this world with ours both historically and universally (waiting has always been like this and always will be). Meanwhile something darker is happening in the sound code as the rusty squeak of the water pump is mixed gradually to crescendo with the mounting score and ultimately the screaming train: a symbolic harbinger and ultimately a bringer of destruction. When the train arrives the action is short and brutal: a couple of lines of clever dialogue and then Harmonica (Charles Bronson) guns down the reception party: so much preparation for so little return. It transpires that they have been waiting for their own deaths.

ACTIVITY

Barthes' Narrative Codes

Screen the opening sequence of a contemporary film or television drama.

Identify and illustrate the following:

- the semic code
- the referential code
- the symbolic code

Are there also examples of:

- the hermeneutic code?
- the prioretic code?

fictions and interactive stories

Technological developments have led to the proliferation of interactive formats that allow readers a much greater degree of participation in the 'fictive act' so that at times the difference between author and reader is blurred. Particularly in 'fan' contexts there is a proliferation of collaborative fictions where fans of a cult television series, for example, write character dialogue (and plot) while interacting with other 'characters' and plots. Equally on-line computer games, particularly experiences like the phenomenally successful *Second Life*, are in one sense experiments in collaborative narrative with the computer generated environment acting as an implicit narrator. While Dickens might have created in words a lawyer's office complete with plaster death masks and a shoulder-height grease line to show where crowds had queued for service, in *Second Life* you may enter such a place and supply your own actions and dialogue. This is partly a tradition that came out of role-playing games of the 1970s, where the role of narrator was passed to a 'dungeon master' who negotiated a story with a group of 'adventurers'.

Figure 5.6 Is life getting you down? Try *Second Life*

ACTIVITY

Interactive Narratives

What are the differences between MMORPGS such as *World of Warcraft* and conventional film or literary narratives?

To what extent are social networking sites such as MySpace or Face Book contexts for 'fictive acts'?

Video games clearly play an important role in the fictional landscape of contemporary culture. Whether we assess the impact of gaming in financial terms or by measuring the time spent in playing games, it certainly looks significant. In November 2008, sales of games reached £4.64 billion – a 42 per cent rise since 2007; and higher than the combined spending on DVD, CD and music downloads (£4.4 billion). Source: http://www.itproportal.com/articles/2008/11/05/games-sales-now-bigger-combined-music-and-video-uk/

A 2008 American survey of 12–17 year olds found that almost all were video gamers, with over half of them playing on any given day. Source: www.pewinternet.org/PPF/r/263/report_display.asp

It seems likely, then, that for many people (especially young people) the video game is one of the predominant forms of fictional engagement. It is certainly an intriguing area for us to examine as we explore the two sets of roles which we identified for fictions on p. 135.

Undoubtedly, there are many ways in which video games communicate to us norms and cultural codes. For example, the male action hero is just as familiar a stereotype in the gaming world as he is in the Hollywood blockbuster and he is likely to carry a similar set of cultural baggage: individualism, use of violence to resolve all problems, limited range of motions, suspicion of anything 'foreign' or 'different' and so on. This type of focus on the somewhat negative and stereotypical character types to be found in the fictional world of certain video games may help to shed some light on cultural influences, but it doesn't really reflect the enormous range, diversity and sophistication of video gaming. From our point of view, an altogether more interesting aspect of video gaming lies in the structuring of the stories and the role of the player as an enactor or initiator of the story.

Interactivity: the case for the prosecution

Let us first set out the argument that the interactive nature of video games is something of an illusion. On the face of it, it seems fairly obvious that the player has a role, a function in the collaborative creation of a fiction. As you play, the format requires your active participation in the creation of a specific storyline from

Figure 5.7 Interactive or just another trip from A to B? *Half Life 2: Episode 2*

a mass of seemingly random variables. But given that so many games consist of cumulative task-based resolutions leading inexorably to a final challenge at the highest level of the game, aren't they just disguised versions of the linear narrative? In other words, whatever the apparent freedom, aren't you in the end merely looking for the path that somebody else has laid in order to take you where somebody else wants you to go? This may be an instructive psychological experience but it's not what's promised on the box (where the size of the explorable environment and the facility for 'freestyle' play are both selling points).

Before the Law

Franz Kafka

Before the Law stands a gate keeper. To this gate keeper there comes a man from the country who asks for admittance to the Law. But the gate keeper says that he cannot grant admittance at the moment. The man thinks it over and asks if he will be allowed in later. 'It is possible,' says the gate keeper, 'but not at the moment.' Since the gate stands open as usual, and the gate keeper steps to one side, the man can stoop to peer through the gateway into the interior. Seeing this, the gate keeper laughs and says: 'If you like, just try to go in despite my veto. But be warned: I am powerful. And I am the meekest of the gate keepers. From hall to hall there is one gate keeper after another, each more powerful than the last. The third gate keeper is already so terrible that even I cannot bear to look at him.' These are difficulties the man from the country has not expected; the Law, he thinks, should surely be accessible at all times and to everyone, but as he now takes a closer look at the gate keeper in his fur coat, with his big sharp nose and long thin, black Tartar beard, he decides that it is better to wait until he gets permission to enter. The gate keeper gives him a stool and lets him sit down at one side of the door. There he sits for days and even years. He makes many attempts to be admitted, and wearies the gate keeper by his importunity. The gate keeper frequently has little interviews with him, asking him questions about his home and many other things, but the questions are put indifferently, patronisingly, and always finish with the statement that he cannot be let in yet. The man, who has furnished himself with many things for his journey, sacrifices all he has, however valuable, to the gate keeper. The gate keeper accepts everything, but always with the remark: 'I am only taking it to keep you from thinking you have omitted anything.' During these many years the man fixes his attention almost continuously on the gate keeper. He forgets the other gate keepers, and this first one seems to him the sole obstacle preventing access to the Law. He curses his bad luck, in his early years boldly and loudly; later, as he grows old, he only grumbles to himself. He becomes childish, and since in his year-long contemplation of the gate keeper he has come to know even the fleas in his fur collar, he begs the fleas to help him and to change the gate keeper's mind. At length his eyesight begins to fail, and he does not know whether the world is darker or whether his eyes are only deceiving him. Yet in his darkness he is now aware of a radiance that streams inextinguishable from the gateway of the Law. Now he nears the end of his life. Before he dies, all his experiences in these long years gather themselves in his head to a point, a question he has not yet asked the gate keeper. He waves him nearer since he can no longer raise his stiffening body. The gate keeper has to bend low toward him, for the difference in height between them has altered much to the man's disadvantage. 'What do you want to know now?' asks the gate keeper; 'you are insatiable.'

'Everyone strives to reach the Law,' says the man, 'so how does it happen that for all these many years no one but myself has ever begged for admittance?'

The gate keeper recognises the man has reached his end, and, to let his failing senses catch the words, roars in his ear: 'No one else could ever be admitted here, since this gate was made only for you. And now, I am going to shut it.'

Unwittingly, Kafka's story provides a telling metaphor for the restrictions of a video game's player environment, and the implications for player pleasure. In many cases exploring the playable environment is akin to visiting a Disney theme park and avoiding all the attractions and rides because you are interested in the spaces between them (the dull bits of a magical world). Conventional video games then, merely give us the opportunity to live in somebody else's imaginative experience and to explore an imagined world from the perspective of a pre-programmed 'trip'. Rapidly evolving gaming technology may have made these trips progressively more visceral and engaging but it has hardly changed the fundamental premise that it is a journey from A to B. This might in a popular game such as *Half-Life* (see Figure 5.7) mean that having escaped the wretched research facility and met up with the troopers who have been sent to rescue you, you then have to spend an equal amount of time climbing back into the same research facility. This time, though, you are pursued by your supposed rescuers who, instead of trying to help you, are now looking to destroy the evidence on the company's behalf. You may in fact find that 'A' and 'B' in this case are very close together. The point is that even with this knowledge the game does not allow you to shortcut the process (the only ways are 'up' and 'down').

Similarly the *Grand Theft Auto* franchise might offer you lots of ways to negotiate a seedy environment but 'lots of ways' is a good deal less than 'free'. In fact where 'free' is significantly addressed, as perhaps in the *Sims* games or in the genuine 'freestyle' of something like the Tony Hawkes franchise, it paradoxically comes to resemble the indecisive, open-ended trial that these computer intensifications are meant to replace. What ultimately might be the difference between skating aimlessly around the precinct with your mates and doing the computer equivalent with your electronic celebrity mates? Like the cyberspace worlds of *Second Life* or *World of Warcraft*, perhaps the fictions of the video game environment are even more susceptible to ennui (that feeling of boredom and pointlessness) than 'real life'.

In Barthes' famous collection of demystifying essays *Mythologies* (which include treatments of the allure of Marilyn Monroe, and the shape of the Citroën car) he attempts what Hawkes describes as 'a remorseless analysis of the myths generated by French mass media' (Hawkes, 1977, p. 110). In doing so, continues Hawkes 'he lays bare their own purposes'. Barthes' introduction to this collection is worth hearing since it should prompt our analysis of computer game fictions (and narratives).

> **The starting point of these reflections was usually a feeling of impatience at the sight of the 'naturalness' with which newspapers, and common sense curiously dress up reality which, even though it is the one we live in, is undoubtedly determined by history . . . I resented seeing Nature and History confused at every turn.**

(Barthes, 1972, p. 11)

With near video-quality graphics the contemporary game acquires a naturalness which conceals its construction process. This is a realism threatening to become a reality. Whether it be the streets of Baghdad or the streets of Laredo these contexts (and their plurality) are imagined and ultimately without depth, an electronic transfer stuck in a bare electronic wall. In an essay entitled 'Myth Today' Barthes proclaimed that 'myth is a type of speech' and further that 'myth is a system of communication, that it is a message'. It seems clear that the computer narrative is a myth in this sense, 'a way of happening, a mouth'. However Barthes went on to explore the character of this speech that is myth or myth is and concluded that 'Myth is depoliticised speech'. Again the original is useful:

What the world supplies to myth is an historical reality
. . .

And what myth gives in return is a *natural* image of this reality. 〞

(Barthes, 1972, p. 142)

For Barthes the act of making natural is 'constituted by the loss of the historical quality of things': 'the function of myth is to empty reality'. It may be that the myths constructed within computer narratives fulfil this function perfectly since they, at the very least, offer an experience without implications. Crudely you can walk 'eye-deep in hell' and no one gets hurt but what happens to your sense of context and perspective? The educational, even the therapeutic function and benefit of role play is to meaningfully explore solutions to problems in a safe and supported context. Shooting bad guys in *Far Cry* for a couple of hours may 'do' tension release but it doesn't do problem solving and it doesn't do historical context: you're reacting not reflecting. This is interesting not as an indictment of escapist computer games but rather as a way of understanding the nature of traditional mythic narratives and fictions. Barthes is very clear what has happened:

The world enters language as a dialectical relation between activities, between human actions: it comes out of myth as a harmonious display of essences. A conjuring trick has taken place: it has turned reality inside out, it has emptied it of history and has filled it with nature, it has removed from things their human meaning so as to make them signify a human insignificance. 〞

(Barthes, 1972, p. 142)

The implication for computer games of Barthes' points are clear. Whether the context is Ancient Rome, The Somme or a far flung future the experience of a computer narrative is visceral and emotional, not reflective and historical. The 'conjuring trick' that has taken place is to dress a number of electronic rooms with one or more doors in a way that suggests they are environments which allow infinite exploration: further that they are 'worlds' which offer a complex experience of a complex reality. In fact they are merely backdrops for the demonstration of the simple truths of a simple reconstruction: a world where complexities can be crudely ironed out by 'sword' and 'pistol'. Barthes again is on the money:

> **In passing from history to nature: myth acts econom- ically: it abolishes the complexity of human acts . . . it organizes a world which is without contradictions because it is without depth, a world wide open and wallowing in the evident, it establishes a blissful clarity: things appear to mean something by themselves.**

(Barthes, 1972, p. 143)

Computer games offer self-sufficient meaning systems wherein a crude, and often brutal, simplicity is the order of the day. It is a world, or series of worlds wherein, however dark the problems, the solutions are blissfully clear.

ACTIVITY

A simple game

Fit your five favourite computer games into the following frame.

Title	Genre	What do you have to do	What's the best way to do it. How do you win.

The simplicity of these contexts is almost touching as if harking back to a less complex world where problems were resolved and meaning was not in doubt. So often history is a reference point, albeit a fairly superficial one as if we are no longer sure what is real and what is not. It would be hard not to read this as a kind of nostalgia thus supporting Baudrillard's claim that 'When the real is no longer what it used to be, nostalgia assumes its full meaning' (1998, p. 354). Here we have arrived at a postmodernist sensibility, a culture in which, Frederick Jameson claimed, real history is displaced by nostalgia. Jameson also accuses the post-modern view of 'pastiche, depthless intertexuality and schizophrenia', according to Storey and of the creation of a 'discontinuous flow of perpetual presents' (Storey, 1998, p. 347). This is a result of the decline of the metanarratives, those 'big' explanations which held everything together. Without them we have some-thing of a free-for-all albeit with increasing concern, where the only 'real' sense is that everything is uncertain. In these circumstances it is perhaps not surprising that we reach back to the imagined certainties of another age when everything made sense (or rather at a time when everyone thought it did). Now, the situation is far from clear, as Barthes asserts in his essay Death of the Author:

> **In the multiplicity of writing, everything is to be *dis-entangled*, nothing *deciphered*, the structure can be followed, 'run' (like the thread of a stocking) at every point and at every level, but there is nothing beneath.**

(Barthes, 1977, p. 147)

Interactivity and video games: the case for the defence

In his book *Everything Bad is Good for You; Why Popular Culture is Making Us Smarter*, Steven Johnson points out that most games offer a very distinctive challenge to players because, unlike board games, they 'withhold information about the underlying rules of the system' (2005, p. 42); just like the plots of of an adventure novel or a Hollywood feature film, video games set up enigmas; mysteries for the player to solve such as 'Who has abducted the princess?' or 'How can I blow that up?' Of course, these are important questions for players but, as Johnson says, 'the ultimate mystery that drives players deeper into the game world is a more self-referential one: how is this game played?'(Johnson, 2005, p. 43).

Most video games, beyond the very simplest, involve solving problems in the pursuit of objectives. These objectives or goals may not be clearly stated — in many games it is the player's task (or the task of the character under their control) to find out what it is that has to be achieved at each stage of the game. In order to open up the game players must embark on a programme of exploration, testing the environment by asking such questions as 'What will happen if I do this?', 'What is this for?', 'What if I click on this?'; the answers to these questions must be accumulated and stored in the memory in order to build up a working knowledge of the game environment. This fund of knowledge is constantly refined as new information comes to light; information that may confirm, refine or refute the player's hypothesis. In order to make progress in the game another set of skills must be added to these 'probing' techniques. Johnson calls this second type of skill 'telescoping' because it involves working out how multiple sets of objectives are embedded in one another, just like the sections of a telescope when it is closed up. Telescoping requires the interpretation of nested sequences of the type 'in order to *x* I must first do *y*'. Here's a short extract of nested sequences in *The Legend of Zelda: The Wind Walker*:

> **With the letter to the Prince, you must now befriend the Prince.**
>
> **To do this, you need to get to the top of Dragon Roost Mountain.**
>
> **To do this, you must get to the other side of the gorge.**
>
> **To do this, you must fill up the gorge with water so you can swim across.**
>
> (Johnson, 2005, p. 52)

Although these tasks may look banal with their references to princes and dragons, Johnson urges us to think of the cognitive challenge of video games rather than the aesthetic quality of the game worlds and their characters. As he reminds us, narratives are built out of events not tasks, so Johnson's argument is that the considerable mental labours employed in video gaming have only limited reference to narrative. Intriguingly, he suggests that video gaming has more in common with 'real life' than with fiction:

> **There's something profoundly lifelike in the art of probing and telescoping. Most video games take place in worlds that are deliberately fanciful in nature, and even the most realistic games can't compare to the vivid, detailed illusion of reality that novels or movies concoct for us. But our lives are not stories, at least in the present tense – we don't passively consume a narrative**

> **thread. [. . .] But we do probe new environments for hidden rules and patterns; we do build telescoping hierarchies of objectives that govern our lives on both micro and macro time frames.**

(Johnson, 2005, p. 56)

This theme is also taken up by another sympathetic analyst of video games and gaming. Espen Aarseth argues that the narrative analysis of literary texts (including film)is not really suitable for video games, even those such as quest games with superficially similar characters and settings.

> **Like people in real life, readers of stories and players of games rely on interpretable elements to make sense of the situations they encounter. These elements can be conflicts, adversaries and allies, desirable objects, overcoming obstacles and tackling challenges, winning and losing. The fact that the basic elements are present in all three phenomena is because the narrative use is secondary. On the contrary, in games, just as in life, the outcomes (winning, losing) are real and personal to the experiencer, unlike in stories.**

(Aarseth, 2004, p. 365)

These 'real and personal' outcomes also influence another aspect of video gaming; the experience of gaming is invariably related as real life experience. As Kiri Miller has shown, players often report their game sessions as if they were tourists or even ethnographic field workers in the imagined world of the game. For example, the cities of Rockstar's *GTA* series are based not only on real cities, e.g. Miami – Vice City, but also on numerous media representations of those cities, e.g. *Miami Vice*. In addition the game creators bring elements of irony, political parody and satire to the environment, giving players the simultaneous pleasures of immersion in violent gameplay and detachment. However, the game experience is not the experience of a detached tourist observer; assuming the identity of a GTA avatar offers opportunities to cross boundaries of class, legality, ethnicity and gender (amongst others). ' With the help of the avatar, player-tourists can pass as natives in gritty urban underworlds; in San Andreas, for example, white middle class players can costume themselves in gang colors and drive around blasting rap music without risking mockery' (Miller, 2008).

Johnson, Aarseth and Miller all suggest that the activity of gaming has much in common with real life. Perhaps one of the attractions of gaming (and explanations for its enormous popularity) lies in the scope to make imaginative and experimental leaps of imagination without the attendant risks of real life.

Fictions and identity

The discussion of video games and virtual environments concludes that the boundaries between fictional worlds and the real world are not quite as clear cut as we may have supposed. Advertisers are certainly well aware of the potential of fictions. The following process is a familiar, tried and tested persuasive technique:

1. Create an alluring and attractive fictional world.
2. Invite your potential consumer to adopt an attractive character within this imagined world.
3. Hint that the acquisition of a product or service may open a door between the real world and the fictional world ('Make your dreams come true . . .').

A 1997 Apple advertisement, 'Think Different', made highly effective use of this technique. Against a collage of black and white slow motion images showing various creative geniuses such as Albert Einstein, John Lennon and Martin Luther King, this message was narrated:

> Here's to the crazy ones. The misfits. The rebels. The troublemakers. The round pegs in the square hole. The ones who see things differently. They're not fond of rules. And they have no respect for the status quo. You can quote them, disagree with them, glorify or vilify them. About the only thing you can't do is ignore them. Because they change things. They push the human race forward. And while some may see them as the crazy ones, we see genius. Because the people who are crazy enough to think they can change the world, are the ones who do.

The ad concluded with the company's logo and the 'Think Different' slogan. No product was shown, but viewers were left to do the imaginative work, painting pictures of themselves as creative nonconformists whose true identity can be unleashed by the purchase of an Apple product.

ACTIVITY

Advertising: Fictions and Identity

Look at the advertisement for Land-Rover (Figure 5.8).

How does this ad display the persuasive technique outlined above?

See if you can find other examples of 'attractive fictional worlds' in advertising, themed shopping malls or adventure parks.

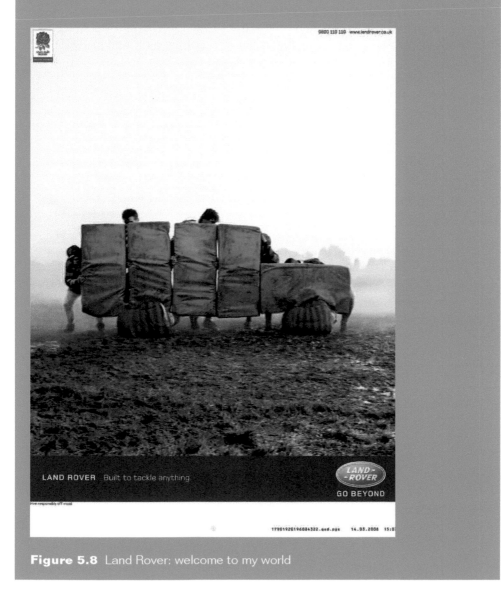

Figure 5.8 Land Rover: welcome to my world

Such fictional worlds into which we can insert our own, imaginatively created, identity are not, of course, restricted to advertising or video gaming. A key pleasure of engaging with fictions of all varieties lies in the identification with unreal characters in unreal situations. The insights offered by fictional texts into fictional characters provide us with many opportunities to gain insight into our own identities. In terms of the Johari Window (Bennett and Slater, *AS Communication and Culture; The Essential Introduction*, 2008, pp. 64–7) fictions enable us to explore the 'Hidden Self'.

We are all aware of the subtle and sometimes painful problems of confronting unfamiliar cultural codes in 'awkward situations': Ian McEwan is an expert observer of the nuances of unshared cultural codes as they occur at the boundaries between different social classes. In the following extract from *On Chesil Beach*, 21-year-old Edward is introduced to the middle class world of his girlfriend in 1961:

> **During that summer he ate for the first time a salad with a lemon and oil dressing and, at breakfast, yoghurt – a glamorous substance he knew only from a James Bond novel. His hard-pressed father's cooking and the pie-and-chips regime of his student days could not have prepared him for the strange vegetables – the aubergines, green and red peppers, courgettes and mangetouts – that came regularly before him [. . .] He encountered for the first time in his life muesli, olives, fresh black pepper, bread without butter, anchovies, undercooked lamb, cheese that was not cheddar, ratatouille, saucisson, bouillabaisse, entire meals without potatoes, and, most challenging of all, a fishy pink taste, taramasalata. Many of these items tasted only faintly repellent, and similar to each other in some indefinable way, but he was determined not to appear unsophisticated. Sometimes, if he ate too fast, he came close to gagging.**

(McEwan, 2008, p. 119)

ACTIVITY

Stories and Identity

How do you react to the situation in which Edward finds himself?

Does Edward's experience tell you anything about your 'unknown self'?

Do you have a story that you relate often because it confirms a part of your identity?

Have you come to know about the identity of others because of stories they tell about themselves?

Nostalgia

The songwriter Billy Bragg referred to nostalgia as 'the opium of the age' in a song despairing of our inability to respond actively to our alienation. It concludes with a line which suggests that 'our place in history is as clock-watchers, old timers, window shoppers' (Billy Bragg: *The Home Front)*. This image of us as history's window shoppers is a particularly powerful one in the current climate wherein 'retro' and 'vintage' are consistent themes and where nothing is safe from the threat of re-make: cartoons, computer games even classic films frame for frame. Why do we need a new *Italian Job* or *Get Carter* when the originals will 'do very well thank you'? Why does *Scooby Do* or *The Incredible Hulk* need re-casting? Clearly our fictions are indicative of our mental state as a society; that 'definitive shape of the human mind' that Hawkes said, 'emerges from our fictive acts…' (1977, p. 58) but what do these increasingly self-referencing cut and paste jobs say about us. What can a *Dark Knight* or *Pirates of the Caribbean* tell us about ourselves?

The postmodernists would argue that they are examples of empty signifiers, that their intertextuality and flexibility are indexes of their essence. These are fictions whose complexities are superficial (to be untangled) and whose ability to represent is falling into disuse because the connection to reality has gone. As the 1990s recovered the 1960s so these early years of a new century have colonized further and more flexibly and, aided by a genuine IT revolution (at last), have produced allusive texts: superficially clever but profoundly empty.

Frederic Jameson has written separately on two kinds of 'nostalgia film' that he sees as symptomatic of the postmodern condition. The first are those films which, rather than being set in the past, recreate the cultural experiences of an earlier period, like the narrative thrill of the old action B movies which became the inspirations for the Lucas/Spielberg products of the 1970s and 1980s. According to Jameson these are purely nostalgic since a film like *Star Wars* 'reinvents the experience in the form of a pastiche: that is, there is no longer any point to a parody of such serials since they are long extinct' (Creed, 1987, p. 362). *Star Wars* is a useful point of reference, as one of the most successful and talked about films of all time, and Jameson's critique is not so much of the film than of what it might tell us about 'the way we live now'. He acknowledges, in fact, that 'it is a complex object' which offers both straightforward adventure and 'to gratify a deeper and more properly nostalgic desire to return to the older period and to live its strange old artefacts through once again' (Creed, 1987, p. 362).

Figure 5.9 *Star Wars* (1977) Lobby card advertising what became one of the most successful films of all time

This is an interesting take on what might otherwise have been seen as epic mythic narratives, concerning 'quests' of varying kinds and the struggle between oppositions, principally good and evil. To see them as 'properly nostalgic' moves the analysis to their function and further sites this in a social-psychological/psycho-cultural domain. It also connects such films as *Raiders of the Lost Ark* with the plethora of comic book films since it is the experience rather than the narrative or structure that concerns us. Of course this deep longing for nostalgia may be described as 'repressed', even infantile and this also puts mainstream Hollywood film and the society it serves under the microscope.

PASTICHE: A work of art that intentionally imitates other works, often to ridicule or satirize (one might think of *The Office* or Peter Kay's *Britain's Got the Pop Factor. . . And Possibly a New Celebrity Jesus Christ Soapstar Superstar Strictly on Ice*)

ACTIVITY

Nostalgia

Identify films and TV programmes that attempt this recreation of 'past cultural experience' and use them to address the following questions:

- To what extent and in what ways is a 'sense of the past' significant to these experiences?
- Can you find examples of *pastiche* in your chosen texts?
- What part do considerations of realism play in our appreciation of these works?
- Do these texts provide viewers with the comforting experience of 'living in the past'?

Jameson also identified 'nostalgia texts' that colonized the immediate past, which are set, as it were, in a recognizable past. In this case what is being attempted is what Jameson called 'a desperate attempt to appropriate a missing past' (quoted in Creed, 1987, p. 261), which he sees as having more significant implications 'as an elaborated symptom of the waning of our historicity, of our lived possibility of experiencing history in some active way'.

According to Barbara Creed, Jameson argues that the preference for films that rely on quotation represents an attempt to construct

> **'intertextuality'** as a deliberate, built in feature of the aesthetic effect and as the operator of a new connotation of 'pastimes' and pseudo-historical depth in which the history of aesthetic styles displaces 'real history'.
>
> (Creed, 1987, p. 362)

What this means in effect is that we are surrounded by nostalgia films, which represent the past in a way that directs us to the representations rather than the historical reality. Thus in films like *Atonement* or even the *Alfie* remake we have a conscious confusion of content and style.

ACTIVITY

Colonies of the historical imagination

Identify film and television texts that offer versions of recent (twentieth century) history and answer the following questions.

- What stories are being told about the recent past?
- How far are these messages being supported by the film's/text's mode of address and reception?
- Does the text refer to other texts either explicitly or implicitly?
- In what specific ways might these texts be deemed nostalgic?

Postmodernism and fictions

The more we look at texts the more we can be moved to address the arguments that postmodernism offers about contemporary representations. Baudrillard and others have argued that in the media-saturated world we live in, representation (which presupposes a relationship between signs and reality) has been replaced by 'simulation' whereby one set of signs is merely predicated on another set. This is the world of the hyperreal and hyperrealism where truth is a relative concept and the difference between 'real' and imaginary is blurred (see also Chaper 2 p. 67). What, for example, is the relationship between an Irish themed pub and an Irish pub or between the *St. Trinian's* films, a set of Ronald Searle cartoons and a girls' public school? *Eastenders* is now more famously a TV soap than the name of a particular inner city working class tribe. Baudrillard characterizes simulation as the binary opposite of representation, talking of a transition from 'signs that dissimulate something to signs that dissimulate that there is nothing' (1998,

p. 354). Baudrillard borrowed the Biblical term simulacrum (pl. simulacra) to epitomize the end point of this process. The simulacrum is a copy without an original, a fourth phase in the journey of the image:

- It is a verification of a basic reality (representation).
- It masks and perverts a basic reality (ideology).
- It masks the absence of a basic reality (substitution).
- It bears no relation to any reality whatsoever (simulation). It is its own pure simulacrum.

The film critic Andre Bazin writes pertinently in this respect on the illusion of film: 'It is a necessary illusion, but it quickly induces a loss of awareness of the reality itself . . .' (Bazin, 1978). Moreover, as we have seen: 'When the real is no longer what it used to be, nostalgia assumes its full meaning' (Baudrillard, 1998, p. 354).Thus we have a world of unanchored nostalgic fictions trading in unsupported stocks and shares at a market of an economy 'based on the production of images and information' (Storey, 1998, p. 347). Moreover, it is ultimately an uncontrolled and uncontrollable market since the information-superhighway is impossible to police. What used to be plagiarism is now bricolage and the channels are always open.

Interestingly in this extremely sophisticated, allusive, technological environment, the most progress is being made socially. What the Internet has delivered, despite the fears of a flood of pornography (which is also there) is a massive extension of interpersonal communication or technically of medio-communication since these connections are achieved through a discrete intermediary. Not only has this extended literate communication in both scope and meaning but it has also put a new focus on the narratives of self: back stories and the paraphernalia of self-presentation. The essence of social networking sites are collaborative fictions, or at least factions, where real issues are thrown around, 'jammed' in often imaginative threads.

ACTIVITY

Drawing the line

Chat rooms and blogs may be a useful place to consider these issues of fiction and 'fact'. The notion of a pure blog is an interaction in which you metaphorically 'speak through your fingers' but how much conscious craft might there be in the following.

- Communication and Culture website
- A fansite
- An open Internet chatroom

All this goes to show is that we are surrounded, beset by fictions of various kinds. Consider the micro fictions which are implied by a million images on a million product packagings: the happy family seated round the kitchen table, the farmer standing in his field, the confident woman negotiating the busy city traffic 'because she's worth it'. These micro narratives are structures that Lévi-Strauss would have understood as mythic, as myths of modern consumer capitalism based on simple oppositions like light and dark, good and bad, desirable and undesirable.

This is obviously easiest to recognize in the pictorial narratives casually activated by the unconscious consumer: the sun-filled fields of wheat that give a context to many breakfast cereals, for example.

However if you choose to see it, the sequential arrangement of elements around a theme to produce a coherent and instructive experience is evident in even the most abstract invitations. Consider for example the micro narrative of this pillar of pinkness (Figure 5.10).

If we leave the specific linguistic analysis to one side and try not to speculate on the shape of the container, we are left nevertheless with a sequence of elements variously displayed. The twin focal points are on the one hand the 'author' and title (L'Oréal and 'ELVIVE') and on the other the dynamic but indecipherable central design which looks a little like an 'escaping radiation warning' but is anchored (if that's the word since nothing is certain) by the legend 'Pearl Protein'. Above and below this 'explosion of protein power' are a series of vaguely sequential elements which add to the mystery while at the same time reassuring us (this is Barthes' hermeneutic code: a productive suspense and an ironic one since we know very well what's inside).

This micro narrative sequence works in the semic code both in its choice of words and in its use of presentational techniques (typeface, highlighting, colouring). Thus 'Nutri-gloss' (whatever that means) works as pure connotation: visually and semantically. It is followed by 'NEW' and LIGHT REFLECTING BOOSTER so that each word and word shape are felt both separately and together and so that the 'explosion' is properly contextualized. This is most evident, though after the visual show in the most modest and therefore most subtly connotative INSTANTLY DETANGLES, MIRROR SHINE, CASHMERE TOUCH

Figure 5.10
L'Oreal Elvive
Nutri-Gloss shampoo

These appear in a common type as if a connected set but this is only possible if we collaborate, linking the mundane 'detangles' (a new word?) with the symbolic 'Cashmere touch' to make even the former pleasurable. All this then bears down on the target/victim/villain of the piece: not us but our hair (and more?) that is dull and lacking energy. Interesting these are just the qualities that the narrative contradicts, being in itself bright and energetic. What is noticeably missing however is the referential code, which connects this pink fantasy to the real world of greasy hair.

If you feel confident enough to read the fictions of a bottle of hair conditioner, then you are certainly ready to take on the task of analysing the fictions that surround us to communicate and reinforce our cultural values. Let us leave the last words to the German film director Wim Wenders who himself ends a piece on his love–hate relationship with 'stories' with these words:

> **And that's really the only thing I have to say about stories: they are one huge, impossible paradox! I totally reject stories, because for me they only bring out lies, nothing but lies and the biggest lie is that they show coherence where there is none. Then again, our need for these lies is so consuming that it's completely pointless to fight them and to put together a sequence of images without a story – without the lie of a story. Stories are impossible, but it's impossible to live without them.**

(Wenders, 1988, p. 59)

References and further reading

Aarseth, E. (2004) Quest games as post-narrative discourse, in M.-L. Ryan (ed.), *Narrative Across Media; The Languages of Storytelling,* Lincoln, Nebraska: University of Nebraska Press, pp. 361–76.

Abbott, H. P. (2008) *Cambridge Introduction to Narrative* (2nd edn), Cambridge: Cambridge University Press.

Barthes, R. (1993) Introduction to the structural analysis of narratives, in S. Sontag (ed.), *A Roland Barthes Reader,* London: Vintage, pp. 251–95.

Barthes, R. (1977) *Image, Music, Text* (S. Heath, Trans.), Glasgow: Fontana.

Barthes, R. (1972) *Mythologies,* London: Vintage.

Baudrillard, J. (1998) The precession of simulacra, in J. Storey (ed.), *Cultural Theory and Popular Culture; A Reader* (2nd edn), Harlow: Prentice Hall, pp. 350–7.

Bazin, A. (1978) An aesthetic of reality: neorealism, *What Is Cinema?* 2: 26.

Bennett, P. and Slater, J. (2008) *AS Communicationand Culture; The Essential Introduction,* Abingdon: Routledge.

Bennett, P., Hickman, A. and Wall, P. (2007) *Film Studies: The Essential Resource,* Abingdon: Routledge.

Bordwell, D. and Thompson, K. (1990) *Film Art: An Introduction,* New York: McGraw Hill.

Carter, A. (1998) *The Bloody Chamber,* London: Vintage.

Creed, B. (1987) From Here to Modernity: Feminism and Postmodernity, in J. Storey (ed.), *Cultural Theory and Popular Culture* (2nd edn), Harlow: Prentice Hall., pp. 358–64.

Crouch, D. and Lubbren, N. (2003) *Visual Culture and Tourism*, Oxford: Berg.

Fiske, J. and Hartley, J. (1978) *Reading Television*, Abingdon: Routledge.

Gillespie, M. (2006) Narrative analysis, in M. Gillespie and J. Toynbee (eds), *Analysing Media Texts*, Maidenhead: Open University Press/McGraw Hill Education, pp. 79–118.

Hawkes, T. (1977) *Structuralism and Semiotics*, Abingdon: Routledge.

Johnson, S. (2005) *Everything Bad is Good For You*, London: Penguin.

Kafka, F. (2008) *The Complete Short Stories*, London: Vintage.

Lévi-Strauss, C. (1963) *Structural Anthropology*, New York: Basic Books.

Longhurst, B., Smith, G., Gaynor, B., Crawford, G. and Ogborn, M. (2008) *Introducing Cultural Studies* (2nd edn), Harlow: Pearson Longman.

McEwan, I. (2008) *On Chesil Beach*, London: Vintage.

Miller, K. (September 2008) *The Accidental Carjack: Ethnography, Gameworld Tourism and Grand Theft Auto.* Retrieved 30 November 2008, from Game Studies: http://gamestudies.org/o801/articles/miller

Silverstone, R. (1981) *The Message of Television: Myth and Narrative in Contemporary Culture*, London: Heinemann.

Stam, R. B. and Flitterman-Lewis, S. (1992) *New Vocabularies in Film Semiotics: Structuralism, Poststructuralism and Beyond*, Abingdon: Routledge.

Storey, J.(ed.) (1998) *Cultural Theory and Popular Culture* (2nd edn), Harlow: Prentice Hall.

Turner, G. (1999) *Film as Social Practice*, Abingdon: Routledge.

Wenders, W. (1988) *The Logic of Images: Essays and Conversations*, London: Faber and Faber.

6 OBJECTS OF DESIRE

> **" The point is, ladies and gentleman, that greed – for lack of a better word – is good. "**
>
> Gordon Gekko in *Wall Street* (dir. Oliver Stone 1987)

> **" Say you don't need no diamond ring and I'll be satisfied**
>
> **Tell me that you want the kind of thing that money just can't buy "**
>
> (John Lennon and Paul McCartney, *Can't Buy Me Love*, recorded by The Beatles, 1964)

This chapter deals with *things*; the things that we possess, the things that we'd like to possess (if money was no object) and the things that other people own or desire. Generally speaking, the Objects of Desire we shall examine are solid, tangible, three-dimensional items that we can see and touch. This is not to say that Objects of Desire must be things we can have and hold, we should also acknowledge the increasing significance of some rather less tangible examples of what we could call *virtual* Objects of Desire. As the two quotations at the head of the page suggest, we are in contested terrain here – an area in which there are many disagreements and disputes. From a Communication and Culture point of view, this is no bad thing. It will give us plenty of opportunities to explore contrasting perspectives as the various debates about Objects of Desire unfold.

Gordon Gekko's notion that 'greed is good' is flatly contradicted by most of the world's religions. Buddhism (according to interfaith.org) is essentially 'about transcending material needs and wants to enlarge upon spiritual growth'. Hinduism defines ignorance as the false belief in independence from Vishnu, manifested as the seeking out of material goods. Similar distinctions are drawn in other religions between the rewards of spiritual engagement and the earthly delights associated with material goods. It's not just the acquisition of material things, but also the desiring of them which tends to be discouraged. One of the Bible's Ten Commandments instructs that 'Thou shalt not covet thy neighbour's house' and greed, of course, is one of the seven deadly sins.

In art and literature, popular culture and high culture it is much easier to find examples of an anti-materialist sentiment than it is to find straightforward endorsements of the idea that it is perfectly OK to desire material things. The paintings of Vincent van Gogh celebrate the beauty and awesome simplicity of nature. Ironically, the canvases themselves have certainly become objects of desire changing hands for millions of pounds, but the fundamental message still isn't entirely compromised. Romantic poets from Shelley and Wordsworth to the beat poets of the 1950s and 1960s have scorned the pleasures of material possessions as unworthy and shallow alternatives to the more lasting and satisfying pleasures of love, friendship and the appreciation of nature. Pop lyrics (like *Can't Buy Me Love*) have also chimed in with the 'Love Over Gold' idea. Perhaps you can think of examples (and counter-examples) of song lyrics that praise the virtues of pleasures that are more important than shopping.

In addition to these influences there is a further set of pressures which may contribute to a sense of guilt associated with Objects of Desire. These derive from a green movement which tells us that over-consumption threatens the environment. 'Do you really *need* these objects?' they may ask, 'Is your purchase really *necessary*? Shouldn't the earth's resources be preserved or, at least, used in the production of *useful* things?' These sentiments are certainly central to the idea of Buy Nothing Day (see Figure 6.1)

ACTIVITY

What are the arguments for and against Buy Nothing Day?

What assumptions does Buy Nothing Day make about objects of desire?

For further information see:

www. adbusters.org

www.buynothingday.co.uk

On the other hand, you don't have to be quite as enthusiastic as Gordon Gecko on the subject of greed in order to gain pleasure and satisfaction from objects of desire. We asked a group of Communication and Culture students to display some of their objects of desire and to explain their importance.

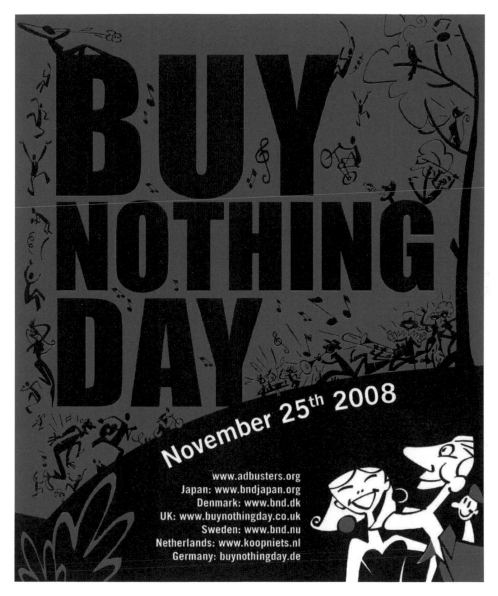

Figure 6.1 Buy Nothing Day poster 2008.

For the students in Figure 6.2, there were many different reasons why they are so fond of their mobile phones and mp3 players. Some stressed usefulness and functionality, others praised design features but all agreed that their device 'says something about me'. Surely, this is a more positive view of objects of desire – one that suggests that possessions are a means of expressing creativity and individuality. Furthermore, our *things*, from clothing to accessories to communication gadgets and even cars and houses allow us mark out our *differences* from one another.

Figure 6.2 Our Objects of Desire

Objects as symbols

We have, then, two very contrasting sets of ideas about objects of desire and the cultural practices of consuming them. Before going on to explore these in more detail (with the help of our theoretical perspectives) we need to remind ourselves of the communicative power of objects. Throughout your studies of Communication and Culture you will have been aware of signs and codes. Signs are the building blocks of meaning, for example a word, a gesture or any of the mobile phones displayed in Figure 6.2. Signs nearly always occur in combination with other signs to create complex meanings, but they are very rarely put together in random patterns. Instead, they are put together in accordance with a set of rules, such as the grammar of a language. These rules only work if they are shared and understood by a group of people; this is what constitutes a set of rules as a cultural code. For more on signs and codes, see our *Essential AS Communication and Culture*, Chapters One and Two (Bennett and Slater, 2008).

In some cases, the symbolic reference of objects is fairly obvious, for example a judge's wig and robes, a police helmet, a wedding ring or a throne. Even in these instances, though, a little further thought can produce alternative or oppositional readings as the table below shows. We have left a few blanks for you to fill in.

Sign	Obvious Reference	Alternative or Oppositional Readings
Judge's Wig	The wearer is a judge	An outdated legal system Over-reliance on tradition at the expense of contemporary values
Wedding Ring	The wearer is married	The patriarchal institution of marriage
Police helmet	The wearer is a member of the police force	
Throne	The power and authority of the person entitled to use it, e.g. a monarch	

Figure 6.3 Signs and their obvious or alternative meanings

From a semiotic point of view, the 'obvious reference' of the object as signifier is the denotation and the 'alternative or oppositional readings' are amongst the sign's connotations.

Objects, on the whole, communicate with us visually. This is not to deny the significance of sound, taste, feel and smell; sometimes the whole basis of an object's desirability lies in its appeal to one or the other of these senses. But it is the visual field that is most likely to be swamped by information from objects. A stroll down the high street, a visit to the shopping mall or a first visit to a new friend's house all offer up hundreds if not thousands of signifying objects to be viewed and decoded. We just don't have the time or the attention span to give careful thought to all of these objects passing through our field of vision and certain skills or strategies are essential in order to get through the day. We process information at a rapid rate, gatekeeping, selecting and de-selecting as we go. Some items may leap to the forefront of your attention whilst others – probably the majority – disappear into a generalized blur. These essential skills may keep us sane, but as Woodward points out, they may also leads us into making 'hasty, stereotypical or discriminatory judgements based on incorrect classifications of people or things as dangerous, or a threat to social order' (2007, p. 58).

In addition to these decoding problems, the consequences, perhaps, of 'sensory overload', there are further difficulties in reading off meanings of the objects of material culture. Just as we noted in relation to non-verbal communication (Bennett and Slater, 2008, p. 38), it is all too easy to make the mistake of assuming that the meaning of objects is *universal*; that all decoders of an object will interpret it in the same way. Furthermore, there are ample opportunities for misinterpreting these objects; we cannot easily tell if our reading of an object is the meaning intended by another. As you will know from your class discussions, the subtleties

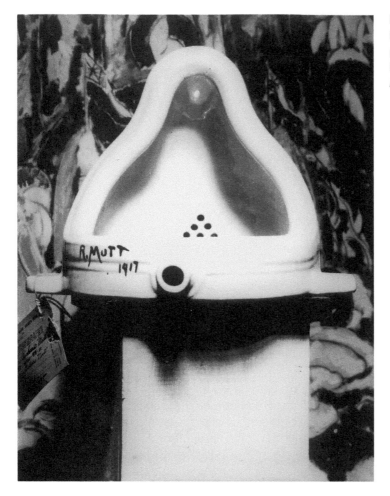

Figure 6.4
Re-educating
perceptions?
Marcel Duchamp's
Fountain

and nuances of meaning available to a group of teenagers when they discuss, say, headgear or footwear or jeans, is often lost on teachers (like us) who just don't have access to the same subcultural codes. Finally, the meaning of any object is highly context-dependent. When objects are removed from their familiar locations, they may become invested with all sorts of connotations not normally associated with them. This 'defamiliarizing' effect has often been exploited by artists who have wanted to make us look anew at certain objects in order to 're-educate' our perceptions. A couple of examples that fall into this category are Tracy Emin's *My Bed* (1999) and Marcel Duchamp's *Fountain* (1917).

To summarize the key points of this section:

- Objects of Desire communicate as symbols.
- In order to read objects we need access to relevant cultural and subcultural codes.
- Objects have ambiguous meanings and can easily be be misinterpreted.

Theory and Objects of Desire

We have already established two distinctive approaches to Objects of Desire; one that takes a very critical position and one that is broadly positive. It would certainly make things neat and simple if we could line these up nice and symmetrically with the theoretical perspectives discussed in Chapter 2. Unfortunately, the theoretical task is a bit more complicated than that. Whilst it is true that Marxist writers, including most of the Frankfurt School, have stressed the degree to which consumerism serves the interests of the ruling class in a capitalist society, there are others, more contemporary writers in a Marxist tradition who have found evidence of the consumer's capacity to resist or evade dominant ideology. Similarly, there are postmodernists who have celebrated the capacity of people to express individuality and diversity through their use of objects and their consumer choices whilst other postmodernists (such as Jean Baudrillard) have taken a rather pessimistic view of the extent to which our desires are manipulated for economic gain. Feminists, too, are divided in their analyses of consumption and the cultural practice of shopping. Of course, all are agreed that gender and power relations are of great significance and that patriarchy is a key concept in the understanding of Objects of Desire. However, it is a matter of some debate whether the emphasis should be put on women as agents of social and cultural change or on the cynical exploitation of gender as a means of selling goods and services. Differences such as these (and there are many more to come!) need to be borne in mind as we investigate the contributions of various theorists and schools of thought to debates about Objects of Desire. As we look at various angles and approaches, we shall attempt to assess their usefulness in understanding contemporary cultural practices and cultural products.

Karl Marx

We all know that Marx offered a sustained critique of capitalism as a mode of production. Perhaps the most important part of this critique was Marx's demonstration that capitalist production is based on the exploitation of workers by bosses who convert the workers' labour into profits for themselves. However, Marx was just as critical of the objects produced by capitalist production as he was of the system by which they were produced. In modern industrial societies, Marx claimed, there is a disconnection between the worker and the object produced. Unlike the craftsperson who invests their time and skill into making an object that they feel proud of, the industrial worker is just part of a giant productive machine.

Remember, of course, that Marx was writing in the mid-nineteenth century, and that the emphasis of his work is much more on the production rather than the consumption of products, or commodities as he called them. Commodities always represent the exploitation of the workers who produced them because the price for which they are sold is always much greater than the production cost. The difference between these two equates to the producer's profit. In Marx's terms this profit is a direct reflection of the degree to which workers' labour has been exploited. The price paid by a consumer for a commodity is the sum of its

Figure 6.5 Charlie Chaplin's 1936 film *Modern Times* satirized the idea of the industrial worker as a 'cog in the machine'

production costs including the cost of labour and the profit element. However, Marx noticed that commodities soon cease to be valued for the labour that has made them. Instead, people forget about the making of the commodity and see its value as *a property of the object itself*.

This belief that value is detached from the labour used in the production of objects is called commodity fetishism. Marx borrowed the concept of fetishism from the anthropological study of primitive religions. It refers to the ways that such belief systems find magical properties or human powers in material objects. Although we may like to see ourselves as modern, rational and scientific, Marx reminds us that our approach to commodities is not so different from the irrational superstitions that other, supposedly more primitive, cultures attach to totems. Capitalism encourages us in the belief that objects have properties above and beyond those that have been put there by people. Largely, this is because we give both labour and commodities a value that is measured by money. The existence of money helps to disguise the social relations of production as we are tempted to see no further than the price of an object when we assess its value.

Let's try to illustrate some of these ideas with a worked through example: the production of a motor car. Needless to say, this is not an example that Marx himself used! The car is built on a production line in a large factory. The owners of the plant have invested capital in land, buildings and machinery. They must also buy in raw materials, parts from other manufacturers and pay for the labour of workers who assemble the cars. The sum of these costs is the *use value* of the car. The workers see their reward solely in terms of the money reward for their labour; they have no particular sense of pride or ownership in the cars that roll off the production line. Only a few of them even see the finished product. This separation of workers' labour and the product itself is what Marxists mean by *alienation*. The price of the finished car is set at a level that will enable the manufacturer to recover their financial outlay together with a profit margin. This is the *exchange value* of the car. As potential consumers view the brand new car in a showroom, they are unlikely to think of the people who have invested their skills and labour into the car's production or the processes and materials used in its production. It is much more likely that they will compare the car's price with the price of other cars on the market, weighing up all the qualities they see in the car. This is the sense in which the car has become a *fetishized commodity* – its value is seen purely as an objective property of the thing itself with no consideration of its use value.

In conclusion to this section, how useful are these ideas in developing an understanding of Objects of Desire in contemporary culture? It is certainly true that Marx paid relatively little attention to *consuming* products – his focus was much more upon the relations of production. It was only with the advent of so-called consumer society that his successors turned their attention to practices of consumption and the stimulation of demand (as we shall see). However, the basic concept of commodity fetishism, as originally conceived by Marx is still helpful in a number of ways. Few manufacturers encourage consumers to link a product that they may purchase with the realities of commodity production. In many cases, manufacturers go to some lengths to disguise the production processes from consumers and it is left to campaigning journalists or lobbyists to draw attention to the worst excesses of labour exploitation. The use of sweatshop labour, especially in the clothing and footwear industries, is often the subject of damning criticism, such as War on Want's *Fashion Victims* campaign (see article below).

In a strange parallel to these efforts to keep the reality of production away from the public's gaze, other manufacturers are at pains to make sure that the labourers who have created the product are fully represented in marketing, advertising and packaging. These workers, though, bear no resemblance to Marx's alienated wage slaves. They are portrayed, typically as 'craftspeople' who have lovingly fashioned the product, using traditional 'time honoured' skills and techniques. It could be argued that approaches like this tend to offer an idealised or sentimentalised view of production rather than an accurate depiction of manufacturing processes.

Retailers accused of ignoring Bangladeshi workers' plight

- *Garment workers 'are paid as little as 7p an hour'*
- *Campaigners say previous factory report was ignored*

- <u>Matthew Taylor</u>
- <u>The Guardian,</u> Friday 5 December 2008

Workers producing clothes in <u>Bangladesh</u> for some of the UK's biggest retailers are being forced to work up to 80 hours a week for as little as 7p an hour, according to a report published today.

The study from War on Want claims that conditions in six factories supplying <u>Primark</u>, <u>Tesco</u> and <u>Asda</u> are worse than they were two years ago when the charity carried out its first investigation. Based on interviews with 115 workers in the Bangladeshi capital, Dhaka, today's report claims many were struggling to survive on meagre wages and some were subjected to physical and verbal abuse.

Some said that they had been forced to work hours of unpaid overtime, adding that factory owners were 'fiercely opposed' to trade unions.

'Primark, Asda and Tesco promise a living wage for their garment makers,' said Ruth Tanner, campaigns and policy director at War on Want. 'But workers are actually worse off than when we exposed their exploitation two years ago. The UK government must bring in effective regulation to stop British companies profiting from abuse.'

Employees in the six unnamed factories calculated that they need £44.82 a month to provide for their families but the report found they were getting less than half that as they tried to turn out the latest fashions and hit 'unrealistic targets'.

Last night Primark said it was committed to ethical sourcing of its clothes and continually audited its suppliers. A spokesman for Asda said it was committed to 'doing the right thing' for suppliers. Tesco said it took working conditions in its supply chain 'extremely seriously' but criticised War on Want which refused to name the factories in order to protect the workers.

'The allegations are unsubstantiated and, as War on Want have again decided not to engage with us on them, we question whether their approach is the best way to tackle the complex issues surrounding the Bangladeshi garment industry,' the Tesco spokesman said. 'We have no history of cut and running from suppliers, and make clear we would work with any suppliers facing problems to help them improve worker conditions and ensure that the interests of workers are protected.'

'Therefore, claims workers are protected by withholding evidence are invalid, and without producing evidence we can neither know whether there is any truth to them nor go about putting right any possible concerns. We take the issue of working conditions throughout our supply chain extremely seriously and insist on high standards, going to great lengths to ensure our suppliers meet them.'

Employees interviewed for today's report said conditions are worse now than they were in 2006. Runa, who makes clothes for Asda and Tesco, is quoted saying: 'My pay is so meagre that I cannot afford to keep my child with me. I have sent my five-month-old baby to the village to be cared for by my mother.' Ifat, who works in another factory, said: 'I can't feed my children three meals a day.'

Campaigners plan a protest outside Primark's Oxford Street store today and one of the study's researchers, Khorshed Alam, has travelled from Bangladesh to attend the annual meeting of the retailer's parent firm, Associated British Foods.

'These companies made promises that they would do something after the last report but two years later we see nothing has changed – in fact it has got worse,' Alam said.

Primark said: 'In Bangladesh we continually audit our suppliers. These audits are often unannounced and always paid for by Primark . . . we have also started a programme of direct engagement with workers and junior management to ensure that they are aware of our commitment to them and to continual improvement. Our customers can continue to shop in Primark secure in the knowledge that the company works hard to ensure that high standards are met.'

Asda said: 'We are working directly with factory owners to create more sustainable businesses by improving factory conditions, improving efficiency in production techniques and therefore reducing working hours and aligning worker pay with these improvements in productivity . . . we would welcome the opportunity to work with War on Want to identify any issues and formulate a structured plan to help resolve this.'

The disguised reality of production? War on Want's *Fashion Victims* campaign.

Consumer society

From the earliest years of the twentieth century theorists were certainly starting to address the relative neglect of consumerism and the cultural practices associated with Objects of Desire. Notable amongst these theorists was Thorstein Veblen (1857–1929) whose book *The Theory of the Leisure Classes* (1899) introduced the term conspicuous consumption. Veblen was interested in the changing habits of the rich, especially the new breed of industrialists whose wealth and status was based on capitalist enterprise rather than aristocratic bloodlines. Marx's analyses and explanations always come back to the influence of the economy; everything in society is determined by the organization of production. Veblen, on the other hand, argued that cultural forces can have an influence on the economy – this is why he put so much emphasis on how and why we consume things.

Veblen examined the affluent elite of American society at the turn of the century, noting their tendency to emulate the styles and habits of the European upper classes. The landed aristocracy of Europe were used to signalling their status through what Veblen termed leisure consumption, 'the ability to distance oneself from the dirty, sordid details of production through living a life of leisure, learning and travel' (Paterson, 2006, p. 19). Essentially, conspicuous leisure involved what you did – flaunting the fact that you did not have to work for a living (see Figure 6.6). Conspicuous consumption was more suited to the display of wealth in urban areas – what you owned rather than what you did. The display of luxury items clearly indicated that the owner did not have to worry about simply sustaining him or herself; these were items of little or no direct usefulness. That was their very point. In many cases the favoured clothing of the upper classes was deliberately anti-utilitarian, demonstrating that the wearer couldn't possibly engage in manual labour. The purpose of conspicuous consumption was to make class divisions and distinctions as wide as possible and also to denigrate labour. As Storey points

Figure 6.6 Not a peasant in sight. Thomas Gainsborough *Mr and Mrs Andrews* (circa 1750) © The National Gallery, London

out, 'the example of the leisure class acts to direct social energies away from productive work and into wasteful displays of cultural consumption' (1999, p. 37), and further, 'the very fact that the leisure class denounces useful work as unworthy of human dignity makes this class a bulwark against what Veblen regards as the natural evolutionary flow of history'(1999, p. 38).

ACTIVITY

Discussion points

Have the phenomena of conspicuous and leisure consumption spread from the superwealthy to other sectors of society?

Veblen's leisure class defined themselves by ostentatious displays of wealth and by the ownership of unnecessary luxury items. Are these practices part of contemporary cultural consumption?

Can you place your own possessions into the categories of 'need' and 'conspicuous consumption'? How is 'need' defined?

Is social emulation (copying the upper classes) a powerful impulse today? If so, who are we trying to emulate?

Are these concepts still relevant and useful? Surely, it is not hard to find evidence of conspicuous consumption today, perhaps even more so than in Veblen's day. His ideas about the symbolic rejection of labour also seem to hold water in many respects. The signifiers of manual work are still rejected by the elite. If we count the following as signifiers of manual work:

- calloused or roughened hands
- practical hardwearing clothes
- sturdy footwear
- sweat (and the smell of sweat)
- well-developed muscles
- weather-beaten skin

then we can attach to each of them a converse signifier of elite status:

- delicate gloves
- fine, impractical clothing
- perfumes, oils and creams
- slightness of build
- smooth, clear skin.

In this way, many of the Objects of Desire that manifest high status are not just unavailable to working people because of their cost, but because it would be physically impossible to display these signs or find time for such leisure pursuits if you have to work hard for a living. Much as contemporary culture reinforces the work ethic and the idea that 'hard work is good', we can also find evidence that prestige and status often involves displays of not having to work. This can certainly be seen in the signifying practices of some of today's celebrities: all night drinking in expensive night clubs, holidaying in exotic locations, ostentatious ownership of more cars and houses than it is possible to use. All of these address us with messages not so different from the *nouveaux riches* of Veblen's day. Also, with the help of the media, these messages are definitely conspicuous. Rather crudely, we could summarize key messages as:

- 'I don't have to go to work tomorrow'
- 'I have many desirable things that you cannot afford'
- 'I have possessions that I don't even need'
- 'I don't have to care what you think of my behaviour'.

Veblen's emphasis on the symbolic significance of objects does seem useful and applicable in many ways as we observe and analyse contemporary cultural practices, but perhaps it would be helpful to have a theoretical framework that also deals with the symbolic aspects of individual identity as well as status, prestige and social rank. We could also raise some doubts about the notion of 'social emulation'; a behavioural characteristic which Veblen seems to regard as being innate. Is it really the case that we have some sort of 'inner drive' compelling us to copy the practices of the rich? There are examples, for sure, of styles, tastes and fashions that have contradicted those of the wealthy or where the direction of influence has gone the other way. Two examples that spring to mind are the cases of denim (the material that jeans are made of) and the pick-up truck. Both of these have strong connotations of manual labour yet both have succeeded in becoming powerful signifiers of a style that is both classic and modern. Jeans are popular not only for their practicality but also for their association with a sort of rugged masculinity and anti-establishment ethos. Why else would supposedly up-market clubs insist on 'No Jeans'? Similarly, the all-purpose, go anywhere pick-up truck makes strong symbolic links to a working class value system; jeans on wheels, if you like. No doubt, supporters of Veblen would point to the existence of fantastically expensive designer jeans and top of the range pick-ups and SUVs like the Cadillac Escalade (Figure 6.7) to suggest that the old distinctions are still around. Agreed, but they do suggest a rather more complex pattern of symbolic practices than is suggested by the social emulation model.

Veblen also observed that our supposed sense of 'taste' or 'beauty' was often nothing more than a reflection of an item's costliness. Having discovered that an object has a high price tag, we proclaim it to be an object of great beauty that demonstrates our highly refined taste. If the same object has a very low price tag, it becomes 'tacky' and banal – the sort of thing that would only be appreciated

Figure 6.7 Dignity of labour? A Cadillac Escalade. Yours for just under $60,000

by those coarse people with no taste at all. This is quite a convincing argument and we would not have to try too hard to find contemporary support for Veblen's argument (quoted here by Sudjic) that if an object previously thought to be hand-made turned out to be a clever machine-built imitation, then:

> ... the utility of the article including the gratification which the user derives from its contemplation as an object of beauty would immediately decline by some eighty or ninety percent, or even more. The superior gratification derived from the use and contemplation of costly and supposedly beautiful products is commonly in great measure a gratification of our sense of costliness, masquerading under the name of beauty.
>
> (Sudjic, 2008, p. 103)

As we have already noted, certain manufacturers do like to place a premium on the idea (and it is often no more than an idea) of handcraft, but as Sudjic goes on to point out, 'by any objective criteria, machines can make most things better than people can, and our eyes, and our hands have become habituated to the standards of finish that machines can provide' (Sudjic, 2008, p. 118). The somewhat bizarre consequence of this is that we face the paradoxical situation of machine-made artefacts 'having imperfections deliberately introduced to suggest quality' (Sudjic, 2008, p. 120).

ACTIVITY

Find as many examples as you can (from cheese to cars) of articles described in their advertising or packaging as 'hand-made' (or one of its equivalents such as 'hand-crafted', 'made in the traditional way').

Do these claims make the objects more desirable and, if so, why?

Are there any attractive ways of describing objects that are not hand-made?

How can manufacturers make their products look non-standard even though they have been mass produced?

Edward Bernays

In a 2002 documentary series called *The Century of the Self*, film-maker Adam Curtis explored the rise of consumer society in the twentieth century. The first of the four films (still available on some Internet sites e.g. source: http://www.informationclearinghouse.info/article12642.htm) is a fascinating account of the career of Sigmund Freud's nephew, Edward Bernays (1891–1995). Bernays, sometimes described as the 'father of public relations' was one of the first to recognize the power of psychological techniques in advertising and persuasion. As Curtis says, he was 'the first person to take Freud's ideas and use them to manipulate the masses'(Curtis, 2002). Bernays showed American corporations how they could make people want things that they didn't need by linking mass-produced goods to people's unconscious desires.

The idea of 'unconscious desires' comes, of course, from the work of Bernays' uncle, Sigmund Freud. In Freud's view we all have dangerous and instinctual desires, often related to sex and violence, which are locked away in our subconscious selves. As we grow up in civilized society, we develop mechanisms to control these urges, but although we can usually succeed in driving them into the area of the subconscious mind, we cannot eradicate them altogether. Repressed as they are, these subliminal urges still find expression in our dreams and nightmares, our jokes and our 'Freudian slips'. Bernays recognized that these subconscious desires could be tapped into by successful techniques of persuasion which could offer acceptable solutions to our innermost fears and primitive drives. He proposed that advertising should not attempt to engage people at an intellectual level by explaining and describing a product's usefulness. On the contrary, advertising should operate entirely at the level of feelings and emotions. The practical usefulness of a product just wasn't the issue for Bernays; he argued that products should make people feel better about themselves by engaging with hidden and irrational emotions.

In a famous campaign of the late 1920s, Edward Bernays accepted the challenge of overcoming the taboos that prevented many American women from taking up cigarette smoking. At the time, women who smoked in public were seen as 'loose women' with low moral standards. There were even laws to prevent such shocking behaviour. Bernays discovered that women saw the cigarette as a symbol of the penis and male sexual power. In March 1929 Bernays staged a carefully organized publicity stunt. A group of young women marched down New York's Fifth Avenue during the Easter Parade, ostentatiously lighting up Lucky Strike cigarettes. Newspaper reporters and photographers were primed to expect the event and their reports made front page news across the country. This was the start of the 'Torches for Freedom' campaign, promoting the cause of women's equality and liberation. The role of Bernays and his employer, the American Tobacco Company, was successfully disguised. The campaign was a great success in promoting smoking amongst women and contributed substantially to the profits of the tobacco companies. Women were persuaded that smoking symbolized their liberty and independence: a powerful illustration of how a product can become desirable because of the way it makes consumers feel about themselves, irrespective of how rational or irrational those feelings may be.

Many of Bernays' subsequent campaigns were equally successful as the advertising and public relations industry adopted his ideas, for example by linking the car to male sexuality and by using bogus experts and dubious 'scientific reports' to demonstrate the health benefits of various products (including cigarettes). Bernays' wider philosophy was that the 'masses' needed to be guided and directed from above even in a democratic society. The ideal way to do this is to stimulate inner desires and then feed these desires with the products of industrial capitalism; a process he called 'the engineering of consent'.

Figure 6.8 Lucky Strike's 'Torches of Freedom' campaign persuaded women that smoking was a blow against 'ancient prejudices'

ACTIVITY

Use an Internet search engine to collect images of cigarette advertising from the 1920s to the 1990s.

Analyse your chosen images in terms of 'inner desires' and their fulfillment.

It is sometimes argued that today's consumers are far too 'media-savvy' and wise to propaganda tricks to be taken in by the sort of persuasive tricks used by Bernays. But are we really so resistant to the ploys of advertising?

It seems to us that Bernays and his associates in the early days of public relations recognized an important principle for the understanding of Objects of Desire: in order to make an object desirable it is much more effective to manipulate the nature of consumer desire than to manipulate the object. The rather cynical idea that 'sex sells' is certainly widespread, even though advertising is more heavily regulated these days and claims that certain products (e.g. alcohol) enhance sexual prowess are forbidden. A 2000 campaign for Heineken beer sidestepped such regulations rather neatly in a TV ad called *Premature Pour* in which a nervous young man watches a beautiful woman immaculately pour a glass of Heineken. When he pours his own, the beer is tipped too quickly, causing it to spill and foam all over the table and himself. The sexual allusion is clear, but witty and understated rather than explicit. The young male consumer is invited to respond to the challenge of proving himself more competent than the 'premature pourer'.

The idea that our inner desires may be exploited by advertisers and propagandists became something of a cause for concern by the 1960s, due, in part, to the influence of a million selling book by Vance Packard: *The Hidden Persuaders* (1960).

The Frankfurt School

The scholars of the Frankfurt School (principally Theodor Adorno, Max Horkheimer and Herbert Marcuse) sought to adapt Marxist theory to the analysis of advanced capitalism in the mid-twentieth century. Although staying within a Marxist tradition, the Frankfurt School (or Critical Theory) paid more attention to psychological and cultural aspects of capitalism. Their particular critique of material culture is that we become entrapped by the very objects we are conditioned to desire. As Woodward puts it:

> The suggestion is that people are mistaken to believe that an object (for example, such as a motor vehicle, a business suit, a computer or a mobile telephone) is

positive in its implications for social progress and individual betterment, or at best neutral in its effects. In deploying such objects, people actually mentally enslave themselves, becoming victims of the ideology which is embodied in the objects of modernity they mistakenly believe liberate them (. . .)

"

(Woodward, 2007, p. 42)

From *One-Dimensional Man* by Herbert Marcuse

We may distinguish both true and false needs. 'False' are those which are superimposed upon the individual by particular social interests in his repression: the needs which perpetuate toil, aggressiveness, misery, and injustice. Their satisfaction might be most gratifying to the individual, but this happiness is not a condition which has to be maintained and protected if it serves to arrest the development of the ability (his own and others) to recognize the disease of the whole and grasp the chances of curing the disease. The result then is euphoria in unhappiness. Most of the prevailing needs to relax, to have fun, to behave and consume in accordance with the advertisements, to love and hate what others love and hate, belong to this category of false needs.

(. . .)

We are again confronted with one of the most vexing aspects of advanced industrial civilization: the rational character of its irrationality. Its productivity and efficiency, its capacity to increase and spread comforts, to turn waste into need, and destruction into construction, the extent to which this civilization transforms the object world into an extension of man's mind and body makes the very notion of alienation questionable. The people recognize themselves in their commodities; they find their soul in their automobile, hi-fi set, split-level home, kitchen equipment. The very mechanism which ties the individual to his society has changed, and social control is anchored in the new needs which it has produced. The prevailing forms of social control are technological in a new sense. To be sure, the technical structure and efficacy of the productive and destructive apparatus has been a major instrumentality for subjecting the population to the established social division of labor throughout the modern period. Moreover, such integration has always been accompanied by more obvious forms of compulsion: loss of livelihood, the administration of justice, the police, the armed forces. It still is. But in the contemporary period, the technological controls appear to be

continued

As we discussed in Chapter 2, the Frankfurt School (particularly Adorno) is highly critical of the Culture Industries that have 'forced together' high and low culture, making the production of cultural objects just another facet of the capitalist machine. In this view the population has become passive and servile, largely due to the machinations of the culture industry. Our tastes and desires, our preferences for leisure activities and entertainment are all manipulated to serve the profit motive of capitalist enterprises. The products themselves, whether films, popular music or consumer items are all 'standardized', i.e. made in pretty much the same way to the same specification in order to keep down the cost of production. Although we may perceive differences from one film to another, from one pop song to another or from one washing machine to another, these differences are no more than illusions of individuality — a part of the con trick that makes us want to consume. Additionally, the ideology of consumerism promoted by the culture industry also serves as a mechanism for social control. Summarizing the arguments of Marcuse's *One-Dimensional Man* (1964), Paterson notes that this ideology 'leads to a depoliticized conformity, effectively limiting our goals and actions only to those realizable within the framework of capitalism, and rendering our political choices fairly meaningless' (2006, p. 27).

So far as a Marcuse was concerned, the desire to consume is simply an expression of 'false needs'; needs that have been created by a cynical advertising industry. These are in contradiction to the 'real needs' of, for example, happiness and freedom. This is what Marcuse meant by 'one-dimensional' in the title of his book: capitalism conditions us to accept a confined and constrained world with only limited opportunity for our full potential as human beings. Our insatiable desire for more and better products has made us malleable and easily controlled whilst our capacity for free and independent thought has just withered way.

Undoubtedly, the Frankfurt School approach to consumerism and Objects of Desire is at the negative end of the spectrum we described in the opening section of this chapter. One of the main criticisms to be levelled at this perspective is that it represents a kind of snobbish elitism: the dopey masses are brainwashed into coveting tacky rubbish whilst the posh intellectuals recognize the value of 'real' cultural experiences. Although this criticism does seem to have some validity, especially in relation to popular culture, it is slightly missing the point of theorists who are trying to understand and analyse the role of culture in a capitalist system from a broadly Marxist perspective. Unsurprisingly, they see consumerism and its associated practices as ideological props to an essentially corrupt, exploitative

Figure 6.9 Clean clothes versus false needs – a Frankfurt School dilemma

system. In some ways this critical position is supported by our discussion of Bernays and the rise of public relations and marketing. Bernays and his colleagues seem to be aiming at precisely the kind of control mechanisms from above that Adorno, Horkheimer and Marcuse are so keen to attack.

Another difficulty for the Frankfurt School assertions is that it is difficult for analysts to bring empirical evidence to bear on the argument; how can we *prove* that advertising creates desire or that it merely responds to the pre-existing desires of consumers? It may be that simple binary oppositions such as this fail to do justice to the complexity of consumer culture.

The concepts of 'false needs' and 'real needs' are also problematic. Who is to say that someone's need for a new electric guitar or a box set of DVDs is false whilst their need for friendship and intellectual stimulation is real? It is rather like being told what is good for you by someone who professes to know you better than you know yourself. As Dominic Strinati puts it:

> The identification and criticism of false needs also seems to rest on the assumption that if people were not engrossed in satisfying these false needs, say watching television (for which they will have more time if they own washing machines), they would be doing something

more worthwhile, satisfying their real needs. But what would this entail? What would the fulfilment of real needs consist of? Would it necessarily exclude owning washing machines and watching television? It is as if Frankfurt School theorists know what people should and should not be doing, but tell them so in a language they can't understand. **"**

(Strinati, 1995, p. 80)

Strinati's last observation here, on language, refers to the rather difficult and obscure style of writing which, some claim, characterizes the Frankfurt School. In spite of the criticisms and problems outlined here, the Frankfurt School and other Marxist approaches are certainly helpful in building our understanding of Objects of Desire, not least because they point us towards a critical evaluation of our own role as consumers and our personal perceptions of 'need'.

Pierre Bourdieu (1930–2002)

Like Veblen, Bourdieu focused on the ways in which differences of *taste* and *lifestyle* are linked to power structures in society. We have already looked at the notion of cultural capital in Chapter 2 and it is certainly a valuable idea in the discussion of Objects of Desire. The desire for certain objects over others – in other words our taste in consumer goods – is a consequence of growing up with and learning the lifestyle of a particular social class.

This lifestyle is not just an accumulation of material things and a pattern of cultural practices, it is also a particular way of looking at the world, a set of predispositions. This is what Bourdieu means by *habitus* (see Key Term Box).

By using the term 'class fraction' Bourdieu points us towards more subtle categorizations of class than those suggested by the broad brush divisions of working class and middle class. Membership of a class fraction is symbolized by the selection and display of goods. However, Bourdieu's argument is that 'taste' is more than just an indication of class position, status and privilege; it is a means of actively creating and maintaining class differences. In this way, members of lower status groups continue to reproduce their class position by their choice of certain objects of desire and their enactment of certain cultural habits. Similarly, high status class positions are systematically reinforced by the tastes and habits of more privileged groups. This distinction is not just a matter of income or even of the expense of consumer goods. The idea of cultural capital explains how certain goods and cultural practices acquire a cachet of 'good taste' that is not necessarily related to their cash price. For example, a glass of fine wine in a city wine bar may be less expensive than a pint of extra strong lager in a public bar, but the two carry very different sets of associations in terms of cultural capital.

HABITUS: This term, extensively used by Pierre Bourdieu, refers to our dispositions (or tendencies) to classify cultural products and cultural practices in ways that relate to our social position. The habitus is not limited to mental perceptions; it also includes our modes of eating, our non-verbal communication and our physical movements.

Although Bourdieu emphasizes social class as the most significant influence on habitus, Longhurst points out that the roles of ethnicity, gender, region, etc. are also important factors conditioning the habitus (Longhurst, 2007, p. 30).

It is matter of debate whether the habitus fully determines our thoughts and actions or whether there is still room for 'human agency', the individual's capacity to think and act independently of habitus.

To observe the ways in which British shoppers casually glance at the contents of one another's shopping trolleys confirms many of Bourdieu's claims about the 'cultural economy of taste'. The weekly food shop at Tesco or Morrison's may seem like a mundane activity but most shoppers could provide an expert and subtle decoding of the product selections that fill our freezers, fridges and kitchen cupboards. Each choice represents a decision making process that inevitably relates to the shopper's taken-for-granted assumptions about identity and class position. For example, delving into Tesco's online grocery site shows that there are eleven possibilities available for that most basic of household items: salt. At one end of the scale is Tesco Cooking Salt at just 78 pence a bag, only 26 pence a kilo. Seems like a bargain, but is it just too, well, cheap? Is there a classier salt available? How about Saxa Fine Sea Salt? Surely it must have something for the discerning salt buyer, after all it is ten times more expensive than Tesco Cooking Salt at £2.60 a kilo. Would it be more 'me' than the own brand product? Perhaps, but wait a moment; also available is Maldon Sea Salt at £2.09, that's £8.36 a kilo – a staggering 32 times more expensive than Tesco's cooking salt. This must be the very pinnacle of the salt buying experience, a true object of desire. But now there's a twinge of doubt. Would it be recklessly self-indulgent or even pretentious to spend so much on salt? Would I seem ostentatious or flashy? Maybe I should scale down my salt buying ambitions a little. How about Tidman's Rock Salt at £2.90 a kilo? Yes, that seems a better selection: tasteful and distinctive but not too over the top . . .

Here we must acknowledge that the average shopping expedition would take hours or even days if this level of indecision accompanied every purchase. Bourdieu's point, though, is that decisions about taste are more or less automatic; a seemingly natural expression and reinforcement of our class position.

ACTIVITY

Habitat's Spring/Summer Kaleidoscope of Colour

Figure 6.10
A kaleidoscope of colour

Tuesday, February 19th, 2008

The new Habitat spring/summer 2008 catalogue launched on 11th February 2008 is bursting with a bold new take on furniture and home accessories.

The collection entitled, 'Our Kaleidoscope' is possibly the brightest and boldest statement Habitat has made in recent years, taking inspiration from the compelling and contrary combinations of colour, texture and pattern found in nature.

For spring/summer 08, Habitat is doing what it does best – encouraging customers to think differently about the places they inhabit and the ways in which they live – Habitat's distinctive attitude towards innovation and creativeness in design are as prevalent as always.

As the season develops from early spring to high summer, consumers will be inspired to style their homes in bold bursts of colour, with three key stories:

Natural – Predominantly white furniture and accessories; this theme is an easy way to brighten living quarters by keeping things simple yet stylish; heralding an altogether purer looking environment.

Neutral – This theme is home to most of the eco friendly products. It incorporates their organic bath collection made from pure cotton, natural oak products and an earthier colour scheme.

Jungle – Using a varied colour palette from warm browns, to bright saffrons, this theme invites people to be more inspirational when it comes to using colours in the home, with a mixture of multicoloured accessories perfect for any room – this is the most daring and unique of the three.

Source:http://www.ukhomeideas.co.uk/ideas/furniture/contemporary-furniture/habitat's-springsummer-kaleidoscope-of-colour

Examine the information about Habitat.

What sort of lifestyles and opportunities for differentiation are offered to consumers?

Look at some other stores and their publicity materials (e.g. catalogues, websites, advertisements) and build some case studies based on Bourdieu's concepts of lifestyle, habitus, distinction and cultural capital.

Useful further reading for this exercise can be found in Mark Paterson's *Consumption and Everyday Life* (2006, pp. 43–57).

The savvy consumer

Mark Paterson makes a distinction between the consumer viewed as a 'sucker' and the consumer viewed as 'savvy' (2006, pp. 142–3). So far, we have mostly dealt with theoretical positions that take the 'sucker' view, but it is time now to consider some more positive approaches to the relationship between consumers and Objects of Desire. What characterizes these savvy consumers and how can they be distinguished from the 'dupes' of consumer capitalism? According to Paterson, they are knowing and,

> **... aware they are manipulated to a certain extent by large corporations and the mass media, but able to reclaim their own sense of identity in some way. The use of mass-produced objects in ways unintended by the manufacturer reveals a sense of irony and creative use ('appropriation') by the consumer, being a tacit acknowledgement of mass media manipulation but simultaneously an unwillingness to blindly comply.**

(Paterson, 2006, p. 143)

Looking back to our Key Concept box on Habitus, you will see that we drew attention to the debates that have arisen in relation to 'human agency'. These concern the degree to which we as individuals are capable of independent thought and action rather than being ensnared within a set of determining economic and social structures. This is a starting point for coming to terms with one of the most important theorists in this territory: Michel de Certeau (1925–86). As the title of his 1984 book *The Practice of Everyday Life* suggests, de Certeau is principally concerned with what people actually do in the situations in which they find themselves. Rather than simply reflecting or reinforcing class position, the every-day cultural activities of ordinary people demonstrate an extraordinary diversity and inventiveness; a view of popular culture not dissimilar from Raymond Williams. This inventiveness is especially true of those with little prestige or status. For them, everyday life offers opportunities to resist or reject the mechanisms of domination. This is not the overt resistance of the rebellion or street riot, it is more the tiny acts of stubbornly independent activity with which people go against the grain. This suggestion will be familiar to us all from our experience of the work-place, school or college. These are the evasions of authority in the extra long tea break or in the class's determination to distract their teacher from the 'official' curriculum.

We could also find de Certeau's version of resistance in those pleasurable activ-ities that take place outside society's power relations: cooking, chatting, informal sports, walking, organizing a reunion or going for a picnic. In spite of Veblen's insights on the relations between price and ascribed value, it is quite reassuring to reflect that many of life's small but significant pleasures cost nothing at all. De Certeau refers to *la perruque* or 'wearing the wig'; an idea that we often adopt simple disguises in our everyday lives in order to 'get away with' minor transgres-sions. This disguise is often a simulated conformity; an appearance of following the rules whilst actually ignoring or breaking them. This is the student who adopts a facial expression of earnest interest in lecture whilst actually day-dreaming or the call centre worker who is apparently totally immersed in the demands of the job, but actually using the work station for personal social networking. It is almost as if we are permanently engaged in a sort of low-grade guerilla warfare in which our enemies are the elephantine forces of 'the system' or 'the establishment'. We know it's a war we cannot win but still take quiet satisfaction in our tiny victories, our pin-pricks of resistance and our general bloody-minded refusal to conform.

Whether or not you are convinced by this restoration of human agency to the enactors of everyday life, de Certeau's ideas are indirectly relevant to our inves-tigation of consumerism and Objects of Desire. In de Certeau's view, consumption is a form of production in which consumers artfully reconfigure the products imposed upon them. Although de Certeau sees this in the fairly prosaic activities of 'making do', other theorists, notably John Fiske, have developed these ideas to suggest a more radicalized version of the empowered consumer.

Fiske concentrates on the power of subordinate groups to transform the meanings of objects and places. As Lewis summarizes his position:

> **The 'weak' select products from the vast array of overly structured and overly invested materials and services on offer. The weak are nimble, deft and creative, while the strong are torpid, culturally and intellectually obese, and fixed in overly rationalized systems of structure. By far the greater majority of all products remain unsold and it is the 'strong' who are left to puzzle over their failure, second-guessing the shifting interests, tastes and sensibilities of the 'weak'.**

(Lewis, 2002, p. 273)

Whilst de Certeau sees the practices and evasions of everyday life more in terms of evasions and indirect resistance to dominant power structures, Fiske sees popular culture as a direct challenge to patriarchal capitalism. This is a stirringly optimistic view of the consumer as a popular cultural activist, though Fiske's supporting evidence, e.g. kids hanging out in shopping malls without buying anything or the personalization of jeans, do seem rather lightweight examples in support of heavyweight theoretical conclusions. Furthermore, this account of the 'power of the weak' does seem to converge with the notion of the 'sovereign consumer'. Laissez-faire liberals defend the 'logic of the marketplace' in capitalist systems by promoting the idea of the powerful consumer. It is the customer, they argue, that determines the success or failure of capitalist enterprises. Producers must compete fiercely with one another to produce goods of a price and quality to satisfy the demands of the customer. Those that cannot meet these demands will fall by the wayside, proving once and for all (they argue) that the consumer wields power in the marketplace; the corporations are our servants not our masters.

Theorists who have developed de Certeau's ideas, including John Fiske and Dick Hebdige, have often been drawn to study the activities of subcultures, particularly youth subcultures. Teddy boys, bikers, mods, hippies, punks, goths, emos, surfers and so on have all demonstrated ingenuity in transforming the symbolic significance of consumer objects, appropriating them for their own purposes. This is a demonstration of what de Certeau terms *bricolage*; the idea that objects have the capacity for multiple meanings and that consumers can exploit this polysemic potential by manipulating the meaning of consumer goods. In *Subculture: The Meaning of Style*, Hebdige examines the ways in which various youth groups co-opted standard items from consumer culture and radically redefined their meanings in the process. Examples include:

Teddy Boys : Edwardian Saville Row suits
Mods : Italian scooters
Punks : Safety pins, bin liners.

To this list we could add more recent examples such as the appropriation of Burberry clothing by so-called chavs and the reinvention of the VW minibus by surfers.

Figure 6.11 Chavmobile in Burberry colours

Business Briefs: Checks and Chavs

What do chavs, Danniella Westbrook and ferrets have in common? All have a penchant for wearing the distinctive beige Burberry-style check! This is bad news for Burberry, which had an altogether more upmarket consumer in mind for its prestigious fashions. All this at a time when the business had been enjoying a resurgence in its fortunes, having successfully repositioned itself away from the staid and middle-aged image of the past. To make matters worse, the market is flooded with fake merchandise and Kate Moss, the 'face' of Burberry, whose association with the brand has been linked to its renaissance, is facing drug-taking allegations.

Burberry is right to be concerned, having invested heavily in creating a brand image which closely fits the aspirations of consumers it wishes to attract. The brand, and how consumers perceive it, are among a business's most valuable assets. When the brand is damaged, its value and sales potential are reduced. The repercussions for the bottom line can be alarming.

At the heart of Burberry's anxieties are the consumers it wants to attract and those that it does not. The enthusiastic adoption of the Burberry cap by chavs was not part of the plan. These young adults with lower class roots and a reputation for hooliganism favour flashy 'bling' jewellery, sportsgear and (fake) designer clothes. They listen to rap, hip-hop and dance music and congregate around fast-food outlets and shopping malls; a far cry from the style-conscious, high-brow target consumers of Burberry's choice. Worries about the reaction of core customers to the brand's chav connections and about consequent damage to its iconic status, are well-founded.

Advertising guru David Ogilvy, a major force in brand thinking, surmised that consumers buy products with a particular personality or brand image. The closer the connection between the brand and those it targets, the better. The word brand derives from the ancient Norse word 'brandr', being associated with the idea of branding (or burning) animals – probably not ferrets – for identification purposes. Current definitions suggest that a brand is made up of a name, term, design, symbol or other features that distinguish one seller's goods from those of others.

A brand's success is determined by consumers: an eclectic bunch with different needs, characteristics and friendship groups, who live their lives and spend their time in a myriad of ways. Their diverse shopping behaviour affects how they respond to and perceive the brands on offer in the high street and elsewhere. The brand and the consumers' image of it are valuable business assets. The value of a strong brand doesn't generally appear on a company's balance sheet and may be difficult to measure exactly. Yet companies invest heavily in developing brand images which appeal to, and fit well with, their targets. The value they achieve is in the desirability of the brand and in the competitive advantage this provides.

Branding experts argue that effective branding strategy improves the chances of business success. In his book on brand leadership, David Aaker extols the virtue of brand leadership, which he sees as central in creating strong brands. The asset value associated with the brands which emerge has been called brand equity, described by Kevin Keller as the 'marketing effects uniquely attributable to that brand'.

Aaker views brand equity as comprising four dimensions: awareness of the brand, its perceived quality, the loyalty of its customer base, and what he calls brand associations. Herein is the problem. Brand associations include anything and everything which links consumers to the brand. This might be the personality attributed to the brand, the situations in which it is used, and even imagery connected with its users. Brand owners like Burberry work hard to develop brand associations which fit closely with the image they wish to create. Associations of Burberry with chavs, Danniella Westbrook and ferrets are definitely not among those sought by the company.

Whatever businesses do to build their brands, it is consumers who determine how the brand is perceived. Consumer perceptions are central to a brand's success or failure. It's the consumer who decides on the brand's image, whether that image fits their personal self-image, and if they will patronise the brand. External factors can shift this brand image and lead to consumers changing their preferences. Nestlé suffered as a result of marketing its infant formula in developing countries. British Airways was recently damaged by the impact of an industrial dispute at the company's in-flight catering supplier. This doesn't mean that large scale changes in perceptions are achieved quickly or for no reason. Consumer views of the best established brand icons tend to be resilient. The image of Porsche as an exclusive brand dripping with heritage, the luxurious associations of Chanel, and the high-fashion status of Prada have all stood the test of time. For these brands at least, the deeply entrenched views of consumers are hard to change.

continued

So has Burberry been permanently tarnished by the chavs, by undesirable furry mammals and by the attentions of Ms. Westbrook? The company denies that a short-term blip in UK sales growth can be attributed to these factors. Chavs, they say, are old news, and the UK anyway accounts for less than ten percent of total Burberry sales. The hope is that the company's long-term brand building efforts will be enough to carry it through these current difficulties. Ultimately, this will be a test of Burberry's brand strength and it is consumers who will decide.

Dibb, S. (2005) 'Business Briefs: Checks and Chavs', Source:http://www.open2. net/money/briefs_20051028branding.html, The Open University

ACTIVITY

Appropriation

Read Checks and Chavs (above) from the Open University website. How do you think that the Burberry company could reappropriate the meanings attached to their products?

Devise your own list of appropriated products whose meanings have been transformed by subcultural groups.

Are your examples confined to youth subcultures?

As Hebdige shows, subcultural styles are often a self-conscious rejection of consumerist values. For example, to be a fully fledged punk or goth requires a dress code that puts the wearer at odds with the requirements of the mainstream labour market. Meanings attached to appropriated objects are not just random alternatives to the meanings of dominant culture but deliberately subversive attacks on 'straight' style. However, Hebdige also notes the capacity of dominant culture to 'reappropriate' the objects incorporated into subcultural sign systems. For example, punk rockers signalled a contempt for consumerism and fashion by displaying anti-fashion regalia: bin liners, bondage pants, razor blades and so on, all designed to symbolize dismissive contempt for straight values. Within a short space of time the oppositional potential of these symbols was annihilated by a process of incorporation. Punk style became chic as tastefully ripped clothes and understated references to bondage appeared first on the Paris catwalks and then in the High Street.

These approaches certainly recognize and even celebrate the abilities of ordinary people to resist the domination of consumer capitalism. They do, however, have their problems. The disproportionate attention to 'spectacular' youth subcultures seems to ignore the consuming habits of those young (and not so young) people who choose not to associate themselves with a subculture group. There is also a danger, surely, of exaggerating or romanticizing the significance of 'resistance through shopping'. We may also ask whether it is possible to be a 'savvy' consumer without necessarily declaring war on consumer capitalism. Most of us are aware of the pleasures available to us in selecting, using and displaying our Objects of Desire; these activities provide opportunities for exploring our identities and creativity as well as signaling our group membership and social position. On the whole, we relish the opportunity to add the communicative power of possessions to our symbolic repertoire. However, this awareness is tempered by the knowledge that consuming (in this sense) is only a part of life and not the essence of life itself.

As we write this chapter, most of the world's economies have been gripped by 'the downturn' and its effects are already being felt on our desire for material goods. Perhaps we are being forcefully reminded that it is unwise to neglect the significance of economic factors in the understanding of cultural phenomena.

References and further reading

Bennett, P. and Slater, J (2008) *AS Communication and Culture; The Essential Introduction*, Abingdon: Routledge.

Curtis, A. (2002) Happiness Machines. BBC Four.

de Certeau, M. (2002) *The Practice of Everyday Life*, Berkeley: University of California Press.

Hebdige, D. (1979) *Subculture; The Meaning of Style*, London: Methuen.

Lennon, J. and McCartney, P. (Composers). *Can't Buy Me Love* [Beatles, Performer]

Lewis, J. (2002) *Cultural Studies – The Basics*, London: Sage.

Longhurst, B. (2007) *Cultural Change and Ordinary Life*, Maidenhead: Open University Press, McGraw Hill Education.

Packard, V. (1960) *The Hidden Persuaders*, Harmondsworth: Penguin.

Paterson, M. (2006) *Consumption and Everyday Life*, Abingdon: Routledge.

Stone, O. (Director) (1987) *Wall Street* [Motion Picture]. USA.

Storey, J. (1999) *Cultural Consumption and Everyday Life*, London: Arnold.

Strinati, D. (1995) *An Introduction to Theories of Popular Culture*, London: Routledge.

Sudjic, D. (2008) *The Language of Things*, London: Allen Lane.

Woodward, I. (2007) *Understanding Material Culture*, London: Sage.

7 INTERSECTIONS

The preceding three chapters have dealt with the cultural sites that form the core of the A2 study programme. You will need to study at least one of these in detail and depth. However, to choose only one cultural site will certainly limit your understanding of Communication and Culture and will also restrict the choice of questions available to you in the COMM3 examination. Clearly, then, there are advantages to be gained from two or even three of Fictions, Spaces and Places and Objects of Desire. These advantages are reinforced by the presence of what could be called a supplementary set of cultural sites:

What are Intersections?

Reading through the Cultural Sites chapters you will certainly have been struck by the breadth of each site and also by the many areas of overlap between the three sites. Overlapping relationships are traditionally represented by a Venn diagram (Figure 7.1) and it is precisely in these overlaps that our intersections lie. The specification acknowledges three Intersections as follows:

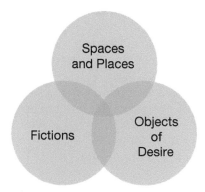

Figure 7.1 Overlapping cultural sites

1. Spaces and Places/Objects of Desire

For example: The property market and the ways in which desirable 'lifestyles' are associated with buildings or places or the use of objects of desire to 'accessorize' places. Both of these phenomena can be found in the publicity material of estate agents or travel agents. Any space or place (or any *experience* of space or place) that is objectified in this way qualifies for consideration in this intersection. Similarly, if the *location* of an object of desire contributes significantly to its meaning, we are in the territory of this intersection.

2. Fictions/Objects of Desire

For example: The association of desirable identities with objects, especially in advertising and promotional material. Many advertisements invite a target audience to place themselves within a story in which objects provide access to 'the person you always wanted to be'. Alternatively, we could look at the ways in which fictional texts are linked to saleable objects, perhaps through merchandising, spin-offs or product placement. This approach includes the packaging of fictions as objects of desire in their own right: the lavishly presented DVD box set or the leather-bound book, for example. In short, this intersection includes any instance of a fiction that is converted into or linked to an object and/or any instance of an object of desire that is 'told' as a story.

3. Fictions/Spaces and Places

The imaginary places of the fictional text from *Mansfield Park* to the Liberty City of *Grand Theft Auto IV* have just as powerful an impact on our cultural perceptions as 'real world' environments. Often, the distinction between the real and imaginary place is blurred. Numerous theme parks, 'lands' such as Legoland and Disneyland, exhibitions and re-creations of fictional places invite us to 'step into' worlds of imagination. Shops, malls, pubs, restaurants and even, on occasions, our own homes invite visitors to place themselves in a narrative. Cyberspace offers endless opportunities to inhabit virtual places; environments where we can lead a *Second Life* with fewer rules or constraints than the first.

Observant readers may point out that there should really be a fourth intersection where all three of the Cultural Sites overlap. You're right, of course – but we think that three intersections are quite enough for the scope of this chapter, though we shall be highlighting a few three-way links. However, if you're feeling ambitious and adventurous, there's nothing to stop you pursuing this rather more demanding route!

The remainder of the chapter deals in some detail with illustrations of each of the three intersections. There should be more than enough here to give you access to the optional Intersections question in the COMM3 exam, but we should stress that they are only illustrations. You are at liberty to explore the intersection

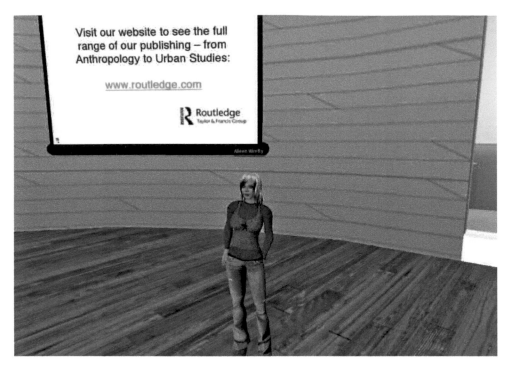

Figure 7.2 *Second Life* is being used by schools, universities and businesses to explore different ways of communicating across great distances

between the sites in any way that you chose as long as you make productive use of the key concepts, theoretical perspectives and analytical toolkits of the COMM3 unit: Communicating Culture.

Intersection One: Spaces and Places/Objects of Desire

We shall start our exploration of Intersections by looking at some areas of overlap between Spaces and Places and Objects of Desire. As noted above, this inter-section includes the ways places and spaces are packaged as desirable things (*commodified* if you wish) and the important role that 'things' (props) have in *accessorizing* locations. Given that consumerism is also principally concerned with selectively allocating meaning (and value) you will not be surprised to find 'fictions' lurking not too far away. Most of the examples suggested here might easily lend themselves to narrative treatment.

An excellent place to look for evidence of the interconnections of sites is across the range of mass media texts: films, television, print advertising, graphic novels and computer games. It is often in the acts of representation and mediation that meaning-making is observed most clearly. The holiday travelogue for example makes explicit the ways in which holidays are invariably packaged as desirable objects.

For most architects and designers of public spaces there is a negotiation of commercial and aesthetic imperatives that leads effectively to the same end result: the building or space that finally emerges from the design and construction process. Pragmatically there are three levels to this.

- The functional/reference that the place or space makes to and in its context (as a bank, a hotel or a public square, for example). This is largely non-negotiable since most public and private work is commissioned. As we saw in Chapter 4, even 'nature' falls under someone's jurisdiction and is just as much a construct as more obviously artificial environments.
- The stylistic (illocutionary) where particular emphases (forces) are given by particular creators in particular contexts. In most realistic contexts these are the designs which need to be 'sold' to the sponsor; the negotiations that take place around the hypothetical space before it is made into a material space.
- The effective/affective (elocutionary) where the real 'sell' goes on in the hearts and minds of those who address, possess, use and inhabit these places. In this negotiation is the point at which 'place' becomes 'object' and where this 'desire' became realized.

Figure 7.3 The Trafford Centre Manchester. A place to shop or a place to visit?

This last level is what all shopping malls aspire to become: places in their own right that escape the generic and become 'specific'. Though this is often attempted through the creating of themed pseudo-narratives, the essence of the process is the objectification of place so that it becomes a thing in itself. The chief sites of all cultures have this 'character'. There is a clear distinction between simply *doing something* (the functional activity of shopping) and *going somewhere* (a trip to a rewarding destination). To be even more specific 'popping out to buy some food' falls into an entirely different category to 'visiting the Trafford Centre' (a huge shopping mall in Manchester). Even in the cash-strapped days of economic recession, retail outlets can rarely afford to compete on price alone. Shops, cinemas, fast food restaurants all present themselves as worthy destinations. A visit involves more than just the consumption of goods and services on offer; it also involves the consumption of *the place itself*.

This notion of the place or space as an object of desire is not, of course, confined to retail outlets. Similar investments are made in High Streets, city squares, museums and galleries, housing estates and country parks. All of them seek to offer rewards (visual, imaginative, emotional, status) that transcend their immediate or obvious function.

The Shopping experience: Product Placement

Shops are spaces in which consumer goods are displayed to best effect. This 'best effect', of course, is relative to the kind of goods being displayed. At one end is the 'pound' shop which 'stacks 'em high and sells 'em cheap'. Here the floor space is almost entirely given over to goods, leaving the customers to find their way through the narrowing aisles of this proverbial Aladdin's Cave (although ironically that was a cave full of jewels and gold). Everything is cheap and cheerful and the £ sign is prominently displayed. Are there any rewards here that 'transcend the immediate and obvious function'? Certainly. This is a place where everything is available; nothing is out of reach. Every shopper can experience the satisfaction of knowing that they can afford anything on view with the added satisfaction of knowing that any acquisition will be a bargain. This is a positive self-image for the shopper: the kind of canny customer who isn't easily fooled and who knows a good deal when they see one. Surveying the products on offer, the savvy shopper may even project forward into a satisfying exchange with a friend. 'Do you know how much I paid for this? Go on, have a guess.'

At the other end of the continuum is the exclusive 'dress' shop where a small number of unpriced items are artfully lit in a self-consciously moody and stylish space. The lack of a price label here is an index of exclusivity and expense: 'if you have to ask the price: you can't afford it'. These shops are never full: their formality deters the casual visitor, inviting a mixture of reverence and awe. Here the 'objects of desire' are given a particular meaning or set of meanings in order that they might be more 'buyable'. The space itself invests desirability into the object. Would that same dress, that same piece of jewellery be coveted just as much if it were exhibited in a different environment? In Chapter 6 we discussed the various factors that contribute to the desirability of an object, recognizing that few of these factors are intrinsic properties of the object itself. Here, we can see that location (a space or a place) can have an important role to play in contributing perceived value to an object.

ACTIVITY

Shopping at the Intersection

For each of the following categories, identify a 'value' and an upmarket brand (for example Aldi and Waitrose). Explore the relationship between the space and the investment of desirability into the objects on display. How does the place present itself as an object of desire (somewhere that is worth a visit in its own right)?

- Supermarkets
- Jewellers
- Entertainment stores (CD, DVD, Video game)
- Furniture stores
- Clothes shops
- Car showrooms

Museums and Art Galleries

With museums and sites of historical importance the situation is very similar, though the designation of values (and the meaning of desire) is rather different. A teenager once described the British Museum as 'an old shopping mall full of bits of old crap'. While it's not the most elegant description I think we can see what he was getting at. For many kids, taken on a school trip in year 10, the British Museum does seem like a rundown London department store (mock classical being a prominent style there too) and what you do there seems not unlike window shopping (without the purchase price). This is a classic case of very similar activities having very different meanings as cultural practices. Thus teachers often forget to tell kids what they are meant to do in a museum (what are you meant to do?). They see people staring intently into glass cases and when they look there's little there of interest so they move on. A determined group of teenagers can clear a museum in fifteen minutes and quite rightly say, when challenged, 'But we've seen everything, sir!'

In what sense are the contents of museums, galleries, assorted stately homes and visitor centres 'objects of desire'? Clearly not in quite the same sense as retail objects that can be bought, treasured and either hidden away or put on exhibition entirely at the discretion of the owner. The visitor to a museum or gallery enjoys a different kind of relationship to the objects on view. What desires are mobilized in relation to these objects? Here are some possibilities, all of them exploited in various ways by exhibitors of precious objects and works of art:

- Projected ownership. Although possession of the objects and works on display is out of the question, we can still enjoy the vicarious pleasure of imagined ownership. These fantasies are often stimulated by forms of presentation that invite you to 'imagine yourself' into some role or other.
- Replica ownership. The value inherent in displayed objects relies, often, on their uniqueness or rareness. This doesn't mean to say that we cannot advertise our good taste in discerning the value of these things by acquiring a 'copy', perhaps a poster to hang on the bedroom wall or a one-eighth size suit of armour, fashioned in brass, to put on the mantelpiece. As noted above, spaces and places vie to provide us with an experience over and above their functional utility. But experiences are transitory – how can they be objectified, made material? The answer, of course, is readily found in the ubiquitous Gift Shop, strategically placed between the exit and the car park, whether it's the tasteful understatement of a set of National Trust placemats or the breezy bombast of a 'We Survived the London Dungeon' tee shirt, all these souvenirs and mementoes are anchored by a caption or an icon that somehow 'captures' the experience of the visit.
- Self-exploration/Self-improvement. Here, the pleasure derived from the contemplation of beautiful or interesting objects lies in the knowledge that the value of the object is somehow transferring itself to me, the viewer. As I allow the items on view to communicate the subtle intent of their creator or the world view of a strange and distant culture, I feel myself becoming a better person: more discerning, more sophisticated, more knowledgeable and more aware. Here perhaps, the real object of desire is not the painting, sculpture or historical artefact, it is *me* the onlooker or, at least, an aspirational version of myself that I can gradually hone and develop through selected cultural experiences.

It may seem that these three explanations all denigrate the activity of visiting the gallery or museum by suggesting that all the associated pleasures or motivated desires are somehow phony. This is not at all our intention. What we are trying to do here is work towards an understanding of a particular set of cultural practices by looking at the intersection between Spaces and Places and Objects of Desire.

Museums have changed considerably in the past twenty years and the old treasure houses of a dominant tradition like the British Museum are more the exception than the rule. Modern museums are much more concerned to bring the public into contact with the 'objects'. One of the issues attached to this democratization of the past is the relative fragility and irreplaceability of the objects. This is after all a measure of their relative value, though 'priceless', as in irreplaceable, refers equally to golden Egyptian death masks and bits of old Roman buttress, and the general public are only likely to get their hands on one of these!

ACTIVITY

Hands on or hands off?

Try to list the ways that modern museums (or traditional museums looking for a makeover) manipulate our relationship with their objects on display. How, for example, is the museum exploited as 'place' and 'space'? What difference does this make to the following:

- Our understanding of the past?
- Our understanding of the relevance or importance of the past ?
- Our understanding of what a museum is?

What's the best museum/historical site you've visited? How traditional was it? How involved were you in the experience of its artefacts?

Curators of art galleries face the same dilemmas both in terms of popularizing art to a broader audience (often a condition of their government funding) and in terms of creating the right contexts and atmospheres for individual art works (where the norm is public display on a gallery wall). One approach is to colonize buildings with no previous connections to Art (with a capital 'A'), for example, the way Bankside Power Station has become the Tate Modern in London. Here the industrial intentions of the original building create a sense of drama and scale which the artwork can inhabit and draw on. It also, if you want to see it this way, makes powerful links between different kinds of making: artistic and industrial. Equally

Figure 7.4 The Bankside Power Station, 1947–81

Figure 7.5 The Turbine Hall, Tate Modern, opened 2000

there is plenty of room, literally and figuratively, to emphasize that the place is still a great source of energy, though this time creative.

The Tate Modern, because of its industrial design, offers a massive and varied set of contexts for the housing of art works. These are often referred to, by those in the know, as 'interesting spaces' (though 'interesting' could be a polite way of saying 'difficult'). Actually the object of the exercise is very simple; we are encouraged to see art work as discrete and unique, so 'interesting spaces' are more likely to surprise us with them. It is as if the acres of white wall are sprouting their modernist (and postmodern) blooms. Nowhere is this contextualization more apparent than in the famous Turbine Hall which visitors overlook as they climb the gigantic ramp at the museum's entrance. This cavernous space which once housed the giant turbine which helped to supply London's electricity has become something of a challenge since it houses giant-size installations, objects on an immense scale. In doing so it fuels the on-going discussion, conducted in tabloid newspapers as well as fashionable galleries, about what art is and what art is for (not to mention what value it has both culturally and commercially).

Figure 7.6 Art exhibition in the Turbine Hall at Tate Modern

Figure 7.7 Mona Lisa in the Louvre

Room with a View

Look at these two images, both in famous galleries, and consider the different meanings of each.

- What is the relationship in each case between artwork and context, object and space?
- Comment on the value of each 'item', in what sense are they 'objects of desire'?
- What is the meaning of each piece?

This house is not a home: property as theft

In the TV programme *Grand Designs*, presenter Kevin McCloud tracks the dream builds and reconstructions of ordinary (if such a thing is possible) folk intent on creating something bespoke, unique and remarkable. Underground burrows, rebuilt medieval castles and nineteenth-century factories feature alongside creations of all kinds in all materials. We see and hear the passion, witness the frustrations as the budget is inevitably exceeded and we then share the sense of triumph as we tour the furnished product, the Grand Design itself. Most interesting, though, is the modest little element that invariably features in the programme's final segment. Beyond the architectural innovation what we are observing is a greater transformation: the metamorphosis of a construction project into a home. We are undoubtedly dealing with Objects of Desire here, but where is that desire most powerfully mobilized? Is it in the bricks and mortar (or bales of straw or cedarwood shingles) that make up that very tangible three-dimensional object which is the house (or 'project', as Kevin McCloud prefers)? Or is it in the much less tangible but more mythically powerful concept of 'home' that is mysteriously assigned to the building as the programme reaches the conclusion of its narrative?

ACTIVITY

Elegant and Well-Appointed: Reading between the estate agents' lines

Match the images to the house agent's description. Identify the key words in the 'sell'. How are these houses being sold?

Figure 7.8 Houses for Sale

A well laid out detached family house with a double garage, gas central heating and a rear garden of approximately 45 × 40ft.

A massive six double bedroom detached house which stands on a large plot at the end of a cul-de-sac.

An exceptionally large five bedroom detached family house with a south facing rear garden of approximately 75ft backing onto part of Hatfield Forest.

A most impressive modern detached house with adjoining annexe set in an established third acre plot with spectacular part wooded garden.

These houses are being sold boldly and bodily as Objects of Desire. This is not subtle, it is 'crash, bang wallop, get a load of that!' These are not so much descriptions (since they do not effectively discriminate between one 'massive' or 'impressive' house and another) as much as designations (of desirability and splendour). The focus at this point is not on the 'inhabiting' but on the 'having': house as valuable object and, perhaps, status symbol rather than house as home.

ACTIVITY

Blankety Blank Supermatch

In the classically cheesy 1980s game show *Blankety Blank* members of the public were rewarded for matching what were effectively collocations with a panel of celebrities. A collocation is a tendency (through usage) of words to go together: purple patch, happy families, etc. On *Blankety Blank* the challenge (in the finale) would be for example, the phrase *Lucky (BLANK)* and the contestant would be challenged to match their response with the response of a chosen celebrity. Considering the collocations associated with 'house' and 'home' will help you to formulate some ideas.

What might be the top three answers here:

■ My (BLANK) house?
■ My (BLANK) home?

What is the difference between them in terms of

■ the kinds of words you have suggested
■ the range of words

Now try it a second time but 'loaded'

■ Madonna's (BLANK) house
■ Kate Moss's (BLANK) home
■ Cristiano Ronaldo's (BLANK) house
■ 50 Cent's (BLANK) house

And moving on (with regret) from *Blankety Blank*:

continued

Having worked your way through these acrtivities, it will be becoming clear that the ideas of house and home are different and distinct. 'Try to imagine a house that's not a home' (Mud, 1974) sang Elvis impersonator Les Gray of Mud in 1973's biggest Christmas hit and followed it up with an analogy to ram home what this almost sacrilegious state might be like: 'Try to imagine Christmas all alone'. That the rich and famous might have price tag houses which fail to meet the basic requirement of homeliness is of some satisfaction perhaps to those of us who are neither rich nor famous. Their houses may be expensive but they are in every sense too, well, too much (too big, too overwhelming, too immaculate, too cold) or, like McCain, they just have too many of them.

I have memories of the England full-back Gary Neville (Beckham's best man) appearing on television in the pointlessly large kitchen of his luxury house in a gated community admitting that nothing had ever been really cooked there. He proved this simply by opening drawers full of still wrapped kitchen utensils. He had no attitude to this but one could sense that average viewers have attitudes of their own. It's the same with *Hello!*, and the MTV *Cribs* we looked at earlier in the book: the rooms which provide backdrops for the celebrity smiling never convince as 'lived in' let along 'homely'. They are classically simulacra, the sons and heirs of nothing in particular, copies of copies. It seems that the desirability of objects can falter when they find themselves in opposition to deeply held cultural myths such as 'home'. As we have seen, myths may be 'triggered off' by the powerful connotations of objects, but myths are rarely simply *about* objects; rather, it seems, they concern our *relationships* with objects.

Home, as all 'real' people know is a state of mind, some would say of grace. It is constituted of relationships, memories and experiences which are merely indexed by the differently crucial objects and their 'boxes'. It bears the signs and strains of life which, as teenagers, we often resent but which, having left we so often value when we return. This is why losing 'your' room in the family household (through 'finally' leaving) is so traumatic and yet symbolic. It is also why losing

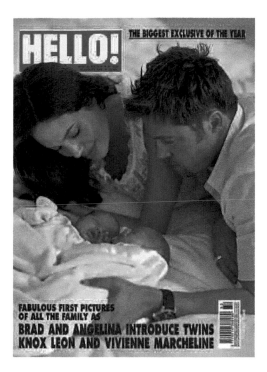

Figure 7.9 Brad Pitt and Angelina Jolie celebrate with *Hello!*

someone is felt so acutely in the 'home' since it is there that some principal identities are 'framed'. Philip Larkin, in typically sombre mood, addresses this very simply and powerfully in ten lines just called *Home is so Sad*, written in 1958.

> Home is so sad. It stays as it was left,
> Shaped to the comfort of the last to go
> As if to win them back. Instead, bereft
> Of anyone to please, it withers so,
> Having no heart to put aside the theft
>
> And turn again to what it started as,
> A joyous shot at how things ought to be,
> Long fallen wide. You can see how it was:
> Look at the pictures and the cutlery.
> The music in the piano stool. That vase.
>
> (Larkin, 1988, p. 119)

ACTIVITY

Is My Home 'so sad'?

Can you identify the physical features of your home (or former home) that trigger these feelings?

What are the familiar objects in your home that carry the same resonances for you?

Intersection Two: Fictions/Objects of Desire

One ring to rule them all
One ring to find them
One ring to bring them all
and in the darkness bind them
In the land of Mordor, where the shadows lie.

(Tolkien, 2001)

The function of precious objects, from magic rings to blood diamonds in narratives of all kinds is a book in itself. Safe to say then that significant props in films and TV narratives and their literary equivalents are all fair game here. Often narratives are driven by these items, whether as a goal or a motivation. The whole of the quiz show genre, for example, is a series of rainbows concealing pots of gold at their ends. The journeys that contestants go on are interrupted by barriers in the form of questions or other contestants but they are kept focused by the prize, that consistent object of desire. Often this prize can be seen accumulating on a screen caption, only to be dissolved away if a question is answered incorrectly.

In other shows the prize might be a material object rather than cash; for example a car. In the plethora of talent shows the 'object' is something more (and more ironic): it is the 'cap' of celebrity, the right to be objectified, to be a 'Leona Lewis' or a 'Will Young'. Is this the greatest love of all: to worship at the cult of your own celebrity? 'In apprehension so like a God', as Hamlet has it. Certainly these prizes have meanings beyond their monetary value, working as they do through extended signification. They are certainly carriers of ideological meaning; not least assumptions about consumerism and consumption. 'Rags to riches' stories are the fairy tales of free market capitalism since they emphasize that 'everything is possible' and that 'anyone can be someone' (without revealing the 'odds'). Moreover the treasure becomes in itself a kind of answer to the ultimate question framed by the quiz: it is, as it were, the ultimate solution. For years you might hate your mundane job and then one day you become a quarter millionaire as a result of choosing boxes on a TV show and your life is transformed.

The game show, the quiz show, the talent show all traverse a similar narrative arc. The story structure reflects that most deep-seated of cultural myths; the idea that the greatest and most prized rewards lie at the end of a quest in which opponents are vanquished. In some ways it could be argued that this reinforces the values of liberal capitalism: compete in order to succeed. Winner takes all and, as Ann Robinson tells the loser at the end of *The Weakest Link*, 'You leave with nothing'. Alternatively, though, these shows and the familiar story that they embody, represent in some ways the antithesis of capitalist values. Hard work and careful accumulation go unrewarded whilst reckless risks, luck and bravado are often characteristics of the victor.

In his surrealist film masterpiece *That Obscure Object of Desire* (1977), Luis Buñuel explores these issues with his customary bluntness and provocation. The title refers to the central character Mattieu's frustrated attempts to penetrate the truth embodied in a young woman Conchita whose 'obscurity' is partly communicated by the fact that she is played intermittently without explanation by two different actresses, one French the other Spanish. To find the pursuit of truth represented in a man's pursuit of an attractive young woman is a common enough artistic conceit and one which Buñuel is keen, as with every other convention, to undermine. The film, like life itself, makes entirely clear that there can be no explanations, that no 'access' is possible. It has the full range of surrealist absurdities from a midget lawyer on a train to a Jesuit Terrorist Group but still it seems we cannot escape the 'desire' for meaning.

Classic collections: the making of Season 3

You can buy Buñuel's *That Obscure Object of Desire* on DVD as part of the Criterion Collection, described as 'a continuing series of important classic and contemporary films'. It may well be that Criterion have made the transition from video to DVD seamlessly since 'classics' (of one kind and another) have always been available in 'special editions' but they are certainly now enjoying advantages that DVDs offer with a plethora of 'extras' on an impressive range of packaged sets. Here the once simple (and physical) packaging of a recording of the film has been enhanced and extended with a set of extras that do much more than enhance the original. In fact they further address the implicit cultural capital in this recording of this surrealist classic. There is an obvious irony of this film, of all films, being subtly transformed into an Object of Desire in itself. You may recall your discussions of cultural value in the AS (Bennett and Slater, 2008, pp. 5–16) and it seems certain that artefacts such as DVDs and books can be given, at the very least, a nudge in the direction of 'classic status' by the quality of their packaging and presentation.

Extra, Extra: DVD bonus discs

Figure 7.10 DVD bonus discs

This need not be a test of memory; just get hold of a selection of commercially available DVDs.

List the range of extras that you regularly find on DVDs and then suggest their purpose/function or just their appeal (for example, Director's Commentary gives an insight into the film's intended meanings and suggests the director has thought these things through).

What other techniques are used to make DVDs (or CDs) desirable objects? (You could include an examination of the language used, e.g. 'Connoisseur Edition', etc.)

DVD is essentially a home cinema format, hence the encouragement it has given to sales of wide screen TVs and surround sound systems. Its advent has turned us all into film students in a process that has turned recordings of films in boxes into film texts presented exquisitely in box sets complete with critical contextualization both on discs and in specially commissioned (and 'free') brochures.

With commentaries, subtitles, even aspect ratios as options, 'play film' is hardly a straightforward command. My DVD copy of Godard's *One Plus One* (1968), the film he made with the Rolling Stones, comes with two complete alternative versions and it is not uncommon to also find deleted scenes and unused footage which becomes material for those legendary 'fan' cuts. It's widely argued, for example, that the best cut of Ridley Scott's sci-fi classic *Bladerunner* (1982, 1997, 2007) is certainly not Scott's! The overall effect is to turn films into 'must-have' items in a way that videos never managed to be; as collectable as the first editions of leather-bound books.

However, the 'fictions' that have been most significantly transformed (among other things into 'objects of desire') are the products of television, both historical and contemporary. And here, expedience and cultural significance go hand in hand. While there had always been some 'traffic' in classic television, it was an unconvincing and ungainly trade. Both the transferable quality and the sheer volume of footage required to see the complete *Sharpe* or *Dallas* or *Only Fools and Horses* (where the complete scripts would take up 5 per cent of the room on your bookshelves of the complete video collection) militated against any recorded television series as a precious cultural archive. The issue of course is to do with the nature of television as a medium, whose relatively low density of information is addressed through its extended episodic nature, where the unit is not the single show but the series (now often called 'the season'). Thus while the immediacy of live action theatre might allow Shakespeare perhaps two and a half hours for *Julius Caesar*, the sheer size and fidelity of *Rome* (reputedly the most expensive television series ever made) needed two series (and more than 20 on-screen hours) to tell the story of Lusius Vorenus and Marcus Pullo. Similarly while actor David Tennant has spent more than three hours 'on the boards' developing his portrayal of Shakespeare's *Hamlet*, this is massively exceeded by his on-screen hours in *Doctor Who*. And even this is dwarfed by Bill Roache's twice and thrice weekly (and now sometimes twice nightly) portrayal of Ken Barlow in *Coronation Street*; a role which he has delivered for hundreds of hours over the best part of forty years.

Television has simply been transformed by DVD with traditional music stores now packed high with TV's back catalogue stylishly packaged to suit all pockets and tastes. Interestingly these objects provoke very different kinds of desire referring not only to the popular and the critically acclaimed but also to the reclamation of your past and those 'texts' that had seemed at the time to be merely ephemera. This final set of reclamations are essentially manifestations of nostalgia, in the spirit, some would argue, of the postmodern age. Whether these are those programmes you watched as a child (for example, *Watch with Mother* Collections) or when growing up they will likely be put to the test by a 'serious' watching and delight and disappointment in equal measure. The owners of moving image 'content', whether film or television, are busily mining a seam that is very familiar to the recorded music industry: the back catalogue. It remains to be seen whether they will enjoy similar success in marketing the same content in different formats such as Blu-ray or whether they will be overtaken by the increasing availability of streamed and downloaded moving images.

ACTIVITY

DVDs as Nostalgia Trip

This requires an examination of your DVD collection and those of your family if you wish. Identify any DVD which you acquired out of affection for watching the show some years ago. Head this list **Nostalgia** and quickly run down this list and designate each item as *Golden Glow* to denote that it was as good as you remember and *OMG!* to denote that memory can be a deceptive facility.

Now take the rest of your collection and create at least two further categories into which they can be divided.

The kinds of categories that you might have chosen to further clarify the way you have acquired (full price or pirated) DVDs might include watered down versions of the High/Popular culture arguments you addressed in AS. in some ways this is entirely the kind of debate that DVD has opened, borrowing from the always more credible medium: film. The packaging is implicitly arguing for television programmes as significant cultural artefacts (where culture has a version of Arnold's designation of 'the best that has been thought or said') in a contested version of their own 'Great Tradition' (the term F.R Leavis used for the literary equivalent). Thus we have landmark and groundbreaking, classic and definitive as defining superlatives. Moreover, the really important shift often goes the extra mile: *The Simpsons* box sets, for example, fully justify both their price tags and their claim to be 'Collector's Editions' by rewarding repeat viewings.

Furthermore, the proof that we're in an intersection between Fictions and Objects of Desire can be found in our responses to an artefact as each of these. While there is an argument that pirate DVDs cost the industry an astronomical amount of money every year, the counter-argument is that legitimate DVD sales are stimulated by 'digital theft'. Although some of us seem to be comfortable to get movies we couldn't quite be bothered to see at the cinema for a couple of quid,

we are still much more likely to buy the stuff we really want in authentic versions. However good the reproduction, including the artwork, 'authenticity' still seems a trump card; we want the thing itself, the genuine article is the object of our desire.

Figure 7.11 The ultimate *Matrix* collection, 10 Disc Box Set

ACTIVITY

Testing the hypothesis. What price is authenticity

Thinking of your own collection of music and moving images, what proportion is in a material form (CD or DVD) rather than a file?

What proportion is an original CD or DVD rather than a copy?

How important is it to own a physical and original version of films or albums?

Would it concern you if your entire collection of books, moving images, music, video games and photos existed solely as files on a memory stick or the hard drive of your PC?

Read the following item on vinyl records. Do you agree with David Hayes' findings?

Teens say they like vinyl records over CDs

April 21st, 2006

A Canadian scientist says teens who used to view CDs as superior to older vinyl records now consider vinyl superior to the newer format.

David Hayes of the Ontario Institute for Studies in Education at the University of Toronto says the growing popularity of vinyl might be a form of resistance against the music industry's corporate taste-makers.

While conducting research for his Ph.D. dissertation, Hayes was surprised to discover the young music enthusiasts he was interviewing were fans of vinyl.

"This made me wonder why they were interested in something that is, for all intents and purposes, a dead medium,' he said, noting the teenagers had switched from buying CDs to collecting LPs, often seeking obscure recordings.

Hayes research subjects said they liked the visual appeal of LP jackets and the challenge of seeking hard-to-find releases.

In yet another turnaround, teens overwhelmingly insisted the sound quality of LPs was superior to that of modern formats. They characterized LPs and the LP artists of the past as more authentic than the barrage of youth-oriented music being aggressively marketed to them today.

Hayes detailed his research in the February issue of Popular Music and Society.

Copyright 2006 by United Press International

Source:http://www.physorg.com/news64807495.html

Figure 7.12 Vinyl LPs. Once an Object of Desire for many teenagers

It has been widely argued, by Walter Benjamin among others, that mass production would ultimately undermine the notion of an artwork/cultural object as a unique and discrete creation. Here though, we're talking about a form of commodification which almost simulates that very discreteness by offering us a physical index of that 'creation'. In the *Twin Peaks* DEFINITIVE GOLD EDITION ('Sights unseen and sights unheard until now') even the show's enigmatic creator David Lynch seems genuinely taken aback by the splendour of the box set. 'I think' he says, 'that this is a great definitive *Twin Peaks* Gold Set'.

Moreover, this is not only a process of rescuing classics from an undeserved obscurity (and recovering those things best left obscured): it is also ongoing. It's quite likely of course that your earlier classifications of your DVDs discriminated between 'the contemporary' (current programmes) and 'the historical' (old ones). Here the packaging has subtlety influenced the existing television formats (like the series/season) and moved them very much in the direction of the 'Season 3' box set. This in turn feeds back into the way these shows are viewed (on screen and in discussions about their character and value). Programmes like *24* and *Lost* are in the vanguard of this transformation but even old favourites like the Russell Davis resurrected *Dr. Who* has used marketing to DVD as both an artistic and a commercial 'tool' (selling instalments and then the Christmas Season box set with extras). As implied above this has also tapped into changes in the way we use television generally, precipitated by multi-channel TV and the digital flexibility of systems like Sky + . Where once the reproductions offered merely the opportunity to revisit programmes you'd enjoyed, many now see the purchase of *Dr. Who* Season 4 as the best way to first see this 'work'. In other words having the whole thing at once is preferable to tuning in at 7.15 every Saturday evening in every sense (not only as a matter of convenience but also in terms of the 'integrity' of relationship between audience and text).

Lunch boxes and action figures: merchandising the narrative

There is a moment in Disney's *Hercules* (1997) when the hero, surrounded by vases bearing his face is confronted by the spectacle of action figures in his image while five female singers blast out the film's big musical number, *Zero to Hero*. As he looks on astonished we are treated to cut scenes which tour the merchandising potential of a major star/star vehicle in a knowing parody of Disney itself, including the obligatory Hercules-shop. Disney stores worldwide extend the Magic Kingdom into almost every household, making Mickey Mouse potentially the most identifiable character in the world, more recognizable than presidents or popes. Disney's merchandising success ensures that their fictions emblazon a hundred thousand nighties and quilt covers, together with lunch boxes and school bags, jotters and jigsaws. In fact part of the budget of many a blockbuster film is predicated on the sell through of merchandise. Of course, different films provide different opportunities, and in some cases perhaps only the book of the film and Collector's Edition DVD emerge. Others like *Lord of the Rings* (2001, 2002, 2003 dir. Peter Jackson*)*, *Star Wars* (1977 dir. George Lucas) (cynically dubbed Star *Wares*) and *Toy Story* (1995 dir. Peter Lasseter) have spawned mini industries of merchandise production.

The success in the late 1970s of the first three *Star Wars* films gave an object lesson in strategic merchandising. *Star Wars* products were made available to suit every income: mass market as well as collectable exclusive. By the time the second trilogy began filming in the late 1990s the new merchandising was already in full swing and there were action figures in the shops long before the ultimately disappointing *The Phantom Menace* (1999 dir. George Lucas) was in the cinema. In the intervening fifteen years these characters had been imprinted on an almost infinite number of items worldwide to the degree that Carrie Fisher, who played Princess Leia, had a nervous breakdown partly prompted, apparently, by being unable to escape her own image on T-shirts and action figures.

In this way capitalism converts the stock and trade of various 'fictions' into consumer goods, proving that everything can be sold with the iconoclastic (think Bart Simpson) just as likely to be prostituting itself as the merely commercial (like Mickey Mouse). I guess one extreme would be to consider the merchandising of our greatest writer, William Shakespeare in the town he spent most of his life avoiding, Stratford upon Avon. Here literature becomes design and his words are decorative additions to calendars and toilet rolls.

This subsection deals with the ways in which Fictions and Objects of Desire interact in the world of advertising. Whereas the merchandising of a film uses consumer goods to promote a central fiction, it is also the case that many advertisements use fictions to promote consumer goods. Often these are subtle, ingenious and elaborate fictions. Marks and Spencer, for example, have for a while been promoting their seasonal ranges through what can only be described as short films, featuring, amongst others, 1960s supermodel Twiggy and singer Mylene Klaas. For Christmas 2008 they paid Take That £250,000 (they gave their fee to Children in Need) to star in their seasonal narrative: the story of a classy M & S Christmas, complete with humour, romance and a little lingerie.

In both the Fictions and the Objects of Desire chapters we have touched on relationships with advertising, so we shall leave you to pursue these links with a couple of activities.

ACTIVITY

Every picture tells a story

What story is being told by this still image?

How is this story advanced by the words?

How does the product being advertised fit into this story?

Figure 7.13 Danica Patrick advertises Tissot watches

ACTIVITY

The stories that we tell to sell

Identify some of the most widely used narratives at work in television and print advertising?

What stories are commonly told to make us *believe* in a product?

What techniques are used by advertisers to invite the viewers to place themselves within the fiction?

Intersection Three: Fictions/Spaces and Places

The default here is a study of the significance of settings to any drama or narrative. Often there is a symbolic narrative told through the settings and their given meanings. This is most obvious in quest narratives like Tolkien's *Lord of the Rings* (Tolkien, 2001) or *Indiana Jones and the Kingdom of the Crystal Skull* (2008 dir. Steven Spielberg), but even the most discursive narratives have their key locations. In fact in genre fictions like the Situation Comedy and the Quiz Show setting is a major factor in generic identity, though in very different ways.

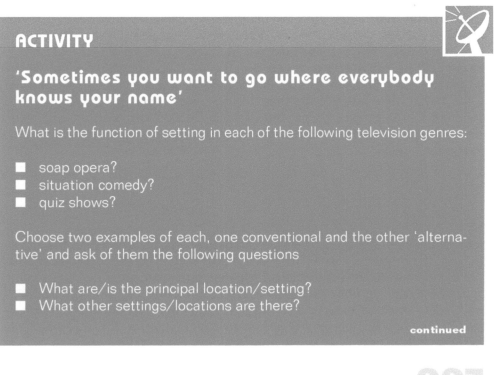

ACTIVITY

'Sometimes you want to go where everybody knows your name'

What is the function of setting in each of the following television genres:

■ soap opera?
■ situation comedy?
■ quiz shows?

Choose two examples of each, one conventional and the other 'alternative' and ask of them the following questions

■ What are/is the principal location/setting?
■ What other settings/locations are there?

continued

Of course, in television production setting is above all a budgetary consideration.
Each different location equates to significant costs in terms of set construction or
location filming, which is why the quiz show with its single studio setting is cheap
TV whatever the prize. This is another significant overlap: the fabrication of places
for film and television 'fictions' which in itself is a 'fictive' act; a deceit, a pretence.
The sumptuous and extensive recreation of Rome for the earlier mentioned BBC
series, which was undertaken at the famous Cinecitta studios in Rome, was largely
constructed as a 'flat'. On one side was the grime and graffiti of the ancient world
while the reverse was merely wood and fibreglass. The *All Roads lead to Rome*
'Making of. . .' documentary in the DVD box set does what any visit to a film set
does: it reinforces the artifice, the essential trick. Remember also that, for actors,
changes of location are also displacements of time, even to the extent that interiors and exteriors are usually shot separately and in different locations.

This brings a particular interest to the notion of the permanent set preferred by
the 'big' soaps like *Coronation Street* and *Eastenders*. Phil Redmond's *Brookside*
set the trend when in the early 1980s, they bought up a Wirral cul-de-sac and
controversially converted some 'real' houses into a usable set. *Eastenders* began
its run in 1985 on a purpose-built set at Elstree studios. *Emmerdale* finally
succumbed in 1998 when the crowds of fans turning up regularly to watch filming
in the real village of Eshott got too much. *Coronation Street* went a step further
in the 1990s when they allowed their updated exterior set (built from reclaimed
Salford brick) to become part of the Granada Studios tour. Visitors could even
take a drink in a replica of the Rovers' Return bar, a genuine simulacrum, a copy
without an original!

Variations on a Theme Park: nature red in tooth and claw

Jean Baudrillard, the second prophet of postmodernism, recognized the importance of the theme park as an index of the postmodern condition. He recognizes
Disneyland as 'a perfect model of all the entangled orders of simulation'
(Baudrillard, 1998, p. 354). He describes theme parks as 'imaginary stations which
feed reality, reality-energy, to a town (. . .)', arguing we need them 'as much as
electrical and nuclear power stations' (Baudrillard, 1998, p. 355). Ultimately he
sees Disneyland as a model of the 'real' America, but of more interest to us here

is his stark analysis of the intersections between two worlds, apparently real and imaginary, but also collective and individual. Rather than focus on 'the play of illusion and phantoms' he focuses on the pragmatics of the experience:

> **You park outside, queue up inside and are totally abandoned at the exit. In this imaginary world the only phantasmagoria is the inherent warmth and affection of the crowd, and in that sufficiently excessive number of gadgets used there to specifically maintain the multitudinous effect. The contrast with the absolute solitude of the parking lot – a veritable concentration camp – is total.**

(Baudrillard, 1998, p. 354)

For Baudrillard Disneyland magnetizes 'the crowd into direct flows', and points them towards a quasi-collective experience, which is largely about a bogus recovering of childhood (or childishness). In doing this, the theme park fulfils a vital function. Baudrillard is blunt: 'Disneyland is presented as imaginary in order to make us believe that the rest is real. . .'. Moreover the infantilism is presented as a similar feint. 'It is meant to be an infantile world in order to make us believe that the adults are elsewhere, in the 'real' world and to conceal the fact that real childishness is everywhere. . .' (Baudrillard, 1998, p. 355). This is not far from W.H. Auden who wrote:

> Lest we should see where we are
> Lost in a haunted wood
> Children afraid of the night
> Who have never been happy or good
>
> (from *September 1,1939*)

Steven Connor in *Postmodernist Culture* addresses the issue of selling experiences as follows:

> **From rock music to tourism to television and even education advertising imperatives and consumer demand are no longer for goods but for experiences.**

(Connor, 1996, p. 177)

Theme parks address these demands in a multiplicity of ways, through gadgets and through thematic integrity but always through the provision of a set of stories around a significant theme. One significant 'genre' in this respect is the safari park which extends to breaking point the intersection between the 'in' and 'out' worlds. It is also co-opts Nature, in its wildest manifestations, into the arena and on to the 'park'.

ACTIVITY

Life with the Lions

What are your expectations/experiences of Safari Parks?

How do they compare, in your opinion, to zoos and animal sanctuaries?

What is there

- to see?
- to do?
- to learn?

What happens after the 'safari'?

At a safari park in the 'wild' West Midlands you get to choose when to fit your 'safari' (tour of the 'reserve') into a day that also includes a meal (picnic or catered), a walk around mini-zoo and the obligatory funfair. At various times in the past ten years this had meant driving amongst antelopes and camels, zebras and giraffes. It has meant peering through car windows into enclosures restraining lions and snow tigers and waiting patiently while monkeys rip the trimming off your car. It has meant marvelling at the size of elephants while the steam trains of the adjacent Severn Valley Railway remind you of a time when travelling circuses paraded wild animals as a spectacle. This, I guess is as 'wild' as the Health and Safety Executive will allow but perhaps less respectful to the lions than throwing Christians to them: perhaps the Romans were more honest about what they wanted from lions. Here they seem more like the famous description of the Monty Python accountant who wants to be a Lion Tamer:

> **Little brown furry things with short stumpy legs and great long noses. I don't know what all the fuss is about. I could tame one of those. They look pretty tame to start with.**

And very little like the 'real' description from the same sketch:

> **You see a lion is a huge savage beast, about five feet high, ten feet long, weighing about four hundred pounds, running forty miles an hour, with masses of sharp pointed teeth and nasty long razor-sharp claws that can rip your belly out before you can say 'Eric Robinson', and they look like this.**

Source:http://www.jumpstation.ca/recroom/comedy/python/lion.html

Clearly it is a little of this latter 'experience' that the safari park promises but cannot deliver. What we get are well-fed lions doing what lions do when they're well fed. Only a terrible accident would ever bring us close to glimpsing the savage beast, which our better off ancestors might have spent time hunting on the earliest safaris. The thrills at the West Midlands Safari Park come on the rides on the rollercoaster, an adrenaline rush to nullify the placid nine to five. This is extreme sports without the hassle, adventure without the ventured and if nothing's ventured can anything be gained?

In Michael Crichton's *Westworld* (1973) the ultimate automated themed experience goes wrong and effectively bites back. Well heeled visitors to the entertainment resort, Delos, are able to live out their fantasies in different themed 'worlds': a medieval world, a Roman world or the wild west of the film's title. Each world is populated by beautiful and sexually submissive androids. But things go wrong. The robotic saloon gals are no longer willing and Yul Bryner's emblematic gunslinger android starts drawing for real. The reaction of the 'guests' is outraged disbelief as the promised interactive experience lives up to its billing. Crichton is entertaining the notion that this postmodern fascination with 'multi-violence' and 'interactivity' conceals an essentially egotistic, controlling and self-indulgent impulse. These may indeed be fictions which reject the assertiveness of the linear narrative but as a result they are cyclical and ultimately futile. On this basis it is not surprising to see the convergence between thrill-seeker rides and virtual reality technology. When the experience of Apocalypse can be simulated by a full body suit and the next generation X box or Play-station, the age of the theme park will perhaps be over. For the best British theme parks the inefficiency of a day out is staggering: for a substantial entrance fee you are allowed to spend the whole day queuing. Baudrillard has it just right: 'You park outside, queue up inside and are totally abandoned at the exit'. What a narrative this is: long hours of boredom for a few minutes of bliss. You end the day with a couple of over-priced photographs and a feeling of unease, which may be the after effects of being rushed through 360° whilst strapped to a sombrero or taken to a great height and just dropped. On the other hand it could be that feeling that you get when you realize that you've just spent the previous 72 hours without sleep playing *Championship Manager*

2009 and despite getting Port Vale into the Premiership you're wondering, 'was it all worth it?'

The past is another country: they do things differently there

One thing that the themed experience often has is reference both explicitly and implicitly to the past, or some version of it. In fact we live in a culture which is more and more interested in the past and yet less and less interested in studying it seriously. Some theorists would, of course, have us believe that this is part of wider repositioning of our relationships to objective truth and what critics have seen as the rejection of the 'Enlightenment Project'. Jürgen Habermas claims that 'Proponents of the Enlightenment (. . .) still held the extravagant expectation that the arts and sciences would further not only the control of the forces of nature but also the understanding of self and world, moral progress, justice in social institutions and even human happiness' (Habermas, 1997, p. 45). Habermas goes on to suggest that this optimistic view of modernity withered away in the twentieth century, leaving us with a much less certain view of progress and the links between past and present.

Now it is claimed, by for example Frederic Jameson, that we live in a culture in which 'real' history is displaced by nostalgia. This is interesting to say the least given that the past fifteen years has seen an unprecedented revival of interest in history and its methodologies. One arm of this, due to the success of TV programmes like *Time Team* is a movement towards the acts of recovering and 'reliving the past': a mixture of archaeology and living history. And this media revival, spawning three or four specialist cable channels and regular spots across the terrestrial schedule, has been matched by the onward march of the history business: *heritage*.

When Blists Hill Victorian Town near Ironbridge (birth place of the industrial revolution) opened in 1973 it set a slow train coming which then gathered speed. It offered (and still offers) a step back into the past complete with 'old' money to spend in the 'old' shops. Others slowly followed suit and now a plethora of living museums/historical 'experiences' exists in all shapes and sizes to service our desire to experience the past. Museums have had to adapt too or disappear, by providing virtual environments and hands on exhibits.

This in turn leads to a further blurring of the line that stands between fact and 'simulation'. Locating the past very much in themed 'events', in spectacles rather than scholarship, has changed our relationship with the past. In the same way the past is continually being simulated and negotiated in historical dramas, on film and television and the two spheres are clearly connected. What is being progressively engaged in by both Blists Hill and the latest recasting of Dickens' *Little Dorritt* is a view of history that is 'bottom up', that is social and economic rather than political, local rather than national. What is sought is an empathetic response to 'the historical', the desire to know what it was like and how it felt rather than

Figure 7.14 Bringing the past to life at Blists Hill Victorian Town

merely 'what happened'. This leads in Jameson's view to a discontinuous flow of perpetual presents and the annihilation of depth, of genuine historical context. In other words the 'living' history movement becomes paradoxically responsible for the end of history since the 'living' cannot be effectively 'past'.

ACTIVITY

Visiting the past

Identify three local or national Heritage sites and comment briefly on their historical importance (where, what, when?)

Identify three to five television or film dramas with significant historical contexts and again describe the historical setting (as much information as possible)

Which of these historical sources is most 'accurate'/authentic/useful when it comes to historical judgements?

How do you know?

What certainly persists is our sense of the past as found in places worthy of preserving and celebrating: ancient monuments, castles, even industrial sites. Each of these is a store of narratives of various kinds but perhaps most interesting is our current metanarrative of the 'past' and its physical legacies. Barely one hundred and fifty years ago Wiltshire farmers were still casually taking stone for their walls from a convenient deposit on Salisbury Plain which we call Stonehenge. What we have fenced off, in nearly every way, they saw as 'accessible', usable and 'over' (as in no longer active). Carrying off the stones would now be viewed as almost sacrilegious even by non-pagans, since the crime would seem to be against history itself. However who is to say that those who encountered Stonehenge as part of a continuous present were not better adjusted to their history. Their making use of this monument asks to be evaluated alongside our own creation of a massive monolithic exhibit experienced only as a kind of historical shop window.

In schools the empathetic movement has passed through, leaving a proper concern for ordinary people (those who Marx said made history by pursuing their own ends) and rightly abandoning the extremes of the 'history in their shoes' approach. Instead the movement is towards historical skills and the interrogation of the evidence on which the lavish media reconstructions are based. Provocative dramas like *Rome* and *The Tudors* have bone fide historical consultants but is it the detail or the gist that we're after. Time and place are in this sense difficult to separate. When Sam Tyler was taken back to 1970s Manchester in the cult 'historical' drama *Life on Mars* a sense of place and time was essential. In fact elsewhere in this text, in a discussion about realism, the film critic Alexander Kluge suggests that reality itself can only be represented as 'the historical fiction that it is' (Bennett, Hickman and Wall, 2006, p. 203).

James Cameron's fascination with that infamous floating 'space' the *Titanic* has led to two very different films and a CD Rom that allowed a virtual tour of 'the greatest luxury liner'. This top-heavy symbol of a class-bound Edwardian world bound for disaster allowed Cameron to create the biggest grossing film of all time (*Titanic*, 1997) around a simple Romeo and Juliet narrative carved out of class rather than family division. However the Cameron *Titanic* film tagged 'ground-breaking' and 'historic' on the Internet is the lesser known IMAX 30 documentary *Ghosts of the Abyss* (1997), which explores the stricken vessel as it rests in pieces on the North Atlantic sea bed. Here the computer reconstruction is almost literally authenticated before our eyes further extending our discussion about reality, simulation and history.

We began this section talking about places made meaningful by their position and function within larger narratives. In doing so we were referring to places like 'The Shire' and 'The Mines of Moria' in *Lord of the Rings*, but our life narratives also have their key locations. Moreover these locations: the family home, your place of work, your school or college, are themselves coloured by representations that have been made and continue to be made of locations like them. Whether it be *The Simpsons* or *Eastenders* these are formative influences so that our perceptions of the world pass through significant filters of expectation. Even seemingly natural landscapes are not free from these interferences. One problem is, of course, that we define nature in terms of living things (grass, trees, birds, etc.) and then find difficulty in seeing these as cultural constructs. In their book *Reading Images* Kress and Van Leeuwen make the point very well, even reminding us of 'landscape's' etymology.

> Each feature of a landscape has a history, as does the landscape as a whole and each is subject to constant remaking. It is here that the etymology of the word landscape is revealing while to a casual beholder a landscape simply *is* and may even have a timeless appearance ('the timeless beauty of the English, or Spanish, countryside'), it is in fact a product of social history, of human work on the land, on nature: *-scape* with its relatives to *shape* in English and *Schaffen* (both 'to work' and 'to create' in German), indicates this.

(Kress and Van Leeuwen, 1996, p. 33)

Much of our 'timeless' landscape is in fact not even 'ancient'. The English country-side went through such significant re-shaping in the sixteenth and seventeenth centuries that very little that we see when walking in the countryside is anything like the views our ancestors might have had. In some cases it is the settlements, the built-up areas, which are most untouched. Remember also that in the Middle Ages most of England was covered in trees. Now, it seems, much of the country is covered in human 'debris' such as concrete and tarmac, though a glance at any Ordnance Survey map shows reassuring swathes of green. The fact is that we don't lack 'countryside' but distinctions between town and country are not so clearly drawn as we might expect them to be. If everything is 'interfered with' where are we going to get 'nature' from, as in 'untouched' and 'untamed'? When Saruman's army sacks The Shire in the *Lord of the Rings*, they defile it by indus-trializing it and this code is still going strong. Purity is more easily found in a field with an adjoining wood than in an industrial setting even if the said 'wood' is full of recently transplanted imported firs and owned by a celebrity's hedge-fund. We're just steeped in the easy symbolism of places and their stories are ours. Undoubtedly, we have created powerful fictions around the spaces that we label the town, the city and the countryside.

References and further reading

Baudrillard, J. (1998) The Precession of Simulacra, in J. Storey (ed.), *Cultural Theory and Popular Culture; A Reader* (2nd edn), Harlow: Prentice Hall, pp. 350–7.

Bennett, P. and Slater, J. (2008) *AS Communication and Culture; The Essential Introduction,* Abingdon: Routledge.

Bennett, P., Hickman, A. and Wall, P. (2006) *Film Studies: The Essential Resource,* Abingdon: Routledge.

Chinn, N. C. (Composer) (1974) *Lonely This Christmas* [Mud, Performer], London: RAK.

Connor, S. (1996) *Postmodernist Culture: An Introduction to Theories of the Contemporary* (2nd edn), London: Wiley Blackwell.

Habermas, J. (1997) Modernity: an unfinished project, in M. Passerin d'Entreves and S. Benhabib (eds), *Habermas and the Unfinished Project of Modernity,* Concord: MIT, pp. 38–55.

Kress, G. and Van Leeuwen, T. (1996) *Reading Images: Grammar of Visual Design,* Abingdon: Routledge.

Larkin, P. (1988) *Collected Poems,* London: Faber and Faber.

Tolkien, J. (2001) *The Fellowship of the Ring: The Lord of the Rings Vol. 1,* Collins Modern Classics.

THE A2 EXAMINATION; COMM3 COMMUNICATING CULTURE

8

We are going to make the assumption here that you have already passed the AS Communication and Culture exam and, in all likelihood, a number of other AS exams, so there is no need for this chapter to be quite as long or as detailed as our chapter on exams in the AS book (Bennett and Slater, 2008). This short chapter is therefore dedicated to the specific challenges presented by a specific exam: COMM3: Communicating Culture. However, it can do no harm (in the sharpest of note forms) to rehearse some general principles.

Passing exams in a nutshell

The process falls into three distinct phases:

1. Revision: which looks at the various ways in which the knowledge gained from a course of study can be recalled, marshalled and reorganized so as to be useful in the examination.
2. Planning: which covers the period from opening the examination paper to starting your first answer.
3. Execution: which deals with different techniques and approaches to answering the question.

Revision

Make sure you know how you are to be assessed. Knowledge of assessment – of what examinations are and what they do – is as important as knowledge of subject.

1. Consider each topic you cover in terms of

   a. its most important content
   b. the amount of information you could reasonably use in about 50 to 55 minutes.

2. Compile the essential information, together with quotations and/or notes, on no more than one side of A4 paper for each topic.
3. Don't forget to practice *applying* what you know. This subject asks us to draw on experience and skill. The more that we try to learn this 'experience', the less like experience it becomes.

Planning

As soon as you turn over the paper and start reading the questions, make the paper your own. You do this by writing and making marks directly onto the exam paper itself. Use underlinings, highlighting, doodles: anything that will help you to interpret the questions and plan your response. These marks are the evidence that you have ruthlessly explored the questions' potential and have identified any potential problems with them.

In the course of this process look for two sets of key words:

- Words that tell you what to do (e.g. 'analyse', 'identify', 'compare and contrast', 'evaluate', 'consider')
- Subject-specific words (e.g. 'ideology', 'discourse', 'mode of address').

Remember that the first group of key words is just as important as the second. Candidates often under-achieve because they haven't used their subject knowledge effectively in the context set out by the question.

Don't be tempted to write too much in this planning phase. Jot down words, phrases, abbreviations, mindmaps, spidergrams, bullet points or whatever it is that you personally find most useful in planning and structuring your response.

Execution

You will have heard the following pieces of advice so many times that they may be becoming meaningless through repetition. As experienced examiners, though, we know that it is these simple hurdles that continue to trip up large numbers of exam candidates, hence the rather exasperated tone of this advice.

- Plan your time properly. Two Questions. Two Hours. I think we can all work that one out.
- Some people will answer all six questions. Don't be one of them.
- Answer the question that has been set, not the one you hoped would be set. (More on this later in the chapter.)
- Select material that is relevant to the question and, just as importantly, de-select material that isn't relevant. The examiner just wants to see enough of what you know to assess your ability; you cannot possibly write down *everything* that you know.
- Write your answers in a fairly formal register. As a student of communication,

you know how important it is to match the *form* of your communication to the *context* of communication.

- Like all academic subject areas, Communication and Culture has its own terminology, its own specialist vocabulary. Use subject specific terms confidently and accurately.
- Don't underestimate the physical demands of writing by hand for two hours. This requires practice. You must be able to write enough (and that means at least three sides of average sized handwriting per answer) and you must write legibly.
- Strike a balance between the *general* and the *specific*. Usually this means starting with a general (i.e. abstract or theoretical) point, then giving a specific illustration or two, then explaining why the illustrated point is relevant to the question or to your argument.
- Your objective is to develop coherent and convincing arguments. This means that ideas need to flow logically from one point to the next. Simply supplying lists of material, however relevant, won't convince the examiner of your ability to *apply* what you know.

Communicating Culture

The title of the unit is, as ever, a key to what goes on in the examination. It is not a reference to the exam, wherein you will be more precisely communicating *about* culture, but rather a reference to the unit content. This unit concerns the various ways in which culture is communicated through the places and spaces, the stories that we tell and the possessions that we collect and covet. It is about the forms and processes of cultural communication and the many competing interpretations and theories of these. Knowing what kind of a thing the unit is about helps massively when preparing for the exam.

What further clues can we get from a consideration of the available evidence? In fact, what is the available evidence? The following will all help to form an appreciation and understanding of the demands of COMM3:

- The specification (pp.17–18)
- Sample papers and mark schemes
- Past papers (and mark schemes)
- Examiner's reports
- The subject specific support provided by AQA

A careful reading of the specification gives a very clear idea of what is required in the COMM3 exam. Moreover, it alerts us to work that can be addressed in all three of the phases we identified above.

- Revision (looking back at what has been done)
- Planning (marshalling this material and your own ideas for use in the exam)
- Execution (having the specific skills to cope with specific challenges)

Revision: what do I need to revise?

Figure 8.1 Revision, revision, revision

The specification states that 'this synoptic unit builds upon the knowledge and understanding developed in units 1 and 2'. Here, from the start, is a specific challenge: to build on the foundations laid in COMM1 and COMM2. What this means here is:

■ Definitions of culture
■ The meanings and practices of everyday life
■ Cultural codes
■ The techniques of critical analysis

It also means an assumption that you will be familiar with a set of key concepts, two of which (identity and power) are developed in A2. It is particularly difficult to get far with COMM3 if you don't have more than a working knowledge of:

■ Culture
■ Value
■ Representation
■ Code

All of these are implicitly extended by the widening of the textual focus from the human form and print examples to the constructed environment and primal narratives. Aside from the identification of these specific cultural sites, the list of 'new' A2 Key Concepts continues the 'texts and meanings' theme. All of the A2 Key Concepts potentially extend the idea that our chief concern in this unit is to act as commentators and analysts of the conversations our society and cultures have with themselves. Consider:

- Ideology (which Althusser described as 'a system of representation')
- Mode of address (which considers the positioning of messages)
- Discourse (the language associated with different communicative forms)
- Narrative (an ordering of data which produces meaning)
- Technology (a primary means by which messages and meanings are exchanged)

Beyond this, the content (i.e. that which is to be tested) is very clear:

- Theoretical Approaches
- Sites of Culture

Both of these components are explicitly defined and yet both also include elements of personal selection at more than one level. This is the point at which so-called revision gives way to the much more significant 'preparation', where theory gives way to practice.

You must be able to show an awareness of the following critical approaches:

- Market liberal approaches (arguments about how free economic markets allied with democratic institutions and legally enshrined personal freedoms provide the best pragmatic model for prosperity and well-being)
- Critical Social Theory (e.g. Marxism: arguments predicated on economic inequalities)
- Feminism (arguments predicated on gender inequalities)
- Postmodernism (arguments based on the premise that we live in a world of 'simulations' and 'hyperreality' in economies based on the production of images and information (rather than the production of things)

And in addition ONE of the following:

- Post-colonialism (arguments predicated on inequalities of race and ethnicity)
- Post-structuralism (arguments which see meaning as a continuing, shifting, unstable and dynamic process rather than the binary oppositions suggested by structuralism)
- Queer Theory (arguments which suggest that the old dichotomy of masculine–feminine distorts what in reality is a social construction)

Similarly, you are only required to study one of the following Sites of Culture

- Spaces and places
- Fictions
- Objects of desire

However there is an explicit encouragement to allow your close study to recognize the interconnectedness of these arbitrary divisions of contemporary experience. What Intersections really imply is 'integration' in a project that might bear the legend 'Everyday life: location, narrative, props'. Here is self-presentation, Goffman-style, on a societal level: persona, performance, role, staging (including props), teams and personal style. Here is *the city* as Barthes imagined it; not only as 'a writing' but also as a set of readings, as location, as character in a tragic fiction, as an object of desire.

In short, we would expect most of you to have studied two Sites of Culture and the associated Intersection. This approach will substantially enhance the range of choice available to you in the exam.

Planning

The information that we have so far gives us ample opportunity for general preparation. The specification offers explicit encouragement for the same kind of critical analytical approach which was fostered in AS: informed active readings, but in this case at a deeper and more sophisticated level. Furthermore we are encouraged to adopt an informed critical approach by the following entreaties:

- To engage with cultural sites (i.e. to actively address them)
- To use relevant key concepts (i.e. to choose those that fit your particular reading)
- To take a comparative approach in the use of theoretical perspectives

All of these are wonderfully enabling since they offer a coherent set of aims for the unit which are completely in tune with the integrated critical approach practised in AS. They are also identified in the three Assessment Objectives (AOs) addressed by this module:

AO1: Tests your ability to communicate in the register of Communication and Culture

AO2: Tests your ability to understand the content and concepts of the subject. You are expected to show your knowledge of relevant critical and theoretical debates

AO3: Demonstrates your ability to apply your knowledge, in this instance by showing analytical, comparative and interpretive skills and by using relevant concepts and perspectives.

Comfortingly AO3 has the greatest weighting in this case. This means that your ability to apply knowledge and understanding in contexts set by the question is the most important in this examination.

Figure 8.2 What to write?

We are now ready to explore the format of the examination paper that is set to address these issues. The basic elements of the COMM3 paper are as follows:

- Externally examined written paper
- 2 hour examination
- 80 marks

Section A (50% of total marks)

- One compulsory question relating to Theoretical Approaches and Key Concepts. Candidates are given a piece of stimulus material comprising written or written and visual material on some aspect of contemporary culture.
- Candidates are required to analyse and evaluate the stimulus material using **at least three** relevant key concepts and comparative theoretical approaches.

Section B (50% of total marks)

- Candidates are asked to choose **one** question from a choice of five: two generic questions which may be answered by reference to any of the

Cultural Sites and three specific questions, each relating to one of the Cultural Sites.

Let's deal with these two, equally weighted sections in turn.

Section A is the place where theoretical approaches and key concepts are formally addressed so do make sure that you use them. The passage(s) provided are intended to 'stimulate' you. Your job is to see in these passages connections with your studies. There will often be two pieces of material for you to take in, each representing a particular position or argument or point of view. You will need to examine the material carefully to see how it 'fits in' with the critical approaches or debates you have studied. The stimulus material will focus on 'some aspect of contemporary culture'. In other words it will be a natural continuation of the course, modelling the kinds of issues and debates you will have been dealing with on a weekly basis. However it may well deal with a topic that you have not encountered before. Don't let this put you off! The examiners aren't testing your knowledge of a specific topic here, but your ability to interpret the arguments being forwarded and to engage in the debate using your knowledge of concepts and theoretical approaches.

Add to this the emboldened quantifiers (**at least three** . . .) and we are faced with a compulsory question on some issue relevant to Communicating Culture, but of which you have no advance knowledge. However, you have (we hope) considerable advance knowledge of the theoretical approaches and key concepts which you must bring to bear on this issue. (This is the stuff you already know.) Thus rather than worrying about trying to second-guess the 'aspect of contemporary culture', it is better to focus on what you already know and to think about how this material can be used and applied. What the exam provides is a tangible area of debate within which you will be able to demonstrate your knowledge and skills. The material will also 'stimulate' your responses; it should guide you towards *relevant* areas of knowledge and skill that can usefully be applied to the specific instruction given on the paper. An example of the sort of instruction you will encounter here is: 'Using concepts and approaches with which you are familiar, compare and contrast the two positions outlined above'.

Section B is even more predictable in its formulation than Section A. As described above, candidates are asked to choose **one** question from a choice of five: two generic questions which may be answered by reference to any of the Cultural Sites and three specific questions, each relating to one of the Cultural Sites.

In fact, there's a little more subtlety here, further adding to your scope. The two generic questions each extend the case for individual readings of cultural products and practices. Question One addresses the intersections between the sites, whereas Question Two focuses on a key concept or critical approach(es) which may be related to any one of the three Cultural Sites. This means that taking an integrated approach in which you study two sites and an intersection gives you the choice of four of the five Section B questions. Studying just one of the Cultural

Sites effectively reduces your choice to just two out of five section B questions. However, you may consider that this reduction of choice is a price worth paying for the extra time, breadth and depth of study you could devote to a single Cultural Site.

Section B, therefore, looks like this:

Question 2: choose **two** of the three cultural sites (Intersection)
Question 3: choose **one** cultural site (generic, based on concept(s) and/or theoretical approach(es))
Question 4: Spaces and Places
Question 5: Fictions
Question 6: Objects of Desire.

In such a configuration the questions will inevitably be fairly predictable combinations of sites and key concepts with theoretical approaches featuring implicitly if not explicitly. These are enabling questions, not questions to catch you out. They are invitations to show what you understand and also to demonstrate the ways in which this unit has grabbed you. These questions are starting points for conversations which you have already been having with your teachers, your fellow students and yourself. They offer simple patterns for you to develop: to challenge, contest, support and in all cases illustrate with your own readings of cultural texts and cultural practices.

Given that both concepts and approaches are explicit requirements, the responsibility that you have is to provide the detail; to identify the texts and contexts, the products and practices. As the questions are generic so the evidence must be specific. In a site as open and wide-ranging as, for example, Spaces and Places there will be lots of opportunities to explore case study examples in your group. These may include the Shopping Mall, the Football Stadium, the High Street or the Village. In addition, these examples should, ideally, persuade you to make your own readings of your own Spaces and Places for the unit to be a success.

You have a great opportunity here to deal with the unit content *and* be entirely prepared for Section B. All you need to do is to take personal responsibility for evidencing your own understanding of the concepts and approaches in the broad context of one of the Cultural Sites (and perhaps beyond it). What you need then is to work on a specific case study (or, preferably, two) which you are going to use to develop your understanding of the content and which will then convincingly address the range of questions set in the exam.

The Cultural Sites are pleasingly and deliberately broad (one might say 'enormous') because they are merely convenient categories within which we may explore the ideas and issues that characterize the unit. As we have demonstrated this task works in tandem with the prescriptive Section A to provide a thorough-going test of your knowledge and ability to apply it. Here, the test is to develop ideas in your own way on your own terms. The relative predictability of the Section B questions is a function of this role.

To take the Spaces and Places Cultural Site as an example, all Section B questions need to recognize the integrity of the site and every Centre and student's right to inhabit it in their own way (which is another way of saying that the openness of the site cannot be compromised). To set a question on a particular place or genre of places would fly in the face of this principle. Often contrasting examples will be requested to further reinforce breadth and choice. (Note, however, that a particular place may appear in the question *as an illustration*. The question could refer to, say, the Taj Mahal or Las Vegas as examples of a general principle, but you would not be expected to confine your response to discussion of these places.) Second, the Spaces and Places question must address one or more of the unit's key concepts and/or theoretical approaches. This means in effect you can expect in the fullness of time, questions on:

- The ways in which spaces and places challenge or reinforce dominant ideology or are carriers of ideology
- The usefulness of theoretical approaches in addressing spaces and places
- The concept of mode of address in relation to places and spaces
- The ways in which spaces and places construct identities for people
- The values embodied in the constructed environment
- The ways in which power is signified by the constructed environment
- The narratives constructed by contrasting spaces and places
- The concept of discourse in relation to spaces and places.

Effectively, the Principal Examiner responsible for setting these Section B questions is simply offering various permutations on the following:

- The Three Cultural Sites
- The following Key Concepts:

  - Discourse
  - Identity
  - Ideology
  - Mode of Address
  - Narrative
  - Power
  - Technology

- Theoretical Approaches (of which only four are compulsory)

From your point of view, what is required, then, is a case study approach that incorporates:

- Contrasting examples from your chosen site (in this case Spaces and Places)
- Awareness of the ways that these examples might connect with at least one other site

- Readings of these examples from contrasting theoretical approaches
- All of the key concepts

This notion of case study is central to the pattern of Communication and Culture. The intellectual project of the course is critical and analytical, its territory is contemporary culture as practice and product. The specification identifies potentially productive locations (sites) for these encounters; landscapes that range from personal language through popular music to body modification and, of course, the three Cultural Sites identified for close study in Communicating Culture.

Given these considerations what your preparation requires is a format, preferably your own, to discipline your response and to pragmatically move preparation from 'doing the course' to 'doing the exam'. Your format needs to be open-ended and electronic to allow for the dynamic interplay between theory and practice, between concepts and contexts. What follows is an example of a grid that could be used and adapted to fit your own needs.

	Mkt Lib	CST	Fem'ism	PoMo	PostCol
Cultural Site					
Case Study					
Example A					
Example B					

	Discourse	Identity	Ideology	Mode of Address	Narr't've	Power	Tech
Cultural Site							
Case Study							
Example A							
Example B							

Figure 8.3 Revision grids for Section B

	Market Lib	Crit Soc Theory	Feminism	PoMo	PostCol'ism
Cultural Site **Spaces and Places**	Pluralism: Different S&P reflect choice and preferences. The property market determines what gets built	Buildings communicate dominant value system of capitalism. Economic power and status manifested by S&P	Spaces are gender coded. Organization of space reflects gender roles	Spaces as simulacra. Playing with architectural styles. Absent sense of history continuity	References to 'exotic otherness' used to give buildings and spaces appeal
Case Study: **Retail Venues**	Consumer sovereignty: massive range of choice for all income levels	Retail spaces encourage consumerism, 'fake consciousness'	Pleasures of shopping: masc and fem shopping experiences	Availability of 'off the peg' identities. Shopping as self-expression	Globalization – inequalities in trading systems. Imported goods disguise low wages, sweat shops
Example A **Midtown High Street**	Clustering of shoe shops: competing for different market sectors. Un-let shop units: couldn't provide competitive service	Job losses as shops close. Aesthetic appeal of the town spoilt by tacky design and garish shop fronts	Shopping as a gendered social activity. Analysis: male and female shop assistants	Bricolage of styles. Efforts to recreate 'historic Midtown'	Midtown celebrates its history – but ignores its role in colonial exploitation
Example B **The Glades Shopping Mall**	Meets consumer demand – car park is always full. People prefer chain stores to local retailers	'Cathedrals of consumption'. Local providers and local retailers annihilated by global brands. Spatial metaphors	Contrast upmarket boutique with mass market clothes shop. Postfeminist fashion	Hanging out in the mall; resistant rituals? Hyper-reality? the 'Egyptian Quarter', 'Bourbon Street'	Rhetoric of diversity, multi-culturalism vs reality of security and policing. Use of the word 'ethnic' in branding goods

Figure 8.4 Sample revision grid for Spaces and Places/Theoretical Perspectives

Needless to say, grids such as these are not the place for recording everything that you know about your chosen Cultural Site. They should serve two purposes:

First, to confirm that you have covered the requisite territory, that there are no gaping holes in your knowledge that could be exposed by the 'wrong' question.

Second, the activity of 'filling in the boxes' is a revision exercise in its own right. If you can discipline yourself to make just a very few, very brief points in each box these can act as triggers to remind you of relevant areas of knowledge as well as your own ideas and insights when it comes to applying concepts and theoretical approaches to your case study examples.

Figure 8.4 shows one of these grids completed for Spaces and Places/Theoretical Perspectives. Needless to say, the points included are not supposed to be definitive; simply an illustration of a possible approach with notes to serve as revision reminders.

This kind of activity is much more useful than honing a carefully prepared Spaces and Places 'model answer' for use in the exam whatever question is asked. Examiners invariably find this technique to be disappointing and irritating in roughly equal measures. It is disappointing because candidates who supply model answers of this sort fail to do themselves justice. By 'covering all the bases' and trying to allow for the eventuality of *any* question, candidates spread their answers too thinly. This means that the highest mark band (Level Four) is virtually ruled out. The answer may be competent, but it lacks the thoroughgoing relevance of the best responses. The answer is irritating because it represents an almost willful disdain for the question that has actually been set. 'Look', the candidate seems to be saying, 'I don't care what question you have asked, *this* is the essay that I'm going to write.'

Examiners, of course, are professionals and they won't allow a little irritation or disappointment to stand in the way of their impartiality. But why not pursue the line of least resistance and give the examiners what they want. And what do they want? They want to see answers that convince them that you have carefully read the question, that you have selected material that is entirely relevant to the question and that you have concentrated all of your efforts on doing what the question instructs you to do. If, in doing this, you have provided evidence of your knowledge, skills and understanding and your ability to apply these relevantly and creatively, you will sail into the top level of marks, leaving the 'model answers' floundering in your wake.

Our final task in this chapter is to look at some sample COMM3 exam papers. You'll be able to find sample papers and past papers on the AQA website (aqa.org.uk). We'll start with Section A. but it is worth making the point that you don't have to answer your two questions in the same order. There may be very good reasons for giving your Section B answer first, moving on to Section A when you are thoroughly warmed up and in your stride.

Material from the paper itself is indented and in black, our comments are in blue

The rubric is the material on the front of the exam paper, a set of general instructions and information that is unlikely to change very much from year to year. The Key Concepts and Cultural sites are listed here and you are reminded of the importance of spelling, punctuation and grammar and the overall quality of your written communication.

SECTION A

There is **one** compulsory question in this section.

The first component of Question 1 is the preamble, which sets the scene. A particular issue or area of interest identified. As there is no expectation that you will have studied this area, it may be the case that certain terms will need a brief explanation in the preamble, as is the case in our first example.

> Both traditional media and new media such as the Internet have made increasing use of user-generated material. This material is contributed by amateurs rather than media professionals and covers every topic imaginable.
>
> Opinion is divided on the implications of this development for contemporary culture.

The topic is clear: user-generated material in this case, but it is also worth subjecting this preamble to some close examination. There are already some helpful pointers towards the areas of debate you will need to address. Binary oppositions are set up between the 'traditional media' and 'new media', between 'amateurs' and 'professionals' and the statement takes it as read that this is a development with 'implications' for contemporary culture. There is an assumption that this phenomenon will inevitably drive forward cultural change of some sort and the assertion that 'opinion is divided' suggests a rift between those who see positive consequences and those who see negative outcomes.

Now the paper goes on to set out two contrasting positions on the issue described in the preamble.

Argument A

'New technology has seen a massive shift of power from producers to consumers, to such an extent that we can say that consumers *are* the new producers. In the bad old days it needed a massive capital investment to produce, record and distribute music, moving images and even the printed word. Today, cheap and easily available hardware together with the capacity of the Internet has given all of us the capacity to be our own music producers, movie makers or newspaper editors.

The creative potential is fantastic and amounts to nothing less than a cultural revolution. It is democratic, liberating and personally fulfilling.'

Argument B

'Recent trends towards user-generated material in cultural production may seem to change the balance of power between producer and consumer, but a close look shows this to be an illusion. Look at how the big corporations have moved in. In 2006, Google snapped up YouTube for £850 million, MySpace became part of Rupert Murdoch's News Corporation empire in a £295 million deal and Friends Reunited was acquired by ITV for £120 million. Meanwhile other corporations and their lawyers circle around, ready to pounce on infringements of their copyright.

Also, there are few if any filters to help us to interpret user-generated material. Is it real or fake? Is it a genuinely amateur product or cunningly disguised advertising? Is it original or ripped off? It is often impossible to tell. We are adrift in an ocean of information without a compass. The shared experiences on which cultural identity is built are being undermined by the mouse-clicking individual grazing on low quality snippets of user-generated entertainment.'

Before we move on to some discussion and analysis of these two arguments, let's look at the final part of Question 1, the instruction that tells the candidate what to do:

Use your knowledge of selected theoretical perspectives and key concepts to evaluate the views of user-generated material expressed here.
(40 marks; Specimen Question AQA 2009)

This final part of the question includes the reminder that theoretical perspectives and key concepts should feature prominently in your answer and the instruction to evaluate the views expressed in Arguments A and B. The ability to evaluate positions involves a fairly sophisticated set of skills and it is one of the most challenging requirements of an A Level examination. In order to evaluate a position or, as in this case, competing positions, you need to establish some sort of criterion against which to make your evaluative judgements. It isn't really good enough to say things like 'I much prefer Argument A', or 'I find Argument B to be the most convincing' unless you can very clearly explain *why* you have reached one or the other of these conclusions. These are the sort of criteria that could be used to evaluate ideas and arguments:

The nature of the evidence. Is any evidence offered in support of the argument? What is the quality of the evidence? Is it empirical or anecdotal? If the evidence is scant, can you supply supportive evidence of your own? You could also consider the terms in which the arguments are expressed, the register. Is the argument a cool and careful consideration or an intemperate rant?

Turning to the content of the two arguments, you should be able to use your knowledge of perspectives and concepts as you start to interpret and analyse the material. This is the stage at which you should be following our advice to 'make the paper your own' by scribbling notes and comments and highlights and underlinings on the exam paper itself.

Argument A takes a highly positive and optimistic view of user-generated material. There are certainly elements here of a market liberal position, particularly in the emphasis on the democratic potential of the developments described. The idea that 'people have power' as both producers and consumers certainly fits with a pluralist conception of society, but it could also be seen as an expression of optimistic postmodernism. You may also recognize elements of technological determinism: the idea that social and cultural changes are a *consequence* of technological developments.

Argument B appears at first sight to be a straightforward statement of a Marxist position on user-generated material. It is typical of a Marxist approach insofar as it puts so much emphasis on economic factors. As we have seen, for traditional Marxists all cultural phenomena can ultimately be explained by the 'contradictions at the point of production', or by who owns what. The idea of 'illusion' or 'disguise' is also characteristic of a Marxist view of ideology. For Marxists, ideology has the function of concealing the reality of power differences by disguising them as 'natural' or 'inevitable'. However, you could detect elements of pessimistic postmodernism in this argument and you may also want to follow more recent cultural theorists in a broadly Marxist tradition who have rejected the idea that the economy determines everything.

SECTION B

Answer **one** question from this section.

EITHER

2 Choose **two** of the three cultural sites. Identify some examples of cultural products and/or cultural practices at the intersection between your two chosen sites. Show how critical theoretical approaches have helped you to understand these examples.

(40 marks; Specimen Question AQA 2009)

Possible case study: Fictions and Objects of Desire – how the cars, clothes, gadgets and other props in James Bond films play a role in the narrative. How women are objectified and objects are sexualized in these films.

OR

3 Choose one of the three cultural sites. Explain why mode of address is a significant concept in the understanding of this site.

(40 marks; Specimen Question AQA 2009)

Here we have something very straightforward and extremely clearly focused. There is opportunity to talk about mode of address across a range of examples, from film and literary narratives to those used in advertising or by us in our negotiations of identity.

OR

4 It has been argued that **places and spaces** 'speak' to us in ways which reinforce our cultural identity. Drawing on contrasting examples, critically evaluate this view of places and spaces.

(40 marks; Specimen Question AQA 2009)

A key word here is *contrasting*. You should make sure that your two case studies are clearly distinct and different. Ideally, one should illustrate the proposition that spaces and places do reinforce cultural identity whilst the other should show a contrary position.

OR

5 'The **fictions** and stories of contemporary culture are the most powerful forces in shaping our identities as cultural beings.'

Discuss this view of fictions in contemporary culture.

(40 marks; Specimen Question AQA 2009)

This is in many ways a very different kind of question since the assertion that fictions and stories are 'the most powerful forces' requires us to consider other shaping influences on our cultural identities. Acquiring a cultural identity is the product (albeit unfinished) of socialization/enculturation. This is enacted through agents such as the family, education and the media. It is most likely that you will see all of these as dealers in fictions of various kinds.

OR

6 'The design and marketing of consumer products tells us all we need to know about power relations in contemporary society.'

Assess this statement using your knowledge of **objects of desire**.

(40 marks; Specimen Question AQA 2009)

This question certainly invites the use of contrasting theoretical perspectives. As each has a different view of 'power relations' it should be relatively straightforward to bring a comparative dimension to your assessment of the statement. Care will be needed in showing that you have attended to *both* design *and* marketing, using suitable examples of each.

And Finally . . .

Here is another example of a COMM3 exam paper for you to discuss and practise.

SECTION A

There is **one** compulsory question in this section.

1. Major international sporting events can have enormous cultural as well as economic significance. In spite of the enormous costs involved, countries compete strenuously with each other for the honour of staging such events. Their popularity is enormous, with media audiences that can reach into the billions. Opinions are divided, though, on the underlying cultural significance of sporting festivals such as the Olympics and the Football World Cup.

Argument A

International festivals of sport such as the Olympics or the Football World Cup are fantastic celebrations of all that is best about the human spirit. Barriers of race, religion and social class are all broken down in the name of true sporting competition. Events such as these remind us that there really is only one race: the human race. We are able to celebrate cultural diversity without any sense that some cultures are 'better' or more advantaged than others.

Argument B

International festivals of sport such as the Olympics or the Football World Cup are sickening reminders of the depth of division between the 'haves' and the 'have nots'. These games are cynically exploited by nation states and multinational corporations in order to promote apathy and consumerism amongst the viewing millions. On each occasion, the host nation uses the event to communicate a thoroughly false and misleading impression of its culture to the rest of the world.

Use your knowledge of selected theoretical perspectives and key concepts to evaluate the contrasting views of international sporting events expressed by Argument A and Argument B.

(40 marks; Specimen Question AQA 2009)

SECTION B

Answer **one** question from this section.

EITHER

2   Choose **two** of the three cultural sites. Use case study material to discuss the relationship between the two sites.

(40 marks; Specimen Question AQA 2009)

OR

3   Choose one of the three cultural sites. Compare and contrast two theoretical perspectives that may be used in the analysis and understanding of your chosen site.

(40 marks; Specimen Question AQA 2009)

OR

4   It has been argued that **places and spaces** communicate and reinforce a culture's value system. Drawing on contrasting examples, explore this view of places and spaces.

(40 marks; Specimen Question AQA 2009)

OR

5   What is the role of **fictions** in communicating cultural information?

(40 marks; Specimen Question AQA 2009)

OR

6.   'Our desire for material objects doesn't come from within us; it is controlled and manipulated by others.' Discuss this view of **objects of desire**?

(40 marks; Specimen Question AQA 2009)

Note

The authors are responsible for all commentary on these questions. This commentary has not been provided nor approved by AQA and it does not necessarily constitute the only possible solution.

9 COMMUNICATION AND CULTURE IN PRACTICE: A2 COURSEWORK

This is the second to last chapter, but probably the most important. Deliberately, we have made coursework the subject of the final chapters because we see this, rather than the examination, as the pinnacle of your achievement in Communication and Culture.

Some of you, we know, will have a rather jaundiced view of coursework. Maybe you see it as a sinister plot designed by the education system for the sole purpose of stealing away large quantities of your valuable leisure time. An understandable view, perhaps, but it is one that we hope to wean you away from in the course of this chapter. It is our hope and belief that you will produce two pieces of coursework that you will look back on with justifiable pride in the years to come. But in order to do this, you really do need to be in the right frame of mind. The coursework materials, the range of topics and the scope for creative self-expression should help to make you feel positive about the process. The next step is to become engaged in the process. If, at any stage, you feel uncertain about what needs to be done or how you should go about doing it − well, this chapter is here to help.

Overview

This brief section explains in outline the processes you will need to go through in order to fulfil the requirements of A2 coursework. The remainder of the chapter will provide more context, in-depth explanations and detailed examples, but this is a section to which you might find it helpful to return for reminders and reassurance that your coursework efforts are on the right track.

Your portfolio of coursework, will comprise two pieces:

Case Study (2000 words)
Creative Work (Digitized multimedia presentation).

Before embarking on these pieces you will need to select a topic from the four that will be available in each year (see Figure 9.1)

Choose one topic from either Site A or Site B		
	Site A: The Person	**Site B: Cultural Practice**
2009 2010	Body Modification Celebrity	Cinema-Going
2010 2011	Body Modification Celebrity	Cinema-Going Holiday
2011 2012	Celebrity Consumer	Holiday Festival (including Olympics)
2012 2013	Consumer Otherness	Festival (including Olympics) On the Street
2013 2014	Otherness The Perfect Self	On the Street Food

Figure 9.1 A2 coursework topics 2010–14. AQA 2009

Once your topic is chosen, you will need to select a title from the list supplied by AQA. Here, for example, is the set of six titles in the topic Body Modification.

Body Modification (Topic in Site A: The Person)		
Title 1	**Title 2**	**Title 3**
Under my skin: implants, piercing, tattoos, skin treatments.	*'Nip & Tuck': cosmetic surgery and reconstructive alterations of the body.*	*Dress to impress: influencing perceptions of our bodies.*
Issues	**Issues**	**Issues**
■ The Illustrated 'Man': tattooing as body art. ■ Implants and/or body piercings: where and why? ■ Fantasy personae. ■ Extreme body modification: what counts as 'extreme'? ■ Skin deep: skin treatments such as tanning or skin whitening.	■ Is beauty skin deep? ■ Total makeovers. ■ Searchers for perfection. ■ Gender difference. ■ Transgender.	■ The search for the perfect look. ■ Fashion and the frame (clothes horse models). ■ Holding back the years. ■ Who are the style police? ■ Accessories. ■ Hair. ■ Putting your face on: the art of make-up.

Body Modification (Topic in Site A: The Person) *continued*		
Title 4	**Title 5**	**Title 6**
Fit for purpose: our bodies at work and play.	*Perfect/imperfect: cultural values and the body.*	*Into the future: technology and the human body.*
Issues	**Issues**	**Issues**
■ Lifestyle and body shape. ■ Looking the part: role and role play. ■ The pressure to compete. ■ Sport and the body. ■ Body fascism. ■ Slimming and body building. ■ Fitness regimes.	■ Physical impairment and disfigurement in films and other fictions. ■ How do ideas about physical (im)perfection reflect and influence our values and attitudes? ■ Physical impairment and cultural difference. ■ Ugliness/beauty.	■ A bionic future? Can we become what we always wanted to be? ■ Fantasy futures: the potential roles and impacts of nanotechnology and developments in genetics. ■ Part human, part machine? Utopia or dystopia? ■ Cyborgs and sci-fi.

Figure 9.2 Body Modification: titles and issues. AQA 2009

As you can see in Figure 9.2, the table shows not only the choice of titles but also a range of issues associated with each title. You will need to give some thought to these issues, preferably in discussion with your teacher and other members of your group. The next stage is for you to devise an individual focus that indicates the issue that you will explore in relation to the title. Here's an example to show this process of refinement:

Site	Site A, The Body
Topic	Body Modification
Title	Into the Future: Technology and the Human Body
Issue	Part human, part machine. Utopia or Dystopia
My Focus	Mutated Bodies in New Wave Science Fiction

You now have the broad parameters for your coursework portfolio. Your next task is a substantial one; the collection of a body of material from secondary and primary sources. To help get you going, AQA will issue a list of stimulus material for each topic (see Figure 9.3). We should stress, though, that this is only a starting point and you will need to compile, analyse and evaluate your own material relevant to your individual sub-title.

The following list of texts can be used as stimulus materials and/or as reference material. It is not to be read as exhaustive in any sense. Teachers will inevitably assemble their own resource and reference ideas. They are likely to be shared via online channels as well.

Non-Fiction Texts

Gelder, K. (2007) Tattoo Communities. *Subcultures*, Taylor and Francis. ISBN: 978–0415379526.

Polhemus, T. (2000) *The Customised Body* (2nd edn), Serpents Tail. ISBN: 978–1852426774.

Toffoletti, K. 2007 *Cyborgs and Barbie Dolls: Feminism, Popular Culture and the Posthuman Body*, I B Tauris. ISBN: 978–1845114671.

Wolf, N. (1992). *The Beauty Myth*, Anchor. ISBN: 978–0385423977.

Weston, S. (1989) *Walking Tall: An Autobiography*, Bloomsbury Publishing. ISBN: 978–0747504993.

Fiction

Bradbury, R. (1951) *The Illustrated Man*, Doubleday; (1995) (Pbk) Bantam Books. ISBN: 978–0006479222.

Carter, A.(1977) *The Passion of New Eve*, Victor Gollanz. ISBN: 978–0860683414.

Dick, P.K. (1968) *Do Androids Dream of Electric Sheep?* Doubleday. ISBN: 978–1857988130 *(book on which Bladerunner was based)*

Forster, E.M. (1909) *The Machine Stops*, Kessinger Publishing. ISBN: 978–1419171116.

Weldon, F. (1983) *Life and Loves of a She-devil*, Hodder & Stoughton. ISBN: 978–0340589359.

Television

Extreme makeover TV documentaries

Liversedge, Marcus, 2008. *Britain's Missing Top Model*, Love Productions for BBC3, Reality Television, 21 November–20 December 2008.

Films

Aldridge, R. 1962. *Whatever Happened to Baby Jane?*, Warner Bros, Film.

Burton, T. 1991. *Edward Scissorhands*, 20th Century Fox, Film.

Butler and Fiore 1977. *Pumping Iron*, Lumiere Pictures, Documentary.

Cronenberg, D. 1983. *Videodrome*, UCA, Film.

Cronenberg, D. 1986. *The Fly*, 20th Century Fox, Film.

Nolan, C. 2008. *The Dark Knight*, Warner Bros, Film.

Scott, R. 1982. *Blade Runner*, Warner Bros, Film.

Sheridan, J. 1989. *My Left Foot*, Universal Pictures, Film.

Tucker, D. 2005. *Transamerica*, 20th Century Fox, Film.

Figure 9.3 continued

Songs

Bragg, Billy 1987. *The Busy Girl Buys Beauty,* from the albums 'Back to Basics' and 'Life's a Riot with Spy vs Spy', Cooking Vinyl.

Dury, Ian *et al.,* 1981. *Spasticus Autisticus,* on the album Reasons to be Cheerful, the Best of . . ., Papillon Records.

Ian, Janis 1975. *At Seventeen*, from the album 'Between the Lines', Columbia Records.

Figure 9.3 Body Modification stimulus material

Now is the time to embark on your 2000 word Case Study. Your teacher will set a deadline for this task, possibly including earlier deadlines for the submission of draft versions. Though not necessarily an 'essay', the Case Study is a piece of formal academic writing. This means that you should observe the conventions of such writing in terms of:

- Style
- Presentation
- Citations and references.

The format of your Case Study should reflect its audience: the teachers and examiners who will assess you. This means that you can assume a certain level of familiarity with the register of Communication and Culture, though not necessarily with the specific focus you have chosen.

The content of your Case Study is likely to include all of the following:

- A coherent response to your title/subtitle
- Examples from cultural products and cultural practices
- Critical readings of relevant texts
- The selected use of theoretical and conceptual material
- References to and from the contributions of others (expert opinion)
- Your own observations, arguments and conclusions.

The last of these will be a very significant influence on the second component of your coursework portfolio: the **Creative Work**. This time, the designated audience is your peers: Communication and Culture students of your own age. Your completed piece of work should demand the full attention of a member of that audience for ten minutes.

In terms of format, you will be working under effectively the same set of criteria as for your AS Presentation. The final piece of creative work must be digitized in a form suitable for web publication, for example a website, a multimedia presentation such as a Powerpoint Show or a documentary style video, or a Podcast.

The content of your Creative Work will respond to the same title and individual focus as your Case Study, but now you will be forcefully and cogently promoting your own ideas, interpretations and arguments. This is the opportunity to use the potential of your chosen medium to engage personally and creatively with your subject. Your task here is not merely to show what others have thought but to make an original contribution of your own.

The Case Study

Now that we have established the outline of what is required for your A2 coursework, we need to consider each of the components in more detail – starting with the Case Study. This is a synoptic piece of work; that is, it draws together the strands of all that you have studied in Communication and Culture, from the beginning of your AS programme.

> **SYNOPTICITY:** Synopticity is defined as drawing together knowledge, evidence and skills in different aspects of the course. The synoptic elements are the threads which bind the course together.

As in the AS coursework, your choice of topic must come from one of two sites, in this case these are:

Site A: The Person
Site B: Cultural Practice

As we have seen, the range of topics, titles and issues is determined for you in advance so, in a sense, you have less freedom of choice than you did in your AS coursework. This narrowing of choice is a deliberate policy that is designed to push you towards carefully focused coursework which achieves a suitable balance between breadth and depth. There is still an important process of decision making to go through. Although your choice is constrained, it still offers you an enormous potential for exploring stimulating and interesting aspects of Communication and Culture. In this respect it is clear that deciding which topic and which question is a process well worth investing time in. Some of the clues for this decision come from the kind of course you have negotiated for yourself both in AS and in the 'Communicating Culture' unit of A2. For example the degree to which you focused on *Spaces and Places* and/or *Fictions* and/or *Objects of Desire* might give you a nudge in one direction or another. However, it is just as important, given the substantial commitment that this unit demands, to focus on an area (and specific issue) that will maintain your interest. Both of these, objective and subjective, elements can be applied across a series of logical stages in order that you arrive at a balanced decision.

In order to elaborate this process, let's take a closer look at a Topic within Site A, The Person for 2009–10: Cinema-going. For this topic, a set of Titles are identified, one of which is as follows:

Title: Saturday Night at the Movies. Explore the ways in which the 'social ritual' of going to the cinema provides social and cultural information about a society, location or era.

Everything about this formulation provides both focus and scope. The scope is in the choices you are allowed to make around the very broad and enabling 'Society, location or era'. Once you have decided this, the 'Explore Ways' and 'Social Ritual' give a helpful direction to your work. Again the specification itself helps since each title is accompanied by a list of Issues. In the case of Cinema as Social Ritual, the list of issues is as follows:

- Girls' Night Out
- The social rules of cinema-going
- Significant demographic factors (gender, age, social class, ethnicity)
- The history of cinema and social change
- Going to the cinema on your own

Figure 9.4 At the Drive-in: social rituals and the cinema

These issues suggest different avenues, all worthy of detailed and fruitful exploration in terms of the overall title. As the major part of A2, the coursework must be substantial in terms of its products but more importantly its process. The chosen topic must be explored and interrogated with the help of the collected wisdoms of the course, with a significant set of tools and theories. As such the titles cannot and will not immediately give up their secrets and are intended to be intriguing prompts rather than transparent and open invitations. Only by unpacking the Topic Guide and your chosen issue layer by layer will you be able to see the possibilities and understand the implications.

For you, of course, the problem is to know how to set about this process of unpacking and decision making in order to ensure that your coursework is brought to a successful conclusion. Perhaps a bit of surreal dialogue between you and the specification can help here.

SPEC: We want you to do some writing and creative work. There are three topics to choose from: Body Modification, Celebrity and Cinema-going

YOU: Cinema-going? What do you mean?

SPEC: Well it's a chance to explore aspects of a cultural practice in which people regularly engage.

YOU: What sort of things could I do then?

SPEC: Well, there are six possible titles. Each title is linked to a set of issues. Choose one title, one issue and then work out your own personal angle, otherwise known as 'My Focus'. Simple really!

YOU: For example?

SPEC: Your teacher has given you a Topic Guide. Look at the page headed Cinema-going. Here's a copy of it.

SPEC: Go on, pick an issue from one of the titles and I'll talk you through it. Choose one at random.

YOU: OK, what about 'Film as Event' in Title 5. Where could I go with that one?

SPEC: Interesting choice! Well, the title refers to the 'ways in which films are packaged as products' so your focus needs to be on the ways in which films are turned into products and made variously available to us in ways other than us actually going to see them. A big West End launch of a film, for example, has so much more going on culturally than it merely being a publicity tool for channelling people into cinemas. The clearly established formalities of the red carpet treatment are crying out for the sharp critical eyes of Communication and Culture students. You could, for example, look at the implications of gender in this context in order to explain and illustrate the ways in which even the most talented actresses are paraded as mere 'talent' to be 'checked out'. You could look at the role played by the celebrity star in film premieres, taking a specific example of a recently launched film. How does the persona of the female star contribute to the event? What is the cultural significance of the different roles taken by male and female stars at such events? These are just a few ideas, but I think that you're beginning to get the general idea.

Cinema-going (Topic in Site B: Cultural Practice)		
Title 1	**Title 2**	**Title 3**
Saturday night at the movies. Explore the ways in which the 'social ritual' of going to the cinema provides social and cultural information about a society, location or era.	*Picture palace or flea-pit. Explore the meanings overtly and covertly communicated by the places in which we watch films.*	*Waiting for the DVD to come out? Explore the impact of film and cinema technology on everyday life.*
Issues ■ Girls' Night Out ■ The social rules of cinema-going. ■ Significant demographic factors (gender, age, social class, ethnicity). ■ The history of cinema and social change. ■ Going to the cinema on your own.	**Issues** ■ Movie palaces and multiplexes. ■ Outdoor and indoor cinema experiences. ■ The cinema foyer. ■ The Americanization of the cinema experience. ■ Art house cinema. ■ Womb with a view.	**Issues** ■ The technology of film and its implications. ■ Digitalization, interactivity. ■ Home movie formats (home cinema). ■ Sound. ■ The consumer as producer.
Title 4	**Title 5**	**Title 6**
That's me! Explore the implications of the dramatization of our lives by film and cinema.	*The Box Set. Explore ways in which films are packaged as products/ franchises and our experience of this.*	*In the back row? Explore the relationships between cinema-going and 'socialization'.*
Issues ■ Film as social practice. ■ Re-defining reality in relation to realisms. ■ The dramatized society. ■ Cinema and personal identity (class, age, ethnicity, physical impairment and gender).	**Issues** ■ Film as event. ■ The launch. ■ The marketing. ■ The merchandising of films. ■ The blockbuster! ■ Award ceremonies.	**Issues** ■ Cinema-going and romance. ■ Film and the way we 'love'. ■ Cinema-going and coming of age. ■ The family film.

Figure 9.5 Cinema-going: titles and issues. AQA 2009

Perhaps that's stretched the dialogue as far as it can go. We wouldn't want to see this as a full-length play (*The Spec and Me* ? Perhaps not). It's just a mechanism for helping you to get your head around the task that lies ahead. In the end, as ever, the desire is for focus and detail. However the point at which you 'swoop' should be the point at which you've satisfied yourself that your target is the best you have on offer. Each of the three titles is a massive landscape of possibilities such that a quick look around is hardly likely to be sufficient. Taking some time out collectively to really get to grips, particularly with the issues, is greatly recommended. Even unpacking topics to which you are not seriously inclined will give you a feel for the task: these are all areas worthy of enquiry and we certainly acknowledge the substantial degree of overlap.

The implication of Case Study is hopefully explicit: you are offering a study of a case (an example) from a chosen context. This case might be the limitations of the multiplex, the provision of special screenings for the grey market complete with free tea and biscuits or the expectations and pressures on boyfriends and girlfriends of sitting on the back row! It might be addressing the difference a bolt through your nose makes to your personal and social identity or the degree to which fame corrupts self-concept. Creating ideas should not be seen as a secret science but rather as a collective art.

ACTIVITY

Generating Case Study Ideas

As a group, try to come up with as many viable case study ideas as possible, using the relevant Topic Guide. Set a target of, say, two ideas for every issue in all six titles in an hour.

The titles offer you a clear pathway for your chosen Case Study. They are all invitations to explore; a term which implies going somewhere (at least in your head) and supporting this journey by the reading and analysis of cultural products and practices. The specification refers to 'source materials' and the Topic Guide provides some examples which might be seen as starting points. Your work with sources must be substantial and you should certainly allow for plenty of time for this stage in your project plan. The 'scavenging for material' that we encouraged at AS Level is still relevant, but this time you will need to complement this with a more methodical approach. This is not a just a search for the conclusion of previous researchers and theorists, no matter how respected they may be. It is also an opportunity for you to make a personal intervention: your own contribution to the debate. For this reason, choosing a case that genuinely needs exploring (or which you genuinely want to explore) is a good starting point.

Figure 9.6 Holiday imagery sells an aspirational fantasy

One of the issues identified in the 'Holiday' topic available 2010–11 is the idea of a holiday as a package which is sold to us and which mixes the real and the 'notional'. In many senses, holidays are offering much more than hotels, flights and food. They are selling a set of aspirational fantasies: tales of adventure in which we are invited to participate. This may lead us to a range of case studies and, subsequently, linked pieces of creative work. You may, for example, want to consider the meanings generated by mass market package holidays, typically to foreign beach-based locations or the very different set of lures implicit in so-called 'A la carte' holidays which seem to be selling the very opposite of packages. Equally your approach may be to focus on the degree to which the balance of the 'value' of a holiday lies in its ability to generate certain kinds of meanings for its audiences or more mundanely on the specific ways in which these meanings are constructed by holiday companies and their advertisers. Each of these is potentially a case worth studying. Looking at the Topic Guide, you will see the relevance of some of these ideas for Title Five *Place yourself in this narrative; the themed holiday* and the associated issue, *Make yourself a better person: the 'learn how to' holiday.* Each of these suggestions clearly has scope for substantial 'exploration' both of primary and secondary sources. All these will be important when it comes to compiling your formal written response.

The specification gives good and clear advice: it makes an important distinction between the act of writing/compiling and 'the candidate's own investigation of source materials related to their chosen topic'. The implication here is that there is work to be done on the topic, title, issue and your individual focus, which includes the need to analyse primary and secondary 'texts'. This compilation of notes and background material constitutes the background work you will need to undertake before embarking on the written work: a 2000 word Case Study. This is what is meant by 'the development of a Case Study': a process which ultimately leads to a product.

As a student of communication, you will recognize that you are now engaged in a task that is itself an act of communication located in the context of your culture. This means that we should be able to bring to bear on the task a good range of conceptual insights and practical advice drawn from communication theory.

Gerbner's general model of communication

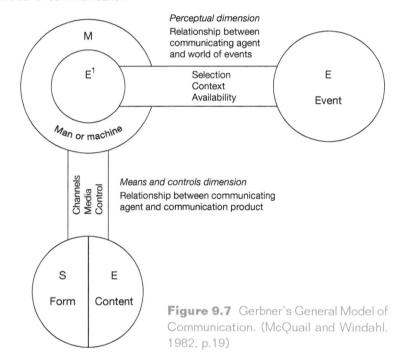

Figure 9.7 Gerbner's General Model of Communication. (McQuail and Windahl, 1982, p.19)

In simple terms the whole of the A2 portfolio is concerned to identify an engaging 'event' (aspect of a topic) and communicate about it to a specified audience (which is different in each case): the Case Study is an academic assignment written for examiners: the Creative Work has an audience of your fellow students. It is expected that their perception (E2) of this issue (E) will have been modified by your own perceptions of it (E1) which will have been 'developed' by your 'perceiving' (reading, analysing, annotating). Working on your Case Study is thus essentially working in Gerbner's 'Perceptual dimension' and is a prerequisite for communicating anything about it. Writing up your Case Study is moving then into what Gerbner usefully calls the 'means and control dimension' since what you are doing is organizing material and presenting it using the best available means (e.g. layout, structure and language, perhaps even images).

In the first phase/dimension Gerbner identifies three relevant issues which he labels:

- Selection
- Context
- Availability

Here are three significant factors which you must acknowledge as you begin to investigate your title and explore your chosen issue. In some ways, for our purposes, this trio works best if reversed since your job is as follows:

- to check the AVAILABILITY of material on your chosen title
- to consider the CONTEXTS of this material and your relationship to it
- to make a SELECTION of those materials, ideas and prompts that will be useful to you in understanding your issue and your responses to it.

The specification gives you some directions, but there is still plenty of room for you to go your own way. The 'suitable material for inclusion' addresses the perceptual dimensions:

- analysis of secondary sources (AVAILABILITY/CONTEXT)
- identification of a specific focus (SELECTION/CONTEXT)
- readings of relevant cultural practices/products (AVAILABILITY/CONTEXT)
- response in terms of concepts and perspectives (SELECTION/CONTEXT).

Much, as usual, is predicated on that most significant of AS concepts, *context*. The key contexts here are various and relate to the sender, sources, issues and perspectives. For example, using theoretical perspectives imposes a context on your enquiry which modifies the way in which the issue is 'seen' and an awareness of this will clearly allow a better overview of your collected data. The focus is not only on *what* you see but also *how* you see. You will need to consider your own, personal context. For example, a squeamishness towards body piercing is likely to act as a significant psychological context for your explanation if you choose this topic. Similarly, a cultural context that does not readily endorse an active courtship will impose certain constraints on your appreciation of 'the back row of the movies'. This is partly about barriers to communication but it is also and more interestingly, about perception, context and ultimately meaning. The idea that to perceive a text is implicitly to take up a position towards it is a good place to start. This is partly the reason that we collect and then report since the ultimate aim is for your product to be analytical, comparative and interpretative. This work invariably benefits from the imposition of a formal deadline and set of goals.

Figure 9.8 Going under the scalpel: what do your peers think?

Before going any further it is also worth describing what this perceptual process is intended to deliver, where all this 'looking' gets you. The specification is very clear about what kind of materials should be considered but less clear on how these will deliver the Case Study as such. The following wish list will hopefully give a better idea of where you should be heading with this; these are the key components you should aim to include in your Case Study.

■ A specific response to the title which is clear and coherent
■ A set of examples taken from 'practice' which support or contextualize your arguments

- A set of readings of relevant texts
- The application of theoretical perspectives
- The opinions and contributions of others, formally or informally, directly and indirectly (think direct quotation, arguments, data)
- A references list of significant sources (books, articles, websites etc.).

At the centre of this enterprise is that *critical* approach that was so prized in AS and that is reinforced here by the theoretical perspectives discussed in earlier chapters of this book. As has been said the key descriptors are 'comparative, analytical and interpretative' so this must be more than a collection of materials that support your arguments. Once again your ability to recognize the complexity of an issue is highly desirable as is an understanding of what the mark scheme calls 'the possibility of alternative readings'. The idea is to pursue the problematic, to be equal to Raymond Williams' claim that 'Communication begins in the struggle to learn'. The Case Study gives a substantial space in which to struggle. The philosopher Plato reminds us that, 'Everything that is beautiful is also difficult'. Or, as the old song has it: 'If you're looking for trouble you came to the right place'.

If you've genuinely engaged with, struggled with, but finally got to grips with your chosen title and issue, the second phase should be relatively straightforward. In Williams' terms, having 'learnt' it you have to describe it, share it, pass it on. This is the dimension which Gerbner labels with 'Means and Control', which answer the questions 'how?' and 'how well?' In this case Gerbner's factors are rather less useful since they focus on access to channels and media which, in your case, are largely given. The channel is academic and a matter of formal assessment and the prescribed medium is the written word. In reality your focus is going to be on the third variable which Gerbner calls 'control'. What comes now is a test of your ability to organize and operate words within these constraints in order to produce 2000 valuable words of response to your title. This is essentially a gatekeeping role which could be expressed by White's Gatekeeping model as shown below.

Little more needs to be said. Yours is exactly the task of moving from 'Incoming information' (or 'source of news item' in White's terms) to 'Selected Information'. However gatekeeping is not just about rejecting and selecting but is also about modifying and adapting information in order that it might be more coherent or persuasive or merely appropriate. At one level it is also about translating 'thought'

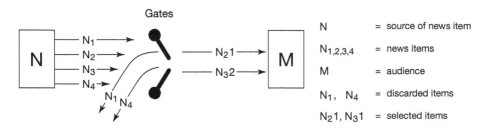

Figure 9.9 White's Gatekeeping model. (McQuail and Windahl, 1982, p. 100)

(what might in this case be cognitive perceptions of your issue) into word. You have 2000 words to write something that is a) academic and yet b) not an essay, at least not in the traditional sense. This is clearly something that has to be carefully planned and constructed rather than merely written up.

All that remains is an explanation of our own of the qualities of the completed Case Study which will attract most assessor approval (a euphemism for 'marks'). The Case Study is allocated up to 40 marks on a grid that describes four sets of qualities which constitute the four Assessment Objectives (AOs) of the specification. In summary they are as follows:

AO1: considers your ability to write effectively as a Communication and Culture student (using the register and terminology of the subject)

AO2: considers your knowledge and understanding of the course's content and concepts

AO3: considers your ability to apply this knowledge

AO4: considers your ability to use the opinions of others effectively in your own work.

This, if you like, is the Communication and Culture agenda, its specific contribution to the big idea of education expressed as a series of active verbs: communicating, understanding, applying and assimilating. These active verbs are certainly worth taking into account as you plan your Case Study. The usefulness of the Mark Scheme doesn't end there though, as the following activity shows.

ACTIVITY

Marking the mark scheme

What appears below is the top half of the Case Study mark grid, that is, the descriptors that apply to the top two mark bands. Of course, this is the level you will be aiming for and we hope that your Case Study will ultimately score at least half of the marks available. It certainly should do so if you follow the advice in this chapter!

The marking grid is a text like any other and as such capable of a number of readings. Our highlights are part of such a reading, they are identifying some key features which might be useful to you in completing your Case Study. Once you have seen them in their context you are invited to consider their connotations.

continued

Level	Overall Marks	AO1: This tests the ability of candidates to communicate in the register of communication and culture.	AO1 Marks	AO2: This tests the ability of candidates to understand the content and concepts offered by the qualification.	AO2 Marks	AO3: This tests the ability of candidates to apply knowledge.	AO3 Marks	AO4: This tests the ability of candidates to work with relevant resources drawn from a range of sources.
4	36–40	Work at this level both impresses and genuinely engages. It is both fluent and technical: accurate and specialist.	4	Sensitive to the scope of their own and others' knowledge and understanding. Evaluative. Sophisticated.	12	Offers a fully supported personal response to a given task, which is exploratory in the sense that it understands the possibility of alternative readings. Insightful.	15–16	Impressively referenced and assimilated piece of writing which clearly evidences the skilful use of relevant source materials. Well informed and scholarly.
4	31–35	Material is well organized including concise use of a technical vocabulary. Written expression is well structured, accurate and precise. Work is confident and detailed.	4	Handles a range of content and concepts. Knowledgeable and specialist.	11–10	Thoroughly analytical in its approach. Applies knowledge in a fully integrated and purposeful manner.	13–14	Evidence of skill and discrimination in the selection and assimilation of source materials. These materials make a telling contribution to the overall piece of work.
3	26–30	Writing enhances the presentation of ideas and arguments. The candidate is clearly controlling the technical code of the discipline.	3	Very good range of specialist knowledge which evidences an engagement with the material. With knowledge comes understanding.	9	Offers informed personal responses which use knowledge and understanding of concepts to create own arguments.	11–12	Makes specific links between own opinions and the opinions of others, even if only by juxtaposition or simple referencing.
3	21–25	Material is clearly organized and usually incorporates neat and purposeful use of a technical vocabulary.	3	Sound understanding of relevant Communication and Culture content and concepts. Shows a good range of specialist ideas.	8–7	Beginnings of an analytical approach, where ideas and techniques are actively used to provide 'readings' of texts and experiences.	9–10	Makes specific, detailed and appropriate reference to primary/secondary sources. Clear understanding of the status of sources.

Figure 9.10 The Case Study Marking Grid, Level 3 and Level 4. AQA 2009

Consider the following words and phrases, highlighted on the Marking Grid (Figure 9.10). What does each one mean for your own writing?

- genuinely engages
- evaluative
- technical . . . and . . . specialist
- sound understanding
- well-structured
- very good range of specialist knowledge
- detailed
- fully supported personal response
- understands the possibility of
- alternative readings
- insightful
- fully integrated
- thoroughly analytical
- well informed
- impressively referenced

The playwright Bertolt Brecht believed that 'showing is more important than being', in other words, that potential is all very well but unless it can be realized it comes to nothing. Having done the looking, the investigating, the discussing and disputing all that's left is the showing. Hopefully the prompts above will have made it even clearer what you need to show:

- energy and enthusiasm for your chosen topic
- knowledge of the subject matter
- understanding of the subject matter
- application of theory to practice
- assimilation of others' ideas
- relevance to the topic at hand.

How you structure the 2000 words is entirely up to you. You may choose to present 2000 words of continuous prose (as long as it seeks to engage with the requirements) or offer a number of shorter pieces, for example:

- Four 'quartets' (500 each)
- The Penny Farthing (1500 and 500)
- Half and half (1000 and 1000)
- Triplets (three even sections)
- Freestyle (any combination you like)

The purpose of these divisions is to allow you the option of compiling a Case Study that consists of distinct and distinctive parts each of which has its own style and function. This is particularly useful for addressing the need to include evidence of critical reading: 500 words on a key text is an attractive option. Equally you may wish to make a distinction between your reflections on your experience (for example of visiting a multiplex) and your musings on the cultural meanings. These choices are best dictated by the nature of your enquiries and analyses. The material you have accumulated and your response to this material will dictate the structure of your Case Study.

ACTIVITY

Test driving case studies, Choosing formats

In this Activity, you're invited to match a possible Case Study structure to a particular issue. Just to help, we've done the first one for you.

Topic: Cinema-going

Title: Explore the ways in which films are packaged as products/franchises (Title 5)

Issue: Film as Event

Personal Focus: *The Dark Knight* premieres

Structure: Four Quartets, each 500 words, as follows

1. History and symbolism of the red carpet
2. London premiere of *The Dark Knight*, a reading
3. The film event as a cultural event
4. Audiences and premieres

Topic: Body Modification

Title: Perfect/imperfect: cultural values and the body (Title 5)

Issue: Physical impairment and disfigurement in films and other fictions

Personal Focus: Two-faced about equality? Disability and disfigurement as a metaphor in *The Dark Knight* and other superhero films.

Structure: That's for you to decide. Try to come up with several alternatives.

Topic:	Celebrity
Title:	Celebrities and fictions (Title 2)
Issue:	The celebrity persona
Personal Focus:	Heath Ledger and fame, fame, fatal fame. Dying young and the celebrity myth.
Structure:	That's for you to decide. Try to come up with several alternatives.

Of course if compilation is not your desire then you can always use a series of headings and subheadings to subdivide your ongoing argument. To help support and encourage a more creative approach to organization, and to discourage the more traditional essay (which you've already proved you can do elsewhere), headings and subheadings are not included in the word count.

Figure 9.11 Heath Ledger in *The Dark Knight*. Penny Farthing or Freestyle?

The Creative Work

'Give me the one fire of an inspiration', wrote Gerard Manley Hopkins, and it is certainly our intention that this final piece of coursework should fire your inspiration in its creation and your audience's inspiration in its reception.

Having completed your Case Study, the Creative Work poses a new and different set of challenges. Your task now is to make a real contribution to the area you have explored in your Case Study. This is your ultimate response to your chosen topic, title, issue and personal focus; an opportunity to communicate your personal observations, arguments and conclusions to an audience of your peers. We should stress from the start that there is a strong emphasis on creativity here (hence the name) and that your work should reflect this in both its content and form. You will want your audience to sit up and take notice of your ideas, so you can be as dramatic, artistic, provocative, thoughtful, ironic, satirical or argumentative as you like!

Here are the guidelines offered by the specification:

- The Creative Work must relate to the theme and title on which the Case Study is based
- The response should 'draw on [your] Case Study'
- The work should 'develop an original and creative idea or argument in relation to [your] chosen question'
- The Creative Work 'must be designed for an audience of the candidate's peers'
- The creative work must be 'in a form that is publishable to the web'
- The creative work should operate in one of the following forms:

  - a web site
  - a multimedia/PowerPoint style presentation
  - a podcast (or vodcast)

- You are required to serve an average Communication and Culture student with ten minutes worth of 'active consumption' (viewing, reading, interpreting).

In this section of the chapter we shall be unpacking these requirements whilst also reinforcing the enormous potential of this task. Although there are, inevitably, a set of constraints and formal requirements, the overall nature of this exercise is one that encourages openness and individuality. The invitation is clearly to make something that will add value to the work you have done in your Case Study. What is envisaged is neither a translation of an element of your Case Study into pictorial form nor merely a continuation of the Case Study's academic analysis in a disguised form. The Creative Work should be conceived as something in its own right; a piece of work that stands alongside the Case Study in a complementary relationship.

The icing on the cake: drawing on the Case Study

The Creative Work and Case Study are ultimately equal partners in the assessment of A2 so it is vital that we establish clearly the relationship between them. Perhaps we might start with a couple of analogies to help tease out the significant aspects of the relationship. It might be useful to see the relationship in the following ways:

- The newspaper and the supplementary magazine. The two components work in different forms and in different ways to deliver an enhanced version of their chosen theme (in this case 'News'). They are separate but also intimately connected. The magazine is not a pictorial version of the newspaper but whereas the paper provides in depth analysis the magazine offers features and opinion led material.
- The icing of a cake. Ultimately the experience of the two together amounts to significantly more than each of them separately, though they work in completely different modes with very different functions. One of the functions of the icing is phatic, it attracts you to the cake. Just like the Portfolio, in which the Case Study is the base, the cake is made first, but equally it may be one of the functions of the Creative Work which, like the icing, makes the reader want to 'partake'.

Both of these analogies emphasize the following:

- The Creative Work is substantially and formally unlike the Case Study (made of different stuff)
- Since the Creative Work is persuasive as well as informative, the form is just as important as the content

Figure 9.12 Coursework: practical, expressive and creative

- One of the functions of the Creative Work is to channel attention to the Case Study (you could conceive of it as a piece of publicity, a trailer, for the Case Study)
- The Creative Work must enhance and be enhanced by the Case Study. The whole should amount to more than the sum of its parts.

Developing an idea or argument

What you should aim to do here is to use your Case Study as a point of departure. If you imagine the Case Study as an establishing shot in the film that is your A2 coursework portfolio, your big decision is whether you 'cut-in' or 'cut-away'.

- The cutting-in approach. You choose to focus on a detail of the Case Study and develop it further. You might pick a fairly small point from your Case Study and then expand this into a further set of ideas or arguments. For example:

Topic	Body Modification
Title	Fit for purpose: our bodies at work and play
Issue	Slimming and body building
My Focus	Eating disorders as wish-fulfilment
Creative Work	Multi-media presentation which juxtaposes images of super-thin, super-confident models with the accounts of anorexics and bulimics and entitled *The Real Size Zero Debate*.
Comment	Size zero is referred to within the Case Study as part of a general context but not explored. Here it becomes the main focus for some high impact work.

- The cutting-away approach. This extends the focus of your Case Study beyond what you have already presented. This may be an aspect of your chosen title and issue that didn't get into your final write-up. For example:

Topic	Holiday
Title	High days and holy days: holiday as communal celebration
Issue	The holiday as a community ritual
My Focus	The decline of community-based and Wakes Week holidays in my part of Lancashire
Creative Work	The local carnival: a documentary-style video (vodcast) on how the revival of the local carnival in my town attempts to connect to traditions of communal celebrations.
Comment	'Carnival' is not addressed within the Case Study itself but this is a perfectly legitimate extension of the arguments about 'people's' holidays and local celebration.

Having fixed the direction of your Creative Work in this way, all that remains is for you to rehearse the argument or development of an idea which will give the piece its structure and its character. This element, the personal response, is the one which carries the most marks, and is addressed under AO3, which tests 'the ability of candidates to apply knowledge'. The application of your knowledge should not be demonstrated by the heavy-handed referencing of Communication and Culture terms and concepts. Rather, it is delivered through the force of the argument advanced or through the genuinely exploratory way in which alternative readings are presented.

Once again, you will find the Marking Grids useful in ensuring that your work is properly formulated. The description of work in the highest band (Level 4) is: 'Applies knowledge in a fully integrated and purposeful manner'. The level of integration and the functionality of the piece are key performance indicators: you are marshalling material which you are then using rhetorically (persuasively) in support of an argument or in the development of an idea.

Ideally, then, you need yet another subheading to indicate the argument or arguments you propose to include. We could extend the examples given above to demonstrate this approach.

Body Modification

Issue   Slimming and body building

My Focus Eating disorders as wish-fulfilment

Creative Work Multi-media presentation which juxtaposes images of super-thin, super-confident models with the accounts of anorexics and bulimics and entitled *The Real Size Zero Debate*.

Argument A The representation of numerous super-skinny models, especially in women's magazines, is dangerous and offensive. It contributes directly to feelings of low self-worth and also to the prevalence of eating disorders.

Or

Argument B Amongst the victims of the media obsession with size zero are those naturally thin but perfectly healthy young women and men who are teased and stigmatized because of their body shape.

Holiday

Issue   The holiday as a community ritual

My Focus The decline of community-based and Wakes Week holidays in my part of Lancashire

Creative Work	The local carnival: a documentary-style video (vodcast) on the revival of the local carnival.
Argument	Even the contrived revival of a long forgotten event is a great boost for the town. It provides a focus for all sorts of local activities and has helped to build a genuine sense of community spirit.
Or	
Argument	The recently revived Town Carnival is a cynical attempt to exploit the area's proud traditions for purposes that have much more to do with commercialism and 'branding' than real community spirit.

The most important thing is to be active and conscious about what you want your creative piece to do. The active verbs 'argue' and 'explore' address this very directly. Both require energy and persuasiveness. While your Case Study has provided a substantial treatment of the title and its attendant issue, the Creative Work is rather a 'feature'; a conscious piece of focused argument on one aspect of your enquiry.

As such these pieces of Creative Work will operate across a range of different modes of address and intentions: opinionated, discursive, controversial (polemical), informative, evocative, narrative, even poetic. There is also room for the satire or parody, though these are particularly challenging options. It is important also that your understanding of 'creative' and 'original' is not confused with notions merely of the 'fictional' and 'narrative'. Much of this work will probably fit more comfortably under the generic umbrella 'Documentary'. This is documentary in the sense of text that does something rather more than simply showing or documenting events; it is the type of documentary that has the explicit intention of persuading an audience towards a certain view or perception of events. This involves, as William Stott puts it: 'the presentation of actual facts in a way that makes them credible and telling to people at the time'. Stott is quoted in an incisive essay on documentary film by Trinh T. Minha-ha who emphasizes the creativity essential in trying to tell the truth:

> **Truth has to be made vivid, interesting; it has to be 'dramatized' if it is to convince the audience of the evidence, whose 'confidence' in it allows truth to take shape.**

(Minh-ha, 1993, p. 96)

These are the truths that you are after in your creative work whatever mode you are working in. You are looking, in Christopher Williams' phrase, to tell your 'truths

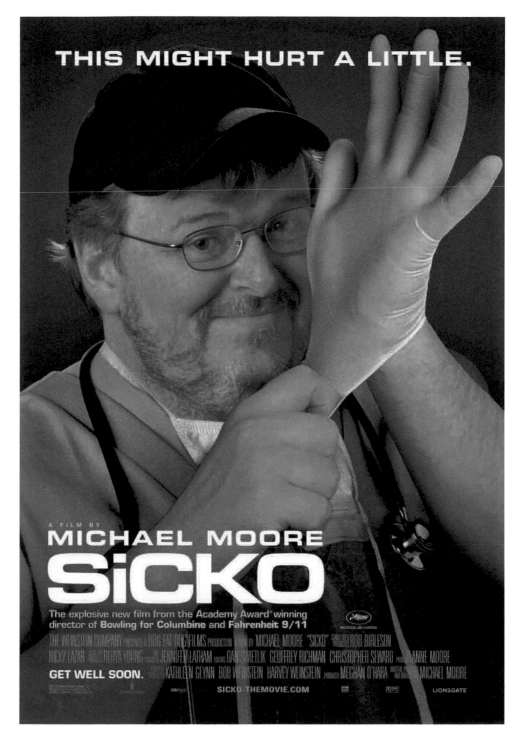

Figure 9.13 Polemical documentaries like Michael Moore's *Sicko* could be a model for your Creative Work

within the framework of the particular set of languages available to you' (Williams, 1980, p. 6). Whether in still or moving images, in caption or voiceover, via archive or live action, your truths have to be vivid and interesting (Minh-ha, 1993).

ACTIVITY

Finding Features

For the following Case Studies suggest alternative creative 'features' and two potential arguments.

Topic	Cinema-going
Title	Saturday night at the movies. Explore the ways in which the 'social ritual' of going to the cinema provides social and cultural information about a society, location or era.
Issue	Social and demographic contexts (gender, age).
My Focus (Case Study)	Chick-Flickery: female bonding and the girls' night out.
Creative Work A	
Creative Work B	
Argument 1	
Argument 2	
Topic	Body Modification
Title	Under my skin: implants, piercing, tattoos, skin treatments.
Issue	The Illustrated 'Man': tattooing as body art.
My Focus (Case Study)	'Read all about': autobiographies on the skin – reading the self from tattoos.
Creative Work A	
Creative Work B	
Argument 1	
Argument 2	

Topic	Celebrity
Title	Celebrities and fictions
Issue	Creating the celebrity persona.
My Focus (Case Study)	'The happiness machine'; case studies of how stars are manufactured.
Creative Work A	
Creative Work B	
Argument 1	
Argument 2	

Sound and vision: the medium is the message

A page or two ago we encountered Christopher Williams' comment about the need to tell your truth 'within the framework of the languages' you have available to you. This rightly identifies that different formats produce different versions of the game and that formats (and media) have frameworks that will, almost unconsciously, shape your responses. The point, as far as possible, is to allow this process to occur; to participate in the formal explorations rather than merely seeing the format as a vehicle for a set of points you have already decided upon. The removal of the need to comment on this process and in particular the need to comment on a fairly formal 'Drafting' process, has not removed the need for drafting; it has merely freed up this analysis so that drafting can be done rather than demonstrated to a third party.

Although the range of forms available to you may seem a rather short list, on closer inspection they are merely generic examples of the key descriptors 'web-based presentation'/'publishable to the web'. In truth this means pretty much the same combination of words, images and sounds that you employed in the AS presentation. The main difference, however, is that this is less prescriptive. Whereas the AS presentation insisted that you employed both sound and visual elements, since in part it was a rehearsal for the creative work, here you are allowed to choose. At the one end stands a web-based slideshow/point and click website, at the other a podcast, with the majority of responses coming in somewhere between 'sound' and 'vision'.

It's probably more important then, to think of components and the relationships between them rather than worrying too much about what the final piece of work may be categorized as. The bullet-pointed options are merely two 'ends' and a massive middle, since 'multimedia presentation' is meant to cover all the possibilities between 'sound' and 'vision' described above. It certainly covers 'short film' which may well be a popular format, particularly with those interested in public opinions on issues or in exploring key locations. The point is that you're being asked to make something and put it 'out there' so your 'showcase' must be consciously and carefully presented. Even more than AS then, this is to be the result of a careful process of contemplating, planning, drafting, scripting, constructing, editing and polishing.

Although there are general indications of the size and scale of the various creative formats (three pages, twelve slides, three to twelve minutes), the key once again is in the concept of 'active consumption'. You are required here to serve an 'average consumer' with **ten** minutes worth of engagement. This is not unlike the way you might rate a new computer game. Partly it's how long it takes to 'complete' but also it's the quality of the experience you're getting. Some games take weeks but frustrate rather than 'stretch and challenge'; others may be cracked in an intensive and memorable couple of days. Ten minutes in this context is meant to represent quite a substantial investment of time and thus a significant challenge to you the creator.

In fact in the context of the way in which the Internet is used, 'surf' hardly being a verb that implies studious concentration, this is perhaps the biggest challenge of all. To deliver ten minutes worth of consumption in such a context certainly

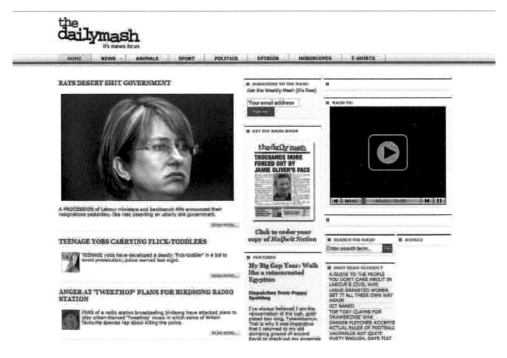

Figure 9.14 Website Homepage: entropic or redundant?

Source: http://www.thedailymash.co.uk/

ups the ante in terms of what might be required. Clearly there will need to be some kind of phatic element to establish contact and a substantial scheme for maintaining interest. This can only be achieved by careful planning, scripting and storyboarding. Once again you are being asked to pack a prospective visual, auditory, intellectual and emotional 'feast' for your audience and as such this 'loaded' advice from AS still seems very relevant. It is, we suggested, for the audience that 'the script and visuals are loaded: loaded with ideas, loaded with interest' (Bennett and Slater, 2008, p. 305).

Potentially these web formats have high levels of entropy. They empower readers to take things at their own pace, and often in their own way and this allows them potentially to be unpredictable and to offer large amounts of new information. In simple terms a website gives you time to view and review information, to work your own way through it and to cross-reference elsewhere if needs be. The key here however is 'potentially' since it requires an insightful creator to provide and organize the material in such a way that the average reader is motivated and able to engage with it. As we all know to our cost many web-based resources merely regurgitate what we already know in a cumbersome way. If you're tempted to imagine that interactivity is the solution to these issues, take a look at the often limited impact this Internet buzzword has across a range of web-resources. There are few experiences more frustrating than gaining redundant, uninspiring information at the end of a tiresome process of 'point and click'.

Rather than look for ready-made solutions or gimmicks a far better approach, as we have implied, is to trust the relationship between form and content and see what develops. Whatever format you choose to work in, the same underlying principles of effective communication and persuasion still apply. This used to be called *Rhetoric* and was a key part of the original classical education. In other words it's as old as the hills. Shakespeare would have been taught it at school in Stratford in the 1570s. Originally, rhetoric referred to the art of persuasive speech, since making speeches in public was an important skill in the ancient world, at least for those who were deemed to be worth educating. Since then rhetoric has developed a broader meaning to encompass all effective communication. As Kenneth Burke has it, rhetoric is 'the use of symbols to induce co-operation in those who by nature respond to symbols' (Nightfly, 2006). As such the movement of meaning has been from the original notion of a method of training effective public speakers towards a method for understanding how humans use discourse to alter or shape reality (Williams, 1980). Discourse in this sense is equivalent to 'discursive formation' – Foucault's term for communication that involves specialized knowledge of various kinds. Every text (website, blog, podcast, PowerPoint presentation, film) inhabits a discursive environment which is effectively a set of assumptions . So must it be with your own creative work.

Do it to yourself? The hardest audience of all

It may have been assumed that 'an audience of the candidate's peers' with the reinforcement 'average consumer (Communication and Culture A level student)' has the implication of a specialist audience.

Such an audience, the argument goes, would be familiar with the specialist terminology and underlying principles of the subject and will therefore provide a convenient (if not expedient) context within which candidates will be able to demonstrate their knowledge (and hopefully understanding) of both. This was after all the context of the AS presentations where the vocabulary of 'critical reading' and the debates about identity were technically engaged. Coursework, after all, and practical work in particular, is a kind of disguised exam. In fact that is probably the basis on which it is justified. As far as A2 Creative Work is concerned, while this is not entirely untrue, it is not primarily or substantially the reason for this audience choice. Academic skills, knowledge and understanding are extensively tested elsewhere in A2, not least within the Case Study. The creative work is rather more about *engagement*, *argument* and *impact*. It assumes a knowledgeable audience and an interest in the issues of Communication and Culture engendered by the course, but this is to be seen as a fertile ground on which to sow (and grow) ideas rather than merely display specialist knowledge. The audience is not specified merely in order for someone to witness your displays of knowledge but rather as an aspect of the ultimate challenge.

These people are not a challenge because they might see through your shaky understanding of, say, 'hegemony' but rather because they (and you) are perhaps the most media-literate generation ever (until the next one comes along). Your peers are entirely aware of what can be done technologically and of the difference between a good idea and a sad attempt. They are a people who are the subject of a massive amount of advertising effort in every imaginable medium, and who are acutely aware of what is being done to them (as Communication and Culture students). They are the so-called 'post-MTV generation': supposedly over-stimulated, but also clever, articulate, confused, emotional, confident and insecure by turns. You should be able to empathize with them because you are one of them. This, we feel sure, only makes you more aware of the challenge.

In order to 'satisfy the expectations of this contemporary audience' you will need to attempt what many have tried and failed to do: to address your peers in a way that engages them and gives them something to think about. I hesitate to use the word 'educate' here, because the connotations are too often of something done by one to another and this is definitely a more participatory exercise. What you are after is something intrinsically interesting (at least to you) and a desire to communicate it which takes proper account of the needs of your audience. As you are aware the 'gutters' of this particular metaphorical 'bowling lane' are called 'boring' and 'patronising' and there are few strikes in this particular game.

On the one hand we have the worthy and tedious, often monotonously text-based and indecipherable which defeats its audience before they've started. I think of a student of mine who described *Hard Times* as 'a big f— off book'. This was not a comment on Dickens but rather of the format: pages and pages of dense text. Since the heyday of the Victorian novel a revolution has taken place in the way in which we access information. The implications of this revolution are not yet fully comprehended. Some have compared the advent of the Internet to the invention of printing or the development of widescale literacy in its impact and significance. Both of these ultimately had an impact on oral and particularly aural skills but it's hard to think that illiteracy is a better way.

However, the other extreme is just as excruciating; perhaps even more so. How many times have you been appalled by advertising materials apparently aimed at students but seemingly more appropriate for infants? In order to avoid the dreaded 'boring' they simply add splashes of colour and set all the text at an oblique angle! It's as if the teenage audience consisted entirely of image-fuelled adrenaline-junkies who constantly require visual stimulation. As if everything that communicates with them needs the 'crash, bang, wallop' impact of *Assassin's Creed* or *Grand Theft Auto*. This cynical audience conceptualization is one that Kurt Cobain recognized in his anthemic 1991 crystallizing of displaced teen con-fusion, *Smells Like Teen Spirit*.

It should not be too difficult, then, for you to construct an Audience Profile, bearing in mind that you are profiling people who are very much like yourself. This is not to say that targeting your audience will be just as straightforward. It is easy to fall into the trap of stereotyping the audience; making assumptions about the sim-ilarities of audience members whilst ignoring diversity.

As we've suggested the formal Audience Profile at least makes things clear and encourages you to find out more. Given your audience is Communication and Culture students there are potentially two audience profiles to consider: one which addresses the generic group nationally, with whom you will theoretically be sharing cyberspace and the second is the Communication and Culture students at your own school or college. This second group is a subset of the first group but how representative is it? Also it may be worth considering how similar or different the Communication and Culture students in your institution are from those students studying other subjects.

ACTIVITY

Facts and speculations

- Use the AQA website to find out the national profile of Communication and Culture candidates (www.aqa.com)
- How do you account for the gender profile of this subject?
- How do you account for the ratio of school, sixth form colleges and further education candidates?
- Find subjects with a different gender profile and explain the difference
- Which subjects are more popular/less popular in selective schools and grammar schools? Why do you think this is?

Moving on to your own school or college;

- How does the profile of Communication and Culture students compare to the national figures?
- How popular is Communication and Culture in relation to other subjects? Why?
- What perceptions do other students have of the type of students who take Communication and Culture? Why?
- Is there such a thing as a 'typical' Communication and Culture student? What are their characteristics?

Finally, having reinforced the importance of audience to you, we should also acknowledge that there is an approach to the audience which doesn't give two hoots about targeting, profiling, stereotyping or, indeed any consideration of the audience at all. Most of that work designated as 'Art' has no particular sense of its audience, rather it just 'happens' and an audience gathers (or doesn't). Interestingly this approach can often produce very successful results in both critical and commercial terms. The problem with this of course is that we only get to see the successful rule-breakers and, we could add, you need to know the rules in order to break them. Thus a writer like Roald Dahl became massively successful by writing for children in a way that ignored all of the rules including the one that says you must always be aware you are writing for children. At its purest this approach is about just writing/composing/filming, etc. without worrying about contexts, consequences or constraints. Although you are unlikely to be in this position, it is still worthwhile thinking about the 'rules' and whether there could be some justification for bending or breaking them. Perhaps the best advice is to think about your audience ... but not too much!

References and further reading

Bennett, P. and Slater, J. (2008) *AS Communication and Culture; The Essential Introduction*, Abingdon: Routledge.

Cobain, K., Novoselic, K. and Grohl, D. (Composers). (1991) Smells Like Teen Spirit. On *Nevermind*.

Heath, M. (2008) *Ancient Rhetoric: an Introduction*. Retrieved 1 February 2009, from Ancient Rhetoric: an Introduction: http://www.leeds.ac.uk/classics/resources/rhetoric

McQuail, D. W. and Windahl, S. (1982) *Communication Models for the Study of Mass Communications*, London: Longman.

Minh-ha, T. T. (1993). The totalising quest for meaning, in M. Renov (ed.), *Theorizing Documentary*, Abingdon: Routledge.

Nightfly (2006) *Kenneth Burke*. Retrieved 25 March 2009, from The Rhetorician Resource: http://nightfly.googlepages.com/kennethburke

Williams, C. (1980) *Realism and the Cinema*, Abingdon: Routledge.

10 A2 COURSEWORK SAMPLES

As the old saying goes, 'the proof of the pudding is in the eating', so now is the time to show you some practical examples of A2 coursework. For obvious reasons, there are no fully worked examples of the Creative Work, since these must be digital productions. However, samples of these will be made available on the AQA and Routledge websites.

Rather than providing you with ready-made Case Studies, this section will work through ideas from coursework topics to provide a rather more developed version of what we've hitherto only sketched out. In doing so we are, as it were, entering the ring, moving from the relative comfort of 'coaching' to the precarious but productive discomfort of 'playing'. Take this, if you will, as an act of faith since it's partly about practising what we preach. We've spent a good number of words describing the potential of the Case Study and implying interest, excitement, challenge, even fun. Now we too will experience the extra difficulty which comes from making the general, specific. Just for once, the authors are in the role of the candidate and you are allowed the luxury of evaluation and judgement.

What this section also attempts is to demonstrate how very different in preparation, process and form Case Studies can be. In doing so we'll inevitably be showing how substantial your commitment must be to the processes of thinking, searching, reading, annotating, planning and performing. Also you will get to see four different ways of organizing the 2000 word write-up. However, what we really hope to get across is the spirit and attitude of work that is genuinely exploratory and individual.

We are well aware that one of the most difficult parts of any coursework is the act of beginning. The dreaded blank page which has reduced even the strongest of us at times to desperate inertia is massively softened by a couple of sub-headers and a grid or two. Although not a formal requirement, it is certainly good practice to get going with a planning framework of some kind. We suggest three stages of development:

- ■ Thinking
- ■ Planning
- ■ Writing Up

The first of these, thinking, is partly an insurance policy, a series of checks that we are doing the right thing. It makes sure that we address a preset topic, title and issue. With these decided, it suggests (and tries to insist) that we carefully consider the implications of these choices. All this hopefully helps us to clarify our focus and provide some kind of descriptive or at least suggestive individual working title; the level of precision previously referred to as My Focus. At this point the ground has been marked out and is ready for the first spade.

Appropriately the planning stage is a personal response to the focus area, an instructive throwing around of ideas and sharing of intentions. 'Your own attitudes and opinions' may include the reason you chose the focus area and any ongoing thoughts you have. In genuine Communication and Culture style this should ultimately lead you to 'sources'. Whose help can ensure your excavation of the area is as efficient and effective as it can be? These are the guides we discussed in the last chapter in the introduction (books, journals, newspapers, television programmes, films, websites, podcasts, personal testimony . . . and any other sources of information you can think of). If 'sender' and 'sources' work you should have no trouble in identifying the salient issues within your focus. This may be a set of provocative questions which sum up the points of contention. The clearer these are (the questions not the solutions) the easier it will be to entertain formal (or informal) critical responses, which is what the final prompt requires. These questions may also help you to identify the sort of contentious debates within your focus area that will be suitable for your Creative Work.

Now you are ready to consider the writing up of your findings, both as a piece of extended writing and as a springboard for your Creative Work. Having ideas about the shape of the project as a whole is useful at an early stage; don't be tempted to set aside all thought of the Creative Work until the Case Study is complete.

CASE STUDY A

Topic	Cinema-going
Title	That's me! Explore the implications of the dramatization of our lives by film and cinema (Title 4).
Issue:	Re-defining reality in relation to realisms
My Focus:	The Camera Never Lies? The use of metaphor in film.

Figure 10.1 Film canister and clapper

HOLLYWOOD

PRODUCTION

DIRECTOR

CAMERA

TAKE

Stage One: Thinking

Sender (Your own attitudes/outlook)

I sense that at the centre of this question there are two strands which might pull everything together (or pull it all apart). One is very much theoretical and sees this argument very clearly in terms of McLuhanite technological determinism: what we're pursing is the simple fact that mass media technology has utterly changed the way we perceive and understand reality. The other is cruder perhaps and more pragmatic and has been touched on earlier in this book when we discussed 'travelling' and 'destinations' (p. 8) In the introduction we refer to de Botton's essay 'On Anticipation' where de Botton points out that there are good reasons why it is easier to learn lessons from films and books than from life: crudely they are simpler in the sense of less complex (which may ultimately mean 'less real'). Anyway the simple points are 'how can reality live up to realism?' and, 'how can life compete with the artful representations and dramatizations which in film terms are bigger, brighter, louder and in some cases more convincing?'

This leads me to think about each of these components in turn: about life and its representations, which are all trying to capture it in their different ways (mental note: don't think 'realism' but 'realisms'). The critic Susan Haywood says that 'Reality produces realisms' to remind us of the priority of 'reality' as the focus of realism. The painter Picasso said that 'Art is a lie that makes us realise truth' which might be useful since there is some evidence that we've heard the lie so often we've lost sight of the truth.

In Tom Stoppard's play *Rosencrantz and Guildenstern are Dead*, there is an actor (character) who talks about the time they organized, for added realism, for the part of the executed man in their play to be taken by a convict awaiting execution. The player (as a character is called) is responding to the accusation that dramatic representations are, in effect, unrealistic: the line is 'You die so many times; how can you expect them to believe in your death?' To which the player responds

> **On the contrary, it's the only kind they do believe. They're conditioned to it. I forget which – so I got permission to have him hanged in the middle of a play – had to change the plot a bit but I thought it would be effective, you know – and you wouldn't believe it, he just wasn't convincing! It was impossible to suspend one's disbelief – and what with the audience jeering and throwing peanuts, the whole thing was a disaster! – he did nothing but cry all the time – right out of character – just stood there and cried – Never again!**

(Stoppard, 1994, p. 84)

Beyond the black comedy I think there's a lot being said here: realism is a code, a set of conventions and the same can be said of reality. Also, Stoppard's fictional points are often reinforced in real life. A friend and former colleague of mine from Belfast once told me he had but one brush with 'The Troubles' while growing up in Northern Ireland. He was walking down the street as a gunman opened fire. Now it would be putting words into his mouth to say that he thought the gunfire 'just wasn't convincing!', but what he did say was in effect that it sounded nothing like a gun! Though many of us, thankfully, have probably never heard gunfire, we all know what a gunshot sounds like, principally from TV and film. George Gerbner famously calculated that by the age of eleven, American children have seen over 400 deaths on TV. However my friend Steve described the gunfire as a sound like a window pane being cracked, almost with the disappointment we all feel when we realize how little horses sound like coconut shells being knocked together!

There is plenty to go on here. This further reinforces my focus, my desire to get to the bottom of this relationship between a camera that proverbially 'never lies' and the texts it produces which offer versions of reality which Picasso simply calls 'lies'. It will be interesting to look at films that operate on the naturalistic end of the continuum and primarily at the way we watch them. There may be a need to talk to some people and listen to some others (a search on 'realism' is a necessity).

There is an influential essay (originally a lecture) by the Marxist literary critic and founder of our subject Raymond Williams which provides one of the prompts for my theme. The piece is entitled 'Drama in a dramatized society' and addresses head-on the ways in which enacted dramas on film and television have transformed the nature of drama and the reality that it relates to and represents. Williams argument is that 'drama, in quite new ways, is built into the rhythms of everyday life and that everyday life can therefore hardly escape being influenced by it'.

Williams raises many issues:

> 1) **'What is it, we have to ask, in us and our contemporaries, that draws us repeatedly to these hundreds and thousands of simulated actions: these plays, these representations, these dramatisations.'**
>
> 2) **'The slide of life, once a project of naturalist drama, is now a voluntary, habitual, internal rhythm, the flow of action and acting, of representation and performance, raised to a new convention, that of a basic need.'**
>
> 3) **'. . . the new kind of Urban crowd, who are physically very close but still absolute strangers . . . had lost any common and settled idea of man and so needed representations – the images on hoardings, the new kinds of sign – to stimulate if not affirm a human identity.'**

(Williams, 1975)

Williams was writing/speaking in 1974 and implicitly about realist/naturalist dramatic representation. He could not have foreseen movies on the mobile phone or even multiplex cinemas and multi-channel TV. In a postmodern context, everything has changed again and new levels of simulation have come in. Gill Branston, writing of cinema realism in 2000, prefers the subtitle 'realisms' to indicate that 'realist forms and connections are under pressure' (Branston, 2007, p. 219). Branston is still tracking Williams but in 2000 there is a lot more to see:

- digital forms have undermined the integrity of realistic cinema: the camera can be made to lie and we all know it
- being unrealistic is a lot more credible: lower status film forms and genres are a fashionable part of the new cultural bricolage

- there is now a better understanding of film form and its operation: we appreciate the artifice more (Branston, 2007)
- seeing is no longer believing: the truth is no longer accessible.

Branston also refers to Corner's argument for two kinds of realism.

- thematic, wherein the complexity of reality is represented by the relationship between that reality and what the text is about
- formal, wherein the shape and size of the representations bears some relationship to those things represented. Corner talks about 'real-seemingness'.

(Branston, 2000, p. 165)

I think perhaps I need to consider some films which successfully address these different realisms and their different impacts. For example,

Formal

- *Nil by Mouth* (1997, dir. Gary Oldman)
- *The Blair Witch Project* (1999, dir. Daniel Myrick, Eduardo Sànchez)
- *Hostel* (2005, dir. Eli Roth)
- *Saw* (2004, dir. James Wan)

Thematic

- *American Beauty* (1999 dir. Sam Mendes)
- *Get Carter* (1971, dir. Mike Hodges)
- *Casino* (1995, dir. Martin Scorsese)

This business of the camera never lying is interesting. Now it's clear that while the camera may never lie, equally it always has a view. Alexander Kluge offers an interesting take on this by pointing out the presence of three cameras in the process, by which he means three levels at which the reality is framed, at which the camera has a view. How and where is the 'real', the truth, being produced? Kluge offers three locations:

1. In the technical equipment
2. In the film-maker's mind
3. In the expectations of the audience generated by the conventions of the genre
(cited in Bennett, Hickman and Wall, 2006, p. 214)

It seems obvious in the case of point 3 that the expectations generated by a film like *Nil by Mouth* (which is brutally naturalistic) will be very different to those generated by, say, *Titanic* (1999, dir. James Cameron). Which then is more real and which more realistic?

- What part does the 'realism'/'reality' of a film play in our appreciation of films.
- What is the status of *cinéma vérité* as a concept. Can film be simply 'true'?
- How does mainstream cinema compare to reality TV in terms of its realism? How important are production values?
- What does watching a film like *The Blair Witch Project* do to our next walk down a forest track? What is the impact of feeling that we could have made the film ourselves? Is genuinely scaring some teenagers for the sake of our entertainment justifiable? What do we gain from the realism of it?
- In what ways has the camera become an important perceptual focus? (think framing, focus, close up). What are the implications of the vocabulary of film becoming part of our everyday language?
- Is it possible that the blurring of reality and realism has resulted in unrealistic expectations of what life can be? Remembering that film 'abbreviates'; are we taking the 'highlights' version as if it was life uncut? I'm reminded of a Jim Morrison poem which includes the lines:

> Did you have a good world when you died?
> Enough to base a movie on?
>
> (Doors, 1978)

Ironically, the poem was set to music after his death by Morrison's band The Doors and the lines also feature in the opening sequence of the biopic *The Doors* (1991, dir. Oliver Stone)

Perspectives

Postmodernism: I guess that much of what has been raised during this developing case study can be read as a straightforward part of a postmodernist reading. Terms like 'simulation' and 'hyperreality' seem particularly apt responses to the blurring of the lines between realism and reality, as discussed in Chapter 2. John Storey's summing up of Baudrillard's postmodernism provides a useful overview of my subject too.

> **Jean Baudrillard defines postmodernism as a world of 'simulations' and 'hyperreality'. The capitalist democracies of the West have ceased to be economies based on the production of things and have become economies based on the production of images and information.**

This last line is challenging but it also expresses a key idea since it potentially gets to the bottom of my central question. What film realism offers us is something that appears to be a literal reproduction of reality, but which is, in fact, a construction of the world, a version of reality. Even a documentary maker like Franju admits 'You must recreate reality because reality runs away: reality denies reality' (Bennett, Hickman and Wall, 2006, p. 214).

The essential deceit is in, ironically, the technology, in the camera that never lies, since its 'recording' is not of an original, but of a 're-creation'. Again in terms of the implications of this, there is a central irony since the processes which make our sense of reality insecure also ultimately undermine the ascendancy of realism. In a postmodernist sense perhaps even realism has ended up as a dysfunctional metanarrative.

Marxism: However convincing the above argument may seem, it is not the only way to read this evidence. Some Marxists, such as Louis Althusser, might argue that the kind of formal realism offered by film is a principal weapon in the operation of the media as an Ideological State Apparatus. Here ideology is not denied but disguised with the metaphor obscuring the method. By presenting the 'way things aren't' as the 'the way things are', a film is borrowing evidence of its hypotheses. By offering ideological representations as if they are historical recordings, film is contributing to the powerlessness of the alienated masses. The confusion between the 'real' and 'fake' and between different varieties of realism do not, in this reading, contribute to a new postmodernist sensibility but rather further estrange the mass audience from the means of their own reproduction.

 **Stage Two: Planning**

My hypothesis is that realism has 'killed' reality which in turn has killed realism and that technology has profoundly speeded up this process.

A set of examples taken from 'practice' which support or contextualize your arguments

■ proposals of marriage to soap characters, television villains confronted in the streets
■ small scale survey amongst my fellow students to ascertain attitudes towards film realism as

1. desirable
2. convincing
3. generic preferences

■ Increase in the speed at which we access information as a result of demand.

A set of readings of relevant texts

Identification of three films representing different approaches to the 'business' of realism, e.g.

■ *This is England* (2006, dir. Shane Meadows): a gut-wrenchingly raw portrayal of skinhead culture in the 1980s.
■ *Die Hard 4.0* (2007, dir. Len Wiseman): the fourth outing for John McClane.
■ *The Blair Witch Project*: Internet-fuelled megahit of the late 1990s. In all kinds of ways this seems a very useful film. Though entirely 'fictional' (whatever that means) this film was improvised on location using actors whose names became those of the central characters. The filming took eight days and produced nineteen hours of usable film (simulating the product of a student documentary) and was then edited down to ninety minutes. This film has a peculiar power (it has been voted in polls as one of the top 50 of all time), which comes from both its naivety and knowingness. Personally I feel that its appeal comes from knowing it's a film we all could have made by going to the woods with our mates and scaring one another. The performance of Heather Donahue in particular has a long-lasting effect precisely because it addresses issues of authenticity in the context of a film that does the same. The degree to which Heather is acting scared or 'merely' being scared cuts to the heart of the realism/reality debate both theoretically and ethically!

The application of theoretical perspectives

I want to pursue as far as I can a postmodernist reading of realism as something of a 'busted flush', a dominant discourse overwhelmed by a technological plurality. John Storey expresses it well when he writes 'In the realm of the postmodern, the distinction between simulation and the "real" continually implodes; the real and the imaginary continually collapse into each other. The result is hyperrealism: the real and the simulated are experienced as without difference' (Storey, 1998, p. 347). If hyperrealism reflects a hyperreality, reality itself is forever lost to us.

In terms of key concepts and terminologies, the semiotic toolkit remains useful in getting to grips with the issues associated with naturalistic representations. Understanding the iconic character of film is only part of this story making, recognizing that film communication is more significantly indexical and symbolic; that its significations are largely second (and third order). Film works through a mythology which is partly its own and which partly derives from its dominant cultures. Entropy and redundancy are also ideas worth recovering from AS.

Chiefly though the conceptual kit is postmodernist with a particular emphasis on two short passages from Baudrillard's the 'Precession of Simulacra', his (Baudrillard, 1998) definitive account of 'simulacra' and the 'hyperreal'. First, we have Baudrillard describing the regressive process by which simulations degrade our ability to relate to 'basic reality'. This is a four stage model:

> **This would be the successive phases of the image:**
>
> - **it is a reflection of basic reality;**
> - **it masks and perverts a basic reality;**
> - **it masks the *absence* of a basic reality;**
> - **it bears no relation to any reality whatever: it is its own pure simulacrum.**

(Baudrillard, 1998, pp. 353–4)

This is the cut and paste world of parody and pastiche which is the modern mass media experience. It is a world in which 'Comic book films' have become a viable (and lucrative) film genre: the reflection of a reflection of a reflection. It is a world in which image and images have lives of their own, unanchored to any 'basic reality', they constitute their own. The second extract speaks, with an increasing accuracy which one might call 'prophetic' of the implications of this process.

> **When the real is no longer what it used to be, nostalgia assumes its full meaning. There is a proliferation of myths of origin and signs of reality: of second hand truth, objectivity and authenticity. There is an escalation of the true, of the lived experience; a resurrection of the figurative where the object and substance have disappeared.**

(Baudrillard, 1998, p. 354)

Here is a sharp reading of our 'retro' obsession, where in Billy Bragg's words 'Nostalgia is the opium of the age'; where our search for 'lived experience' merely takes us to the simulations of previous generations where we mistake an absence of production valves for a purer (more naive) take on the truth.

A list of significant sources (books, articles, websites, etc.)

The sources used in Case Study A can all be found in the references section at the end of this chapter. In addition, the following websites have been invaluable:

- Wikipedia http://en.wikipedia.org (a vital starting point, but do remember that Wikipedia is not always a definitive source and should be treated with care)
- The Internet Movie Database www.imdb.com (a mine of information on everything related to film)
- Cultsock www.cultsock.ndirect.co.uk (Mick Underwood's site with everything you need to know about everything – almost!)

 ## Stage Three: Writing Up

Having got this far it feels very much like editing *The Blair Witch Project* – nineteen hours filmed for a ninety-minute broadcast. The preparation for the Case Study has been a challenging exploration of an area of the topic aided by the tools and concepts of the Communication and Culture course. Now comes the challenge of completion: the selection, adaptation and development of a focused response. This is so much more than cut and paste since the dynamic is not so much 'compilation' but rather 'process'. Looking back the focus (My Focus) seems intact (pleasingly) though I am now tempted to move towards a refinement of my original idea by adopting a new one as follows:

My Focus: 'The Camera never lies anymore, because there's nothing worth lying for': hyperrealism and the hyperreal.

Don't be afraid to modify your focus in this way if the process of preparation has suggested a refinement or a slight change of direction or, best of all, an even tighter focus.

The bulk of my Case Study preparation has focused on film (and television) realism and the ways in which it might impact on our idea of what 'reality' is. This ought to be my central argument or thrust. At the same time I have unearthed *The Blair Witch Project* as almost a case study within a case study and certainly an interesting way to both exemplify and extend these arguments. It would be good to give some dedicated space to this work. Looking at the 'off the peg' models on p. 273, the shape that best suits my needs is probably the 'penny farthing' since it can offer the bulk of the wordage to the discussion of realisms and hyper-realisms whilst maintaining an investigation's worth of words for the 'Blair Witch' project.

The reading of *Blair Witch* and its issues can effectively be slotted into the piece any time after half way so as to allow some gathering of its points afterwards. Subheaders can help this process to be smooth and effective. The Blair Witch piece can also be developed discretely, a place to start or finish?

CASE STUDY A: THE FINAL VERSION

'The camera never lies anymore, because there's nothing worth lying for': hyperrealisms and reality

> However powerful its effects realism is only a convention.

Nicholas Abercrombie

> There isn't any *cinéma vérité*. It's necessarily a lie from the moment the director intervenes – or it isn't cinema at all.

George Franju

Figure 10.2 The camera never lies any more

This Case Study looks at some aspects of the problematic relationship between film realism and our individual and collective understanding of what the reality of our lives is like. Film as, arguably, the 'hottest' contemporary medium exerts a powerful influence on our hearts and minds. It does this partly because of its cultural position but also because it is an essentially photographic medium, apparently showing things as they are. This 'verisimilitude' or lifelikeness, is very much at the bottom of all the issues, positive and negative, which surround film as a medium and what the critic Andre Bazin called its natural mode of address, realism. Abercrombie talks about realism as a 'window on the world' yet also points out that 'there is no way in which any description of reality can be the only pure and correct one, just as people will give very different descriptions of what they see outside of their kitchen windows' (Raynor, Wall and Kruger, 2004, p. 55).

Realism and reality: nature and artifice

Realism is not a style, it is the basis of all cinematic representations in a relationship that Bazin described as 'necessary' and 'unacceptable' (Bennett, Hickman and Wall, 2006, p. 207). The paradox is that film is technologically striving for a reality that its very existence will always frustrate. The camera may never lie but it always has a view. On the one hand it simply shows what's there, hence Susan Haywood's assertion that, 'As far as the film camera is concerned, it is not difficult to see why it is perceived as a 'natural' tool for realism, since it reproduces what is there (that is the physical environment). Film as cinema makes absence presence, it puts reality up on to the screen' (Bennett, Hickman and Wall, 2006, p. 205). In semiotic terms we are talking about a form of communication that is highly motivated and principally iconic. This aspect is what John Corner called a 'formal realism' or a way that texts seeks to achieve a real-seemingness in their look. It is not however the whole story, though it may be the level at which we are as audience members most affected.

Subjected to the heightened and extended experience of the modern cinema's multi-sensory onslaught, it is easy to see the potential influence. Despite Abercrombie's insistence that the 'window' is not transparent, this is 'clearly' how it is most often perceived (as in 'taken as read'). When, in the early days of *Eastenders* the character Michelle initially opted for a termination of her pregnancy, the NHS reported a significant increase in requests for terminations. This may be alarming but it is certainly evidence that these naturalistic representations of ordinary life have an extraordinary power. Raymond Williams famously concentrated on the dramatization which is central to these televisual and cinematic events. He talks of drama as 'habitual experience' and one that has become 'necessary to stimulate if not affirm a human identity' (Williams, 1975). He also talks about drama's 'experimental, investigative' function, whether this be via the social realism of a film like Shane Meadows' *This is England* (2008) or via the values of a Hollywood blockbuster like *Die Hard 4.0* (2007, dir. Len Wiseman). In other words these lifelike representations are providing us with the evidence of a sort of life-based research, against which we can measure ourselves. In fact as technology improves to offer us much more available 'drama' (and ways of accessing and interacting with it), this function becomes more dominant even though the 'artifice' can hardly be ignored.

Thematic realisms and the degrading of reality

The counter-argument to the seductive naturalism of film lies in the unacceptable and necessary fact that as Bazin simply says, 'realism in art can only be achieved in one way: through artifice'. Even for documentary film makers, 'Truth has to be made vivid, interesting'. For Alexander Kluge, who claimed it must be possible to represent reality as the historical fiction that it is, it is principally about the way reality is framed, not in one camera but in three:

- 'in the technical equipment
- in the film-maker's mind
- in the expectations of the audience generated by the conventions of the genre'
  (Bennett, Hickman and Wall, 2006, p. 214)

With this 'triangulation' a more complex relationship is developed between the material and the reality. This is what Corner calls a thematic realism, which proposes 'a relation between what a text is about and reality' (Bennett, Hickman and Wall, 2006, p. 219). Interestingly this crudely corresponds with the critic Georg Lukacs' call to arms on realism: 'Thus realism means three-dimensionality, an all-roundness, that endows with independent life characters and human relationships' (Bennett, Hickman and Wall, 2006, p. 203). The key here is endowing characters with life rather than recording their apparent reality. Semiotically, it is a significant difference since it stresses the indexical nature of these signs as manifestations of associated meanings.

Drama may have been 'raised to a new convention, that of a basic need' (O'Connor, 1989, p. 5): the degree to which it is critically addressed is surely related to how we understand the way it is constructed and transmitted to us. A Marxist reading of this would stress the way in which lifelike images naturalize the relationships that are represented in and through them as a classically ideological deceit. The media theorist, De Fleur, talked about the way that the media present 'social values' dressed up as social reality (Bennett, Hickman and Wall, 2006, p. 252), but in an increasingly complex decentralized technology-driven context, these explanations seem a little unconvincing. Surely movies accessed on mobile phones or iPod screens are very clearly identified as 'artificial': they cannot overwhelm us with their 'verisimilitude'.

An alternative interpretation is offered by postmodernists, in particular Baudrillard. There are clues, for example, in the Marxist Raymond Williams, who refers repeatedly to 'these hundreds and thousands of <u>simulated</u> actions' (O' Connor, 1989, p. 5) and in the film criticism of people like Bazin whose insight provides another path to follow. Talking of the 'unacceptable and necessary illusion which is at the centre of film realism' he writes: 'It is a necessary illusion but it quickly induces a loss of awareness of the reality itself, which becomes identified in the mind of the spectator with its cinematagraphic representation' (Bennett, Hickman and Wall, 2006, p. 207).

The Precession of Simulacra (Baudrillard, 1998)

This 'loss of the awareness of the reality itself' is central to Baudrillard's recasting of the Biblical term 'simulacrum' to imply a baseless image, what Storey describes as 'an identical copy without an original' (Storey, 1998, p. 347). This is a central concept of postmodernism and one that goes a long way to addressing the tension between realism and reality. Concerned about the implications, Baundrillard warns us that 'simulation threatens the difference between "true" and "false", between "real" and "imaginary" ' (Baudrillard, 1998, p. 351). Realism, in film terms, has to sit within these simulations as stimulant perhaps for a process in which reality is degraded. Baudrillard talks of four successive phases of the image

- ■ 'It is the reflection of a basic reality
- ■ It masks and perverts a basic reality
- ■ It masks the *absence* of a basic reality
- ■ It bears no relation to any reality whatsoever: it is its own pure simulacrum.'
(Baudrillard, 1998, pp. 353–4)

In some ways the above 'model' is a model of a process of alienation from a productive relationship with reality. Baudrillard also argues that simulation is diametrically opposed to representation, which is an interesting thought; this is a transition from 'signs that dissimulate something to signs which dissimulate that there is nothing' (1998, p. 354). What is created from this, of course, is a hyper-reality, a reality referenced only by simulations. Thus we long for a time when we did have an unproblematic relationship with reality. As Baudrillard suggests 'when the real is no longer what it used to be, nostalgia assumes its full meaning' (1998, p. 354). Looking at film and television schedules 'retro' is in full flow, as it is in all other media, from fashion to home furnishings. Here is a desire to rediscover the 'real' acted out in yet further simulations whose watchwords are 'real', 'authentic', and 'objective'. The most significant is the hopefully named 'Reality TV' phenomenon, spearheaded by a show in which thirty-seven cameras attempt to find (and film) a reality. This lived and observed experience has proved ultimately unconvincing and *Big Brother's* manipulation of the format has failed also to whet jaded appetites. All that remains, living and breathing, is a celebrity franchise which further blurs the boundaries between the 'real' and 'imaginary'.

The Blair Witch Project: mixing fiction and faction

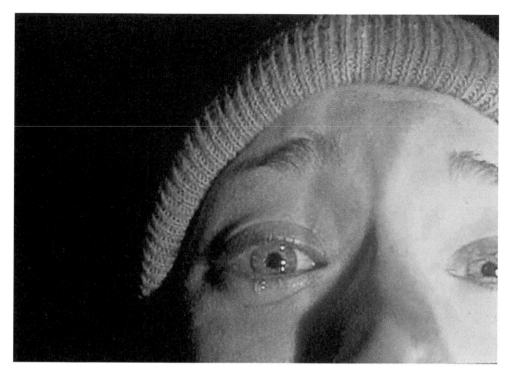

Figure 10.3 *The Blair Witch Project* (1999)

The Blair Witch Project (1999, dir. Daniel Myrick, Eduardo Sànchez) was a surprise hit, making $258 million on an outlay of $35,000. This was partly the result of a whisper campaign on the Internet but more significantly it was to do with production values that matched its budget and challenged its generic identity. Here all postmodern identity crisis elements are in place but not irony or playfulness. Here the bricolage is more mundanely a literal case of 'do-it-yourself' as actors playing themselves filming themselves scaring themselves.

Particularly in the case of Heather Donohue it is hard to doubt the authenticity of this fear, more reaction than performance. Even the people in the local town who unwittingly 'fessed up' their knowledge or ignorance of the entirely invented Blair Witch legend don't seem to know it as any more than a student film. The filming took eight days and furnished nineteen hours of material to be used in the final ninety minute edit. The edit is packaged as if it is the tape recorded by these kids before their disappearance, which gives us every reason to watch it until the end!

What *Blair Witch* demonstrates is a productive uncertainty about what is 'realistic', about the notion of 'authenticity'. This is not likely, in the context of this low budget film, to be a result of a knowing, ironic playfulness. It seems much more likely to be a symptom of a situated unease, proving essentially that realism is not a position a text takes up but rather a discourse which is continuously negotiated. Frederic Jameson suggests that postmodernism is typified by pastiche, depthless intellectuality and schizophrenia and these are present to some extent in *Blair Witch*. To return to Kluge's 'three camera' model, what you see in each case supports and challenges and contradicts the others. Thus, in a barely conscious way, we have a found location, photographed by a sensibility steeped in the traditions of low budget horror serving up an often crude emotional 'ride'. This is naturalistic and entirely contrived, motivated but also profoundly conventional, iconic but also significantly symbolic. It may function then like Disneyland in Baudrillard's famous interpretation 'as a perfect model of all the entangled orders of simulation' (Baudrillard, 1998, p. 354) and as a powerful statement about the way we live now.

Postscript

Postmodern theorists have tended to view the postmodern condition as a cultural Disneyland where everything is parody and nothing is better or worse. This view emphasizes the unanchored nature of signs in a culture where simulation has usurped representation and where the signifier–signified connection is merely temporary. This is a culture in which contexts have replaced context, where surface has replaced depth, where a perpetual present has replaced any significant historical sense (Jameson argues that 'real' history has been displaced by nostalgia). Gill Branston, in her book *Cinema and Cultural Modernity* (2000), suggests that with the development of digital forms 'anything can be simulated on screen: nothing is necessarily true'. In crude terms seeing is no longer believing, which clearly will have implications for our increasingly visual culture, though perhaps representationally the issue has always been the same. After all Minha-ha's assertion that 'Truth has to be made vivid, interesting' (Bennett, Hickman, and Wall, 2006, p. 212) is not a million miles from Keats:

> 'Beauty is truth, truth beauty, – that is all
> Ye know on earth, and all ye need to know.
>
> (John Keats *Ode on a Grecian Urn*)

(2075 words)

Case Study A: possible Creative Work options

■ How real is realism? How natural is naturalism? A multi-media presentation which juxtaposes the 'walking in the woods' footage from *The Blair Witch Project* with some home-made footage of a similar walk recorded with a camera mounted on a character's head. Asks the question 'Is it possible to divorce the act of filming from the generic conventions of film?'

■ The codes of realism. Explores the idea that the same event, the same object can be represented in many ways. This is a short film which takes the filming of a simple object or location and demonstrates the different meanings that might be assigned by camera movement, framing, sound, lighting in order to develop the question 'which is most real?'

■ The hyperrealism of the Blockbuster special effect movie. An enhanced PowerPoint presentation which explores the relationship between cutting edge film special effects and our ideas about verisimilitude. Where is the realism of *The Dark Knight* or even *Die Hard 4.0*?

CASE STUDY B

Figure 10.4 *Britain's Missing Top Model*

Topic   Body Modification

Title   Perfect/imperfect: cultural values and the body (Title 5).

Issue: How do ideas about physical (im)perfection reflect and influence our values?

My Focus: Natural Selection? Redefining the search for perfection.

Stage One: Thinking

Sender (Your own attitudes/outlook)

I'm prompted in this case by stopping to think about the implications of 'beauty' and 'perfection'. If body modification is mostly an attempt to move in the direction of bodily perfection, sometimes synonymous with beauty, what of disability? It's a disturbing thought rather like considering those who don't fall into the 'gifted and talented' category in schools; are they the 'cursed and talentless? This could take us in a number of directions such as:

■ What are the underlying implications of the different attitudes towards cosmetic surgery for the able bodied and for the disabled?

■ What does the difference between those born disabled and those disabled as a result of illness and accident add to this debate?

- Some have argued that conventional (geometric) beauty is a sign of good genes. Is beauty a case of natural selection?
- What is the particular nature of the abiding taboo about recognizing the sexuality of disabled people? Are they doing 'it' wrong in some way?

Sources (where you get information and opinions from)

- A principal resource is the website which continues to support the *Britain's Missing Top Model* television (Wolf, 1998) programme and project at http://www.bbc.co.uk/missingmodel/

This is a magnificent resource for a case study: so many issues addressed in images, comments and quotes. This is a regular model 'contest' which also raises wider questions about women's beauty as a passive spectacle. Also there are issues of invisible/visible disabilities and the degree to which the show pulled punches.

- A definitive statement about conventional representations of female beauty can be found in John Berger's *Ways of Seeing* (Berger, 1990). He argues that, 'according to usage and conventions which are at last being questioned but have by no means been overcome – men act and women appear. Men look at women. Women watch themselves being looked at.' (p. 45)
- A famous feminist take on this was published by Naomi Wolf in 1991. Entitled *The Beauty Myth: How Images of Beauty are Used Against Women*, it explores how a kind of body fascism is used to undermine and belittle women, seeing men as success objects and women as sex objects. This seems a useful juxtaposition to the parade of semi-nude disabled women in the programme above.
- An interview with brittle-boned actor Nabil Shabon, described as 'once Mr Super-Crip', talking frankly about his severe disability and his sexuality. Nabil faced a storm of criticism in the early 1980s when a documentary he made, in which he talked frankly about his sexuality, featured semi-pornographic images of able-bodied women. (Source: http://uk.geocities.com/jinghiz53/Inside 57_interview.html)
- JG Ballard's novel *Crash*, originally published in 1973, uses our profound unease about disability and sexuality to make powerful statements about his own unease about contemporary Britain. The central character, Vaughan (the nightmare angel of the expressways) is an anti-hero fascinated (to the point of arousal) by injuries and mutilations caused by car accidents. Ballard described it as 'an extreme metaphor for an extreme situation' (Ballard, 2008).

Arguments, Debates

- How does 'Beauty' work as an idea? A striving for perfection? A metaphor for moral worth? Healthy body = healthy mind?

- What is beauty for? Is it to get us loved and laid? Are we meant to be genetically matched?
- Does disability challenge ideas about beauty or extend them or confirm them? What about the terminology? Is 'perfection' more acceptable than 'imperfection' as a subject for discussion?
- What part does 'beauty' play in our understanding of human sexuality? Why is disabled sexuality largely invisible in a contemporary reality in which the pornosphere is rapidly expanding?
- How does the meaning of cosmetic surgery change when disability is added to the mix?

Perspectives (the different ways of viewing the world)

1   Anti Disabledism: whatever you chose to call it, this considers the prejudice meted out to disabled people and suggests the reasons for it. An example of this is 'Fragile Body Syndrome': able bodied people feel uncomfortable with disabled people because they are thereby reminded of their own frailities and limitations (Vic Finkelman) (Source: http://127.0.0.1:4664/cache?event_id=900528 & schema_id=6&q=%E2%80%98Fragile+Body+Syndrome%E2%80%99&s=hGF9Sycei3TXTsP11wlzwNiXBW8)

2   Feminist readings of 'beauty' are often revealing. Betty Friedan's 1963 book *The Feminine Mystique* dealt, in part, with ways of looking and being perceived (Friedan, 1992). Gaye Tuchman's notion of 'the symbolic annihilation of women' is based on a reduction of a woman's worth, particularly by the mass media, to her appearance through the processes of omission, trivialization and condemnation (Strinati, 1995, p. 164).

3   Marxists would conversely see all of these issues as ideological and ultimately peripheral. They might argue that the problems for disabled people are economic: they have low status as both producers and consumers.

Stage Two: Planning

A specific response to the title which is clear and coherent

Statement: all arguments about body modification, cosmetic surgery and the search for perfection are thrown into confusion by the 'arrival' of disability. The taboo 'disables' our critical faculties.

A set of examples taken from 'practice' which support or contextualize your arguments

There is an opportunity here to do some interesting if challenging and sensitive research which asks able bodied and disabled people to address the whole business of perception and expectation. Also, we need to consider the part played in this process by the media.

A set of readings of relevant texts

Britain's Missing Top Model and *Crash* (either the novel or the 1996 film (dir. David Cronenberg)) are possibilities for close reading.

These readings could be added to survey evidence and your own arguments.

The application of theoretical perspectives

There will be an implicit feminism at work in all that I do since conventional ideas about beauty are clearly ideological. A broader analysis of the operation of ideology will also be used to uncover the levels of disadvantage which affect all aspects of a disabled person's life. This will be related to the operation of dominant ideology, which may be seen to represent the interests of the 'strong'/powerful against the powerless. Partly this is economic since disability can be seen as 'using' resources rather than providing/producing them.

The opinions of others, formally or informally, directly and indirectly (a list of significant sources: books, articles, websites, etc.)

In addition to the texts already mentioned could be added

1   Lars von Trier's film *The Idiots* (1998)
2   Interview with Nabil Shabon in *Insiders* magazine issue 57 about disability and sex (source: http://uk.geocities.com/jinghiz53/Inside57_interview.html)
3   Beauty and Perfection as part of an age old discourse which metaphorically represents goodness, truth, etc.
4   Billy Bragg – *The Busy Girl Buys Beauty*

> **What will do you do when you wake up one morning to find God's made you plain in a beautiful person's world?**
>
> (Bragg, 1987)

5.   Yvonne Roberts (*Observer*, 2 May 2004): '. . . females have always been strongly conditioned to believe that beauty is a large part of a woman's worth' . . . She talks of 'the most vital of beauty secrets: cash conquers all'.

 **Stage Three: Writing Up**

There is an awful lot here and many ways in which it might be structured, depending on a final decision about the focus. *Britain's Missing Top Model* alone might furnish a number of challenging Case Studies. However I want the final Case Study to reflect the diverse material I have been able to gather and explore. As a result I have plumped for the 'Four Quartets' option, held together by ideas about disability and beauty:

My Focus: Natural Selection? Redefining the search for perfection.

Structure: Four 500-word 'investigations' headed:

a) *Britain's Missing Top Model*: making disability sexy. The programme, its mission and its issues.
b) *Crash* and Bang: disability, sex and the ultimate taboo. From sexy to sex and from sex to symbolism.
c) Do Androids dream of electric sheep: disability and sexuality; Nobil Shaban's wet dreams and the representation of desire.
d) Disability, beauty and 'cash conquers all': the search for perfection. Here come the girls: but where are they going?

Possible Creative Work options

1 Beauty and the Golden Mean. A website or PowerPoint presentation which investigates claims that beauty can be described geometrically. What are the implications for disabled people?
2 The end of imperfection? A short film which documents the responses of both disabled and able-bodied people to the eradication of 'bodily abnormalities'.

CASE STUDY C

Topic   Celebrity

Title   How celebrities make objects and places desirable (Title 1).

Issue: Celebrity endorsement: the various uses made of celebrity involvement in marketing strategies.

My Focus: Getting what you deserve (because you're worth it).

Figure 10.5 Jennifer Aniston

 **Stage One: Thinking**

Sender (Your own attitudes/outlook)

This study was prompted by a certain kind of unease (in the pit of my stomach) I feel every time I see some pampered overpaid celebrity trying to convince me to shop at, say, Asda, take life insurance or buy an expensive cosmetic (because I'm worth it).

This seems to me to ask very important questions about the character and function of the celebrity in contemporary culture. This centres around our identification with celebrities, and they with us, as if we are the same (or at least made from the same stuff). What this identification seems to deliver, however, is simply consumption and an ideological conceit. L'Oréal's 'because you're worth it' campaign exemplifies this by delivering a pseudo-feminist message which ironically delivers a continuation of the idea that a woman's value is related directly to her appearance.

Sources (where you get information and opinions from)

- Turn on the TV or leaf through a magazine for the latest celebrity endorsements and select the most surreal, e.g.
- Kerry Katona at Farm Foods (discount food shop)
- The Spice Girls buying Christmas presents
- Desperate Housewife Eva Longoria or actress Andie MacDowell offering cosmetics because they're worth it. (Look also at the archive – Henry Cooper and Kevin Keegan splashing Brut 33 all over)
- The Beckhams' underwear (both David and Victoria have featured in Armani campaigns)
- Ellis Cashmore's *Beckham* (2002). A classic study of a classic celebrity
- Cashmore's *Celebrity/Culture* also includes a chapter (Buying/Sales) on celebrity endorsement (2006).

Arguments, Debates

1. What is the nature/character of the fictions we are being offered in which celebrities are complicit?
2. What is our role? Are we dupes or participants in some kind of postmodern irony?
3. What is being exchanged? What is being sold?
4. What is the relationship between celebrities and the kinds of things they endorse?
5. Explore the ways in which celebrities are used to channel personal aspirations and to validate traditional ideological roles.
6. What part might gender play in this process?
7. How is 'value' defined in these contexts?

Perspectives (the different ways of viewing the world)

This seems a good study for entering a theoretical 'crossfire'. Celebrities fit so squarely into the postmodernist confusion of fact and fiction and simulacra while also providing ample evidence for the operations of dominant ideology. Marxist accounts of consumerism, commodity fetishism and commodification are all relevant here. Althuser's concept of interpellation is at work here and, in terms of gender, is relevant to feminist accounts. In the worst cases (think L'Oréal) advertisers are using the focus and aspirations of the women's movement to sell back to them the means of their exploitation: anti-wrinkle cream, expensive eyeliners and lipsticks.

Stage Two: Planning

A specific response to the title which is clear and coherent

Celebrities are involved in transferring value/values from products to people and vice versa. They willingly promote false needs while at the same time satisfying them since their own existence is potentially unfounded. For women this is significantly worse since celebrity promotes a clearer 'stereotype' and women are sold a success predicated on cosmetics.

A set of examples taken from 'practice' which support or contextualize your arguments

The key evidence is the association of some celebrities with products such that there is a relationship very like Barthes' notion of myth, for example, the Beckhams with Emporio Armani or Jamie Oliver with Sainsbury's. At the same time the language of the celebrity endorsement becomes part of the everyday language of the culture. 'Because I'm worth it', for example, has a life of its own and one that often confuses a certain kind of selfishness with a certain kind of empowerment. Like 'Girl Power' whose iconic item was a Union Jack mini-dress, being worth expensive cosmetics is at least problematic. The feminist writer Angela Carter suggested that any woman wearing high heels was letting the side down. What she would have made of L'Oréal is an interesting thought. Such expectations of women are often presented by female celebrities who have already (seemingly) acquired an effortless confidence.

A set of readings of relevant texts

The focus must be on sharp evidence from representative advertising and promotional campaigns such as:

a) Celebrities endorsing retail outlets: e.g. Kerry Katona in Farm Foods or, more surreally, the Spice Girls in Tesco or, more subtly, Twiggy and Mylene Klass in the Marks and Spencer ads.
b) 'Because you're worth it': the dubious spectacle of the privileged and beautiful telling us that we're worth it, while demonstrating what Yvonne Roberts calls 'the most vital of beauty secrets: cash conquers all'.

Ultimately this will lead to a reading of 'celebrity' as a set of codes and conventions.

The application of theoretical perspectives

The argument that I am developing sees celebrity as merely a little oil for the ideological state apparatus that is the media. What are being promoted are false needs and a consumerist agenda (and mood). Ironically the values that are being promoted (from the elusive glamour to a 'Just the same as I am' ordinariness) are essentially economic, they are lures for the unsuspecting consumer.

At the same time there is an even more cynical 'trick' being pulled in the context of gender. First, the female celebrity seems significantly more hedged in ideologically only to be even more persuasively passing this on to her 'sisters'. The reduction of a woman's value to her looks seems today to be breathtakingly regressive. The famous L'Oreal slogan cynically exploits the aspirations of feminism, for freedom and self-worth, to produce the perfect symbolic annihilation (in Tuchman's terms): I am what you see ('I'm pink therefore I am').

The opinions of others, formally or informally, directly and indirectly (think direct quotation, arguments, data)

A list of significant sources (books, articles, websites, etc.)

1 'In our factories we make lipstick, in our advertisements we sell hope' Charles Revlon (of Revlon cosmetics)
2 'We now have a generation hooked on the irrational pleasures of celebrity watching or, more accurately, celebrity fantasising'
3 'Consumption is the new phoney egalitarianism in which anybody can be somebody'
4 'It's a culture that nurtures, maintains and protects our right to be consumers' (Ellis Cashmore, 2002, p. 195)
5 'Because you're worth it' (L'Oréal)
6 'Modern celebrity… is a product of media representation' (Turner, 2003, p. 8.)
7 'They are living out narratives that capture our interest' (Neal Gabler, p. 5.) Source: http://www.learcenter.org/pdf/Gabler.pdf
8 'Celebrity taps some of the deepest contradictions about who we are and who we'd like to be' (Neal Gabler, p. 15.)
9 Concept of *Celebricacy* (Michael W. Jackson). Accessed at http://blogs. usyd.edu.au/theoryandpractice/2007/01/celebricracy.html
10 Readings of TV ads featuring celebrities.

 Stage Three: Writing Up

What has developed here is a connected (and hopefully coherent) argument. It begins with our general attitudes towards celebrities and theirs to us and progresses to close readings of celebrities themselves in particular promotional contexts. It ends with a close and critical analysis of the L'Oréal campaign and its underlying principles. In this case, the form that best fits and appeals to me is the format of a single extended piece.

My Focus: Because that's what we're worth: Going shopping with our celebrity friends.

Structure: Single 2000 word 'polemic' (consciously argumentative). The piece will be punctuated by three or four subheaders, for example:

1) **'God makes the stars': our love affair with celebs.**
2) **'You're just the same as I am': recognition and identification.**
3) **'The Busy Girl buys Beauty': Is it worth it?**
4) **'Headlong into harm': Into the *celebricacy***

Possible Creative Work options

1 The Anatomy of Celebrity. A mini-Cashmore style reading of a specific celebrity. Pod-cast
2 Spoof fan-site. A series of 'as it were' TV ads which parody L'Oréal-style campaigns.

CASE STUDY D

Figure 10.6 Gap years and grand tours

Topic	Holiday
Title	Gap years and grand tours; is it really better to travel than to arrive? (Title 4)
Issue:	'Travel broadens the mind'; travel as education/self-improvement
My Focus:	The Gap Year: self-improvement or self-indulgence?

 Stage One: Thinking

Sender (Your own attitudes/outlook)

This case study was prompted by my own plans to do the student 'thing': take a year out after A levels and 'travel'. Partly I was interested by the different responses I got from different people: some who reacted as if it was a great idea and others who just wondered 'why!'? I also have become aware that there is a lot riding on where I decide to go and for how long. There is no confusing 'travelling' with 'holidaying'; only the first broadens the mind.

This led me to further examine the vocabulary of journeys: the difference between 'travelling in' and 'travelling to'; the graduated danger and potential benefit from expeditions/adventures/excursions/trips/holidays. Also, I wanted to look at travel as a metaphor and as a multi-layered experience (cultural, historical, emotional, physical).

I will be able to draw on the experiences of two of my friends who have travelled in the Far East (Thailand, Vietnam).

Sources (where you get information and opinions from)

1. Articles, supplements, features on 'the gap year' from newspapers and magazines. Internet search of 'gap year', 'grand tour', 'student travel', etc.
2. Brochures, leaflets and websites advertising the gap year. A number of commercial organizations promoting 'guided' gap years or working holidays send promotional material to the college.
3. Historical accounts of the Grand Tour (the trips made by the well-to-do to get an education, especially in the eighteenth and nineteenth centuries).
4. Travel and tourism texts as listed in the Holiday Topic Guide.
5. Travel books and films: once again, starting with those in the Topic Guide.

Arguments, Debates

1   'Everybody hates a tourist', travel as a form of one-upmanship, one person's travel is another person's tourism. Travel/holiday as an indicator of social status/class (defined by destination, activity, context).
2   The search for the last wild place/the perfect beach. The confusion of activity and metaphor. Are we running towards or away from the 'truth' (or just running?)

3   The Gap Year as rite of passage: is this merely a bourgeois (middle class) ritual? What do working class kids do on their Gap Year?
4   Travel as 'education': icing on the cake/finishing school.

Perspectives (the different ways of viewing the world)

1   Liberal pluralist: regulated capitalism has meant an increase in standards of living which have implications for lifestyles, attitudes and aspirations. Many more people are able to enjoy foreign travel and its many (perceived) benefits. This has resulted in a society that is more open to cultural difference/appreciative of other people's cultures (food, behaviour, customs). Competition for our spending on travel has kept prices down and quality up.
2   Marxism: 'Holiday' is just another site in which you can read a society riven by inequalities based on social class. The classic package holiday is a 'commodity' for which a 'false need' has been created. 'Travel', on the other hand, requires cultural capital (Bourdieu) since it draws on your personal resources (e.g. an appreciation of historical contexts, fine wines, museums, art galleries, etc.)
3   Post-colonialist: interesting and problematic issues here. Think 'essentialism' (and Orientalism) where, for example, South East Asia becomes a stereotypically semi-mysterious destination for new age pilgrimages by those who have little or no experience of indigenous South East Asian communities in Britain. An investigation into how travel is often represented and marketed as an opportunity to accumulate 'exotic' experiences.
4   Feminism: the gendering of tourism, particularly the ways in which different types of gap year experiences are sold on the basis of male or female target groups.

 **Stage Two: Planning**

A specific response to the title which is clear and coherent

My Focus (revised): Mind the Gap. An enquiry into the personal and cultural meaning of the Gap Year between school (or college) and university.

1   The theory: travel broadens the mind; perfect preparation for university; take some time out; open yourself to new experiences; work your way; bring something worthwhile back.
2   The practice: certain kinds of kids go to certain kinds of places to have certain kinds of experience which gives them further confidence and cultural capital. Others work in B and Q and go on holiday with their mates to Magaluf.
3   Conclusion: 'travel' is a signifying system which communicates social and cultural values.

A set of examples taken from practice to support your arguments

1   Survey of intentions of students at my college (perhaps linked to parents' professions/jobs to pursue my argument about social class).
2   Analysis of advertisements aimed at Gap year students: who is the audience for these ads?
3   E-Journals of my friends Nike and Nat, two working class friends from the Black Country who 'did' the Far East.

A set of readings of relevant texts

1   The Gap Year as cultural practice: at the centre of my work is the understanding that 'Gap Year' is a value-laden construct which needs some deconstructing
2   Alex Garland's bestseller *The Beach* (Garland, 1996) and the subsequent film (2000, dir Danny Boyle) that present an ironic take on the search for the perfect destination (the truth). Since the central plot twist is based on the misheard mutterings of a drug-addled traveller (it was in fact never 'The Beach' but rather 'the bitch'), there are also links with those other 'mind-enlarging' trips such as Tom Wolfe's *The Electric Kool-Aid Acid Test* (Wolfe, 1969) and Hunter S. Thompson's *Fear and Loathing in Las Vegas* (Thompson, 1973).

The application of theoretical perspectives

Part of my argument is classically Marxist in that it seems a cultural practice in terms of its ideological function, which is to present as 'natural and essentially human' an experience which is a packaged privilege of the middle classes. In this sense the Gap Year alienates those who have no real access to it, by subjecting them to the accompanying sense of loss.

Gramsci presented a more subtle version of this process when he coined the term hegemony to contain all of these ideological negotiations.

There is also the sense in which, at least from Victorian times, the migration of travellers to the next beach has been as much 'away from' as 'towards'. Here, as everywhere, power is visibly on display, from the crowded beaches of Magaluf to the private beaches of celebrity-owned Caribbean islands. This is about consumerism and commodification, about what it is feasible and acceptable to buy and sell (transport and digs seem fair enough but the spiritual stuff might not stand the journey).

An alternative (but not oppositional) focus might be provided by a consideration of gender in this particular 'development'. Though gender cannot be entirely disconnected from social class in matters which are in some ways essentially economic, there is a sense in which 'the Gap Year' has been a way for many young women to confront and negotiate restrictive gender stereotypes. The idea of striding into the world, even on a carefully designed and well-supported itinerary, is a rite of passage unthinkable for most women a generation ago.

The extent to which this is a genuinely challenging dominant patriarchal ideology is perhaps best found, darkly, in reports of female backpackers who are attacked or abused. There is still, in the face of statistical evidence that young men are much more likely to be the victims, a common assumption that the warning voices were right.

The opinions of others, sources, etc.

1. 'If our lives are dominated by a search for happiness, then perhaps few activities reveal as much about the dynamics of this quest – in all its ardour and paradoxes – than our travels' (Alain de Botton, *The Art of Travel*, p. 9).
2. 'The concern to be always moving through a place, to see it never primarily as a place-in-itself, but always mediated by its connection to one place in the east and another to the west, produces a sense of space which is defined always by this linear movement' (J. Barrell, *The Idea of Landscape and the sense of place 1730–1840*) (is this the essence of travelling?).
3. 'For the twentieth century tourist, the world has become one large department store of countrysides and cities' (Schivelbusch, 1986, p.197).
4. 'Tourism is a complex form of consumption . . . It is the consuming of images, representations and predominantly visual experiences at first hand, yet also involves the consumption of a vast supporting network of resources in order to facilitate this gaze' (Paterson, 2006, p.118).
5. Urry talks of the 'tourist gaze' which has two 'flavours':

   a   the 'romantic': solitary, personal spiritual
   b   the 'collective': the mode of mass tourism (quoted in Paterson, 2006, p.119).

6. 'The tourism industry provides a structure within which tourists view, experience and interact with nature' (Alex Wilson, quoted in Paterson, 2006, p.132).
7. 'But still we feel the need for pristine places, places substantially unaltered by man. Even if we do not visit them, they matter to us' (McKibben, 1989, p. 55).
8. 'If contemporary Western society no longer holds a valid myth...then that might be why people search other cultures – to discover that which may be lost in their own' (Zurich, quoted in Paterson, 2006, p.134).
9. It is better to travel hopefully than arrive (proverbial).

 **Stage Three: Writing Up**

As ever there are, in reality, a number of Case Studies here. Gender and social class would, on their own, be worthy focal points. However, I am keen to maintain the integrity of both my hypothetical hunch and my genuine discoveries, which point to a dictotomy between either 'theory' and 'practice' or opposing perspectives (or maybe even 'Innocence' and 'Experience'). In short there are lots of reasons why a desire to travel is a positive inclination, but it isn't quite as simple as that. I'd like to present the two sides independently, as 'half and half' and let the reader decide but I realize that the order gives advantage to the second view offered.

My Focus: Mind the Gap. An enquiry into the personal and cultural meaning of the Gap Year between school (or college) and university.

Structure: Two equal parts (approx.1000 words)

Part A The Gap Year as rite of passage: Go East, young (wo)men

- the symbolic journey of the hero
- the search for independence
- the gendered gap year

Part B Let Nature by Your Teacher. Not!

- the world as finishing school
- we are what we consume (I am what I can buy)
- Travel and tourism: an ideological conceit

Suggested Creative Work

1   Critical reading of Gap Year presented as an informative 'how to' website. Gap year as a cultural practice for Communication and Culture students.
2   'What I did on my gap year without going to Thailand': a short documentary film about what students did on their year off before university which did not involve 'finding themselves'.
3   'What was the Grand Tour?' An illustrated podcast/photostory and historical documentary on the original 'tour': route, itinerary, purpose, glories and downfalls.

Hopefully these examples will have clarified the challenge and given some indication of the freedom you potentially have to make this the best part of the course. In the future these topics will change but the essence remains the same: pursue your interests, present your arguments and then bring it all to life with your expertise as a communicator.

References and further reading

Ballard, J. (2008) *Crash,* London: Harper Perennial.

Baudrillard, J. (1998) The Precession of Simulacra, in J. Storey (ed.), *Cultural Theory and Poular Culture: A Reader* (2nd edn). London: Prentice Hall, pp. 350–7.

Bennett, P., Hickman, A. and Wall, P. (2006) *Film Studies: The Essential Resource,* Abingdon: Routledge.

Berger, J. (1990) *Ways of Seeing,* Harmondsworth: Penguin.

Bragg, B. (Composer) (1987). *The Busy Girl Buys Beauty.* [B. Bragg, Performer] On *Back to Basics*. Cooking Vinyl.

Branston, G. (2000) *Cinema and Cultural Modernity,* Oxford: Oxford University Press.

Branston, G. (2007) Realisms, in P. Bennett, A. Hickman and P. Wall (eds), *Film Studies: The Essential Resource*, Abingdon: Routledge.

Cashmore, E. (2002) *Beckham,* Cambridge: Polity Press.

Cashmore, E. (2006) *Celebrity/Culture,* Abingdon: Routledge.

Finkelman, V. (nd.) Accessed at http://127.0.0.1:4664/cache? event_id= 900528&schema_id=6&q=%E2%80%98Fragile+Body+Syndrome%E2%80%99 &s=hGF9Sycei3TxTsP11wlzwNiXBW8

Friedan, B. (1992) *The Feminine Mystique,* London: Penguin.

Gabler, N. (nd.) Toward a New Definition of Celebrity. Accessed at http://www.learcenter.org.pdf.Gabler.pdf

Garland, A. (1996) *The Beach,* London: Viking.

Greer, G. (1971) *The Female Eunuch,* London: Paladin.

Hill, A. and Martin, N. (Composers) (1982). *My Camera Never Lies*. [Bucks Fizz, Performer] Polydor.

McKibben, W. (1989) *The End of Nature,* New York: Anchor Books.

Morrison, J. (Composer) (1978). *An American Prayer.* [T. Doors, Performer] On *An American Prayer*. Elektra/Asylum Records.

O' Connor, A.(ed.) (1989) *Raymond Williams on Television*, London, Routledge.

Paterson, M. (2006) Consumption and Everyday Life, London, Routledge.

Raynor, Wall and Kruger (2004) *Media Studies the Essential Resource*, London: Routledge.

Schivelbusch, W. (1986) *The Railway Journey. Trains and Travel in the Nineteenth Century*, Oxford: Blackwell.

Shabon, Nabil (nd.) Interview. Accessed at http://uk.geocities.com/jingh1253/ Insides57_Interview.html

Stoppard, T. (1994) *Rosencrantz and Guildenstern are Dead*, New York: Grove Press.

Storey, J. (1998) *Cultural Theory and Popular Culture; A Reader* (2nd edn), London: Prentice Hall.

Strinati, D. (1995) *An Introduction to Theories of Popular Culture*, London: Routledge.

Thompson, H. S. (1973) *Fear and Loathing in Las Vegas*, New York: Random House.

Turner, G. (2003) *British Cultural Studies: An Introduction*, London: Routledge.

Williams, R. (1975) *Drama in a Dramatized Society: An Inaugural Lecture*, Cambridge: Cambridge Unversity Press.

Wolf, N. (1998) *The Beauty Myth: How Images of Beauty are used Against Women*, London: Vintage.

Wolfe, T. (1969) *The Electric Kool-Aid Acid Test*, New York: Bantam.

INDEX

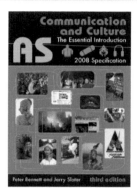

AS Media Studies: The Essential Introduction for AQA

Third edition

Philip Rayner and Peter Wall

AS Media Studies: The Essential Introduction for AQA is fully revised for the 2008 specification with full colour throughout, over 100 images, new case studies and examples. The authors introduce students step by step to the skills of reading media texts, and address key concepts such as genre, representation, media institutions and media audiences as well as taking students through the tasks expected of them to pass the AQA AS Media Studies exam. The book is supplemented with a companion website at www.asmediastudies.co.uk featuring additional activities and resources, further new case studies, clear instructions on producing different media, quizzes and tests.

Areas covered include:

- an introduction to studying the media

- the key concepts across print, broadcast and e-media

- media institutions

- audiences and the media

- case studies such as *Heroes*, *Nuts*, and the *Daily Mail*

- guided textual analysis of real media on the website and within the book

- research and how to do it

- a production guide and how to respond to a brief

AS Media Studies: The Essential Introduction for AQA clearly guides students through the course and gives them the tips they need to become proficient media producers as well as media analysts.

ISBN13: 978–0–415–32965–1 (hbk)
ISBN13: 978–0–415–32966–8 (pbk)

Available at all good bookshops
For ordering and further information please visit:
www.routledge.com

AS Film Studies: The Essential Introduction

Second edition

Sarah Casey Benyahia, Freddie Gaffney, John White

AS Film Studies: The Essential Introduction gives students the confidence to tackle every part of the WJEC AS level Film Studies course. The authors, who have wide-ranging experience as teachers, examiners and authors, introduce students step by step, to the skills involved in the study of film. The second edition follows the new WJEC syllabus for 2008 teaching onwards and has a companion website with additional chapters and resources for students and teachers that can be found at http://routledge.tandf.co.uk/textbooks/9780415454339/. Individual chapters address the following key areas, amongst others:

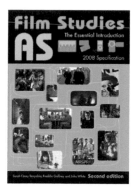

- British stars – Ewan McGregor
- Genre – Horror
- British Production – Working Title
- Social-Political Study – Living with Crime
- US Film – Westerns
- Film form
- Spectatorship
- The practical application of learning

Specifically designed to be user friendly, the second edition of *AS Film Studies: The Essential Introduction* has a new text design to make the book easy to follow, includes more than 100 colour photographs and is jam-packed with features such as:

- Case studies relevant to the 2008 specification
- Activities on films like *Little Miss Sunshine*, *Pirates of the Caribbean* and *The Descent*
- Key terms
- Example exam questions
- Suggestions for further reading and website resources

Matched to the new WJEC specification, *AS Film Studies: The Essential Introduction* covers everything students need to study as part of the course.

ISBN13: 978–0–415–45433–9 (pbk)

Introduction to Communication Studies

Second edition

John Fiske

How can we study communication?

What are the main theories and methods of approach?

The discipline of communication studies is now firmly established in the academic market-place. This now classic text is a lucid introduction to the main authorities in the field, aimed at students coming to the subject for the first time. It outlines a range of methods of analysing examples of communication, and describes the theories underpinning them. Thus armed, the reader will be able to tease out the latent cultural meanings in such apparently simple communications as news photos or popular TV programmes, and to see them with new eyes.

This second edition includes new material on the theory, methods and applications of structuralism, ideology and audience ethnography.

ISBN13: 978–0–415–04672–5 (pbk)

Available at all good bookshops
For ordering and further information please visit:
www.routledge.com

An Introduction to Language and Society

Second edition

Martin Montgomery

In this new edition of a classic textbook, Martin Montgomery explores some of the close connections between language and social life. He explores the ways in which children learn language in interaction with those around them, learning at the same time through language how to make sense of their world. He considers the social implications of accent and dialect as well as the broader interconnections of language with social class, ethnic group and subculture. He explores the role of language in shaping social relationships as part of everyday encounters and looks at the ways in which our habitual ways of interpreting the world may be shaped by the categories, systems and patterns of our language.

Despite the rapid development in new electronic technologies of communication, everyday language remains the most fundamental and pervasive communication technique. This book provides an ideal introduction to how language works in a modern society.

This new edition includes:

- a new chapter on gender and language
- new material on register, the speech community, language and subcultures and language and representation
- detailed suggestions for further reading and practical work.

ISBN13: 978–0–415–07238–7 (pbk)

Available at all good bookshops
For ordering and further information please visit:
www.routledge.com

The Media Student's Book

Fourth edition

Gill Branston and Roy Stafford

The Media Student's Book is a comprehensive introduction for students of media studies. It covers all the key topics and provides a detailed, lively and accessible guide to concepts and debates. This fourth edition, newly in colour, has been thoroughly revised, re-ordered and updated, with many very recent examples and expanded coverage of the most important issues currently facing media studies. It is structured in four main parts, addressing key concepts, media practices, media debates, and the resources available for individual research.

Individual chapters include: Interpreting media * Narratives * Genres and other classifications * Institutions * Questions of representation * Ideologies and power * Industries * Audiences * Advertising and branding * Research * Production organisation * Production techniques * Distribution * Documentary and 'reality TV' * Whose globalisation? * 'Free choices' in a 'free market'?

Chapters are supported by case studies which include: Ways of interpreting * *CSI: Miami* and crime fiction * J-horror and the *Ring* cycle * Television as institution * Images of migration * News * The media majors * The music industry, technology and synergy * Selling audiences * Celebrity, stardom and marketing * Researching mobile phone technologies * Contemporary British cinema.

The authors are experienced in writing, researching and teaching across different levels of pre-undergraduate and undergraduate study, with an awareness of the needs of those students. The book is specially designed to be easy and stimulating to use with:

- marginal terms, definitions, references (and even jokes), allied to a comprehensive glossary
- follow-up activities, suggestions for further reading, useful websites and resources plus a companion website to supporting the book at **www. routledge.com/textbooks/0415371430/**
- references and examples from a rich range of media forms, including advertising, television, films, radio, newspapers, magazines, photography and the internet.

ISBN 13: 978–0–415–37142–1 (hbk)
ISBN 13: 978–0–415–37143–8 (pbk)

Available at all good bookshops
For ordering and further information please visit: www.routledge.com